Turbo Pascal
Precisely

Turbo Pascal
Precisely

Judy Bishop

University of Southampton

ADDISON-WESLEY

Harlow, England · Reading, Massachusetts · Menlo Park, California · New York
Don Mills, Ontario · Amsterdam · Bonn · Sydney · Singapore
Tokyo · Madrid · San Juan · Milan · Paris · Mexico City · Seoul · Taipei

© 1992 Addison-Wesley Publishers Ltd
© 1992 Addison-Wesley Publishing Company Inc.

Pearson Education Limited, Edinburgh Gate,
Harlow, Essex CM20 2JE, England.

The programs in this book have been included for their instructional value. They
have been tested with care but are not guaranteed for any particular purpose. The
publisher does not offer any warranties or representations, nor does it accept any
liabilities with respect to the programs.

Many of the designations used by manufacturers and sellers to distinguish their
products are claimed as trademarks. Addison-Wesley has made every attempt to
supply trademark information about manufacturers and their products mentioned in
this book. A list of the trademark designations and owners appears below.

Cover design by Chris Eley.
Cover printed by The Riverside Printing Co. (Reading) Ltd.
Typeset using MicroSoft Word Version 4.0 on an Apple Macintosh SE with camera
ready copy produced on a QMS-PS™ 800+ laser printer by the author.
Printed and bound in Great Britain by Biddles Ltd, *www.biddles.co.uk*

British Library Cataloguing in Publication Data
A catalogue record for this book is available from the British Library.

Library of Congress Cataloguing-in-Publication Data
Bishop, J. M. (Judith Mary), 1951
    Turbo Pascal precisely / Judy M. Bishop.
      p. cm.
    Includes bibliographical references and index.
    ISBN 0–201–54449–0 : $30.00 (est.)
    1. Pascal (Computer program language).   2. Turbo Pascal/Computer
program)   I. Title.
QA76.73.P2B574 1992
005.13´3–dc20

12 11 10 9 8
03 02 01 00

Trademark notice
MS-DOS™ is a trademark of International Business Machines Corporation.
Turbo Pascal™ is a trademark of Borland International Incorporated.
Apple Macintosh SE™ is a trademark of Apple Computer Incorporated.
MicroSoft Word™ is a trademark of MicroSoft Corporation.
QMS-PS™ is a trademark of QMS Incorporated.

The publishers wish to thank the following for permission to reproduce material:
Ordnance Survey and the Cartographic Department of the University of
Southampton for the map of the University of Southampton in the colour plate
section; and Elliot B. Koffman for the syntax diagrams in Appendix G, reproduced
from his book *Turbo Pascal* 3rd ed. © 1991 by Addison-Wesley Publishing
Company. Reprinted with the permission of the publisher.

Preface

Turbo Pascal Precisely heralds a new era in Turbo Pascal books in that it actually introduces the real features of this rich Pascal dialect, such as strings, graphics, windows and objects. It aims to teach programming through examples, both human-based and computer-based. The whole of the Pascal language is covered, and the standard of programming is based firmly in the modern style of structured, readable, and user-friendly programs.

Turbo-ness

Turbo Pascal Precisely is based on the earlier texts *Pascal Precisely (1989)* and *Pascal Precisely for Engineers and Scientists* (1990), but is essentially a new book, breaking away completely from the strictures of 1980 Standard Pascal, and making full use of the exciting Turbo facilities. The power of Turbo Pascal is evidenced in the fact that many of the programs included from the other books have reduced considerably in size and complexity. For example reading a string is done in one statement, instead of a ten-line procedure as before.

The book assumes that Turbo Pascal is being run on a personal computer which supports elementary screen handling facilities, if not enhanced pixel graphics. Thus screen-handling, windows and cursor control are introduced right at the start and all but the smallest programs are presented with decent window-based, menu-driven user interfaces. The book also takes the reader through the development of a proper file-choosing unit which delves into the intricacies of DOS in the controlled way that Turbo promotes.

Of course, not **all** of Turbo Pascal's extensions can be covered in an introductory text, but the book chart (page xii) and the appendices should provide an efficient *entré* into the comprehensive Turbo Pascal on-line help and manuals.

Approach to programming

The approach of the *Pascal Precisely* books is to teach by example. Each of the chapters tackles a few features of the language, and exercises them to the full. The order of the material does **not** mimic the Turbo Pascal manual and the traditional text book style. These start with expressions and simple types, move on to control statements, and only then tackle procedures and structured types. Instead, *Turbo Pascal Precisely* takes a holistic approach, with most of the chapters evenly divided between attention to:

- program structure,
- data structure,
- control structure,
- input/output,
- Turbo specialities.

To assist the reader, a chart of the book along these lines is provided. Our experience has shown that this integrated approach to the order of topics has tremendous benefits for motivation and understanding, and that students are able to get ahead and accomplish more in a shorter time, without compromising their assimilation of the principles of Pascal and programming.

Examples

The book uses both short explanations of new features, and fully worked examples. Each of the examples goes through the six problem-solving steps of:

- problem,
- solution,
- example,
- algorithm,
- program,
- testing.

Many of the examples have a 'real world' flavour, which reinforces the need for a programmer to understand the user's problem, and to write programs in a user-friendly way.

The book subscribes to the belief that Pascal is an excellent teaching language, and that it is in a different class to its competitors, C, Fortran and BASIC. It teaches Pascal properly, with procedures, parameters and subranges coming in right at the beginning. As soon as a new feature is introduced, it comes firmly into the repertoire of tools, and the improvement in style that is obtainable thereby is constantly emphasised. Thus the examples in later chapters are longer and more challenging, reflecting the growing experience and maturity of the student.

Programming vs problem solving

It is no longer sufficient to teach coding – the means by which explicit algorithms are translated into statements in a programming language. The expectation of today's scientists and engineers is that the whole computing milieu will assist in the solution of day-to-day physical problems. In addition to explaining syntax and the construction of a well-formed program, the modern programming text book has to include techniques for problem solving.

Turbo Pascal Precisely is indeed such a modern text book. Every worked problem – and there are over 60 of them – is introduced with a typically inexact statement. This is then refined in the process of devising a solution. Where applicable, the appropriate technique is selected from those previously discussed, and then we proceed to algorithm development. As an additional aid, algorithms are illustrated with structured diagrams, and important techniques are discussed, highlighted, and identified for reuse later on. The important programming paradigms of:

- structured programming,
- data abstraction,
- modularity,
- object-oriented programming,
- software reuse, and
- polymorphism

all receive attention, and examples are carefully chosen to show, as far as is possible in Pascal, how these techniques can encourage correctness and efficiency.

Who the book is for

The book is intended for students learning to program for the first time in Pascal, who have access to Turbo Pascal 4.0 or later on a PC. Students would normally be in their first year at a university or college, and could be in the science, engineering, commerce or liberal arts faculties: the examples are sufficiently wide ranging to cater for all. The book does not require mathematical experience, and would certainly be accessible for school pupils taking computer science in senior years. Because there is an emphasis on facts and examples, rather than long discussions, the book would also be suitable for experienced programmers or hobbyists who wish to pick up Pascal quickly.

The book is based on courses given to science and engineering students at first year university level since 1980. Included are many of the class-tested examples and exercises from these courses. The Turbo Pascal extensions were newly tested on first year computer science students in 1991, using Turbo 6.0 in the lecturer's office and Turbo 4.0 in the laboratories.

Learning aids

There is a whole range of these! Specifically, the book offers:

- helpful **hints** and reminders in the margins;
- succinct **summaries** at the end of each chapter;
- ten-point self-check **quizzes** for each chapter, with answers;
- over 60 worked **examples** with complete programs;
- four large **case studies** of real computing problems;
- over 100 set **problems** to suit a wide range of abilities and interests;
- **answers** at the back to a selection of the problems;
- separate sections on **key Turbo Pascal features**;
- several **appendices** summarising Turbo Pascal features.

Acknowledgements

My thanks are due to the students at the University of Southampton and the University of the Witwatersrand for their enthusiasm and insightful comments; to Peter Goddard for his valuable input at the start of the project; to Martin Sykes who skilfully digitised the campus map; to the members of the Addison-Wesley editorial and production teams, especially Simon Plumtree, Stephen Bishop and Susan Keany for their very professional support; and to Nigel for his unfailing and very real assistance throughout my preoccupation with the book.

Judy M Bishop
November 1991

Contents

Chapter	Structure	Data	Control	Input-output	Methodology	Techniques	Turbo Pascal
2 Beginning with Pascal	programs procedures value parameters	subranges	for loops expressions	write writeln	meaningful indentifiers good layout software reuse generalising	counting loops self-contained procedures	standard units screen handling Crt unit windows colour
3 Changing and choosing	begin-end	const var	assignment if-then-else	read readln dialogue user interfaces	comments globals and locals initialising controlling input	swapping averaging highest number generating test data	constant expressions gotoxy clreol random numbers
4 Types and looping		integers booleans reals	while loops repeat loops standard functions	input trailers field widths	logical expressions arithmetic accuracy	conditional loops graph plotting pixel graphics	extended integer and real types keypressed Graph unit – lines, pixels
5 Character processing		characters strings text	case statement	text files eof eoln	input/output streams	drawing borders menu handling with windows	extended key characters string routines Graph unit – fonts, input
6 Functions and arrays	var parameters functions	type statement subranges again arrays			functional decomposition procedural interfaces secure programs	array processing integer conversion data-driven drawing	array constants Graph unit – shapes
7 User-defined types	with	enumerated records variants sets		menus in windows	state indicators abstract types debugging data abstraction	decoding data searching roots set manipulation	record constants defining units cursor control
8 Advanced topics	recursion	procedure types general files		file read and write	nesting scope and visibility user interfaces	sorting access tables based numbers	DOS unit – date, time and directories cursor tracking
9 Dynamic data structures	objects	pointers objects			object-oriented programming	linked lists stacks, queues	Graph unit – animation

Turbo Pascal Precisely Chart of the contents

List of examples

List of problems

Answers are provided for problems marked with a §.

Projects

1

Computers and programming

In this initial chapter computers are introduced and the various tasks involved in problem solving, algorithm development and programming are discussed. Some of this material will be revision for those who have encountered computers before. The chapter ends with an introduction to the Turbo Pascal environment.

1.1   Computers

What is a computer? A straight answer might be:

A computer is an electronic machine.

This does not tell us very much – no more than saying that a refrigerator is an electric machine. If we ask 'what is a refrigerator?', the answer would be:

A refrigerator is an electrothermal machine for
making and keeping things cold.

This defines the object in terms of the *function* that it performs – in this case, it is a built-in function to cool things. The difference between a computer and most other machines is that a computer is not confined to performing a specific built-in function. Functions are supplied by means of **programs**.

1

Let's try again: what is a computer?

> A **computer** is an electronic machine which can be programmed to perform a variety of functions.

What functions? Look around and you will see computers in most walks of life these days. If one had a brain-storming session in class and asked everyone to name one use of computers, the list could well be something like:

banking	airline reservations
controlling spaceships	controlling washing machines
solving equations	newspaper publishing
pay-rolls	controlling chemical plants
advising doctors	calculating engineering constraints
stock control in shops	marking examinations
playing games	monitoring heart beats

Computers = hardware + software + devices.

and so on. Computers in general have a seemingly endless range of functions, but there are limits to what any one computer can do, and these limits are imposed by:

- the **hardware** of the computer, whether it is extensive or minimal, fast or slow;
- the **software** that is provided in the form of programs;
- the **devices** to which the computer is connected, such as automatic money dispensers, cash registers, optical card readers, chemical equipment, volt meters, laser printers and so on.

Thus, any one computer cannot perform any function – it must be suited to the task in terms of its hardware, and it must have the appropriate devices and software.

Classes of computers

The vocabulary of computers is many and varied. What follows is a guide to the most common computer terms.

Mainframes

Large corporations have mainframes.

Mainframe computers are usually large in terms of their memory and the number of devices that can be connected to them. They are usually very fast, and are used by hundreds or thousands of people in big organisations. A mainframe computer can be located in one city, and by using **tele-communications** via land lines or satellite, it can receive and transmit data to and from **remote** sites or devices in other cities. Examples of such computers would be those used by banks, with their automatic tellers all over the country, or by a university, with **terminals** all over the campus.

Large machines are **multiprogrammed**, in that they can deal with several functions and many users seemingly all at once. Of course, there is still only one computer, but it is so fast that it can share its time between tasks, without humans noticing this sharing process – at least most of the time. When one does notice degradation in the visible performance at any one device connected to a mainframe (such as a wait before a balance slip is printed) then it means that the computer could well be getting congested, with too many things to do.

There are two different kinds of large machines, depending on the tasks that they mainly perform. By far the largest number of computers in the world are concerned with **information processing** (formerly **data processing** or **DP**), and the applications they are involved in tend to use very large amounts of information stored in a **database**. For example, a bank keeps a database of all its accounts, their owners' names and addresses, recent transactions, balances and so on. The other kind of mainframe is used for very complex and lengthy calculations such as weather prediction or nuclear physics research. These **supercomputers** are extremely fast at numerical computations and usually employ several processors working at the same time using **parallel processing**.

Minicomputers and microcomputers

For the past three decades, computer hardware has been getting smaller and cheaper, thus bringing computers within the range of individuals, for their businesses, home organisation or pleasure. **Minicomputers** were the first of the affordable computers and they tended to be used by 10 to 20 people, performing much the same tasks as a mainframe, but on a smaller scale. They were thus often found in small businesses or university departments.

Computers for the individual.

Next came the **microcomputers**, which were distinct in that they were intended to be used by one person at a time – enter the **personal computer**. Personal computers meant an explosion in usable, friendly software, with games, word processors, and spreadsheets being the most popular. Nowadays, microcomputers often have very sophisticated devices for performing graphics, high quality typesetting or even speech synthesis.

Following on from the micros are the **workstations**, which have hardware that rivals that of many mainframes, but that are still meant to be used by only a few people. Their function was originally to provide the increased power demanded by more sophisticated applications in research and software development, such as expert systems or image processing. However, workstations are increasingly replacing microcomputers as standard desk equipment.

Microprocessors

Mainframes, minis and micros are quite visible – one can walk into an office or computer room and see the metal cabinets containing the electronic

Chips with everything!

machinery. Probably far more populous are the computers which reside inside other machinery – often known as **microprocessors** or even just **chips.** Such a computer is manufactured with its software built in, and this would consist of a dedicated program for performing a specific task, such as controlling a washing machine or an arcade game.

Microprocessors are relatively cheap to manufacture, but they are not intended for use by people directly. They are embedded in the machine they control and essentially form part of it. The software for embedded computers is developed on some other, larger, computer, and then may be **down-loaded** to the chip. It could well be that the chip in a household machine or a car is the same as one in a microcomputer – the difference is that the microcomputer has additional devices that enable it to communicate directly with people, and to be programmed afresh to carry out new tasks.

Networks

Power for the future.
Computers of different makes and capabilities can be connected together to provide communication or to enhance the capabilities of one by using the facilities of another. Networks can be created within a small area such as a building or a campus where the physical connections between the machines can be made relatively easily (these are known as **local area networks** or LANs), or, on a larger scale, computers can be connected right around the world using satellites, provided a common **network protocol** is observed during communication.

The beauty of networks for the ordinary user is that communication is often initially via a telephone, so that very little special equipment is needed. Of course, it is not legal to gain access to another computer unless one has permission, and this is the area of concern of **computer security**.

1.2   Hardware and software

The machinery of a computer is known as the **hardware**. When learning to program, one is most often faced with the hardware of a microcomputer, for use by one person at a time, or a terminal connected to a mainframe being used by many people. We shall describe a microcomputer here, since it includes all the important computer components. The situation for a terminal would be similar, but some of the devices of the computer may be in other rooms.

Figure 1.1 shows a typical microcomputer. While the arrangement of the boxes may vary, virtually every microcomputer will have a keyboard, screen, processor, memory, disk drive(s) and access to a printer. The mouse is optional, but is becoming increasingly popular. Let us look at each component in turn.

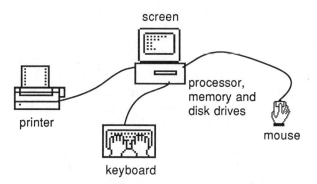

Figure 1.1 Components of a typical microcomputer

1. **Keyboard.** The keyboard enables one to type in instructions, programs and data to the computer. It resembles a typewriter, but has many more keys. The keyboard is an **input** device.

2. **Screen.** The screen enables one to see what is typed on the keyboard, and is also used by the computer for presenting results, messages, and so on, in the form of text and graphics. For the text, screens usually allow 80 characters across, and some 25 lines down. Modern screens also allow **graphics** (pictures) to be shown. For this, the screen is treated as rectangular grid of dots or **pixels**. The brightness and colour of each pixel can be controlled. The detail which can be shown depends on the size of the pixels – the smaller the size, the greater the detail. On IBM and compatible personal computers the size depends on the **graphics adapter** used. A range of adapters is available, including CGA, EGA, VGA and **Hercules**. The screen is an **output** device.

    VGA = Very high resolution Graphics Adapter.

3. **Processor.** The processor performs the actual work of the computer, calculating or processing data according to instructions, and producing results. Processor throughput can be measured in Mips (millions of instructions per second) and typically a microcomputer might run at 0.5 to 1 Mips. This figure will depend on the underlying speed of the computer's clock which is measured in Megahertz (MHz), with typical clock rates being 8 or 16MHz.

    Mips = Millions of instructions per second.

4. **Memory.** While it is working, the processor keeps the current program and much of the data and results in its memory. Memory is usually volatile in that the contents are erased when the power is switched off. Memory is measured in terms of **bytes** consisting of 8 binary digits (**bits**) and may in addition be organised in units called **words** which may be 16 or 32 bits long. Typically a microcomputer will have 1Mbyte (where M stands for Mega or $1\ 048\ 576 = 2^{20}$). Some memory is termed RAM (**randomly accessible memory**) and can

    Megabytes = Millions of bytes.

be used freely by a program; other memory known as ROM (**read-only memory**) is used by software provided with the computer and cannot be overwritten.

5.   **Disk drives.** In order for programs and data to be reusable, they must be stored on some permanent medium. **Disks** are the most suitable magnetic medium, though some larger computers may use magnetic tapes as well. A microcomputer will have a **hard disk drive** built in, which will be capable of storing from 40Mbytes upwards. On the hard disk will be all the system software and spaces for the user to put applications and data. The hard disk can be partitioned into sub-disks, and these would be known by the letters C drive, D drive, E drive and so on. For saving software and data, and for moving it from one computer to another, the most popular method is to use small removable **diskettes**. Most microcomputers have one or two such diskette drives, and they come in two sizes: 3.5 inch and 5.25 inch. The older 5.25" disks are usually known as **floppies** because they are encased in a flexible cardboard cover, whereas the newer 3.5" disks have a hard plastic cover and are sometimes known as **stiffies**. The amount of information that can be stored on a disk depends on the density and quality of the magnetic covering and most floppies and stiffies can store over a megabyte.

6.   **Printer.** Printers produce the **hard copy** of programs or results that can be taken away and studied. The printer may be connected directly to a microcomputer, or it may be shared by several over a network. The two most popular types of printer are:

- **dot matrix printers** which give reasonable quality printing, and are versatile in being able to output a reasonable selection of fonts and graphics;

This book was printed on a laser printer using output from a microcomputer.

- **laser printers** which can produce output of typeset quality, complete with font changes and graphics.

7.   **Mouse.** A mouse is a pointing device which acts as an assistant to the keyboard. It enables parts of the screen and the instructions that manipulate it to be selected more easily. To operate a mouse, one rolls it around on a flat table top, and the motion is reflected on the screen. When the correct place is found, a button on the mouse is clicked, to indicate that the computer can go ahead and perform the selected operation. Some mice have one button, some have two or even three.

Software

As **hardware** is the name for the electronic components discussed above, so **software** is the name for the programs that reside in the computer. In

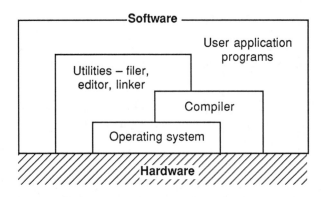

Figure 1. 2 Layers of software

addition to hardware, computers also possess resident software, and additional software can be obtained and written. Figure 1.2 gives an impression of the different layers of software.

The main piece of resident software in a computer is its **operating system** which controls all the peripherals and provides an interface to the user. It generally handles access to the compiler and to utilities which can include an editor, a filer (or finder), and a debugger.

The computer's controlling program.

The **editor** is a program that enables one to type in a program, store it on a disk file, edit it, and add to it at will. The **filer** is there to keep track of all the names and properties of the files and disks being used. On a multiprogramming system, further components of the operating system keep track of the amount of time and resources consumed by each user. Sometimes these are budgeted to users, and one has to take care to keep within one's allotted budget since the system could deny access if a budget is exceeded.

Utility programs.

A system may have several **compilers**, one for each computer language. The compiler's task is to translate a program into a form that the computer can then execute. In the process, it checks the program for incorrect spelling, grammar and usage and reports any errors to the user.

Computer language translation programs.

As you gain practical experience with using a computer, you will become familiar with the features for your particular computer. Although operating systems for different machines are superficially different, underneath they all provide the same sorts of functions, and after a while it becomes relatively easy to move from one computer to another.

The examples and problems in this book are based on the use of an IBM (or compatible) personal computer, running **Turbo Pascal**. The underlying operating system is **MS-DOS**. Turbo Pascal provides its own editor and compiler, plus some other useful programming tools, and is therefore described as a **programming environment**, rather than just a compiler. The Turbo Pascal environment is introduced in Section 1.6.

1.3 Problem solving

As we have already discussed, the crucial difference between computers and other machines is that computers can be **programmed**. What is a program?

> A **program** is a set of ordered instructions which can be understood by the computer.

The purpose of the program is to provide a new capability to the computer – a capability to solve a new problem. The process of developing the program is called **programming** but in reality it involves all the skills relevant to **problem solving** as well.

In the context of programming, problem solving involves several stages, each with its own particular difficulties and skills. The stages are:

Seven steps to solving a problem.

- defining the problem,
- outlining a solution,
- developing an algorithm,
- programming the algorithm,
- testing the program,
- documenting the solution,
- maintenance.

Problem definition

The first step is naturally to define the problem. This is surprisingly difficult in practice. Problems that are intended for solution by a computer can be phrased at any level from the wishful:

'Theatre reservations are too slow in this town.'

to the specific:

'What is the standard deviation of the following 100 numbers?'

The purpose of the problem definition phase is to pin down the problem more exactly. To do this, we try to define what the **data** will look like, and what the expected **results** will be. It is often useful to work through an example with the person who set the problem, thus bringing to light any misconceptions or misunderstandings.

For example, suppose one is asked to arrange a file of student records 'in order'. The questions to be asked would include the following:

- What is the basis for the ordering – surnames or student numbers or years and then surnames, or whatever?
- Must the old file be replaced by the new one, or must it remain?

Despite the importance of this phase of problem solving, it is nevertheless the case that a problem can seldom be completely defined a priori. There will always be aspects which only become clear as a solution is being worked out, and this is quite acceptable. It is actually better to leave some questions open until more information is available, rather than to make pre-emptive assumptions which may spoil the solution at a later stage.

Problem solving is evolutionary.

Outlining a solution

The very first question to be asked is 'Do we need a computer at all?' There are times when using a computer is not appropriate, although it seems attractive at first. For example, deciding to put one's car mileage, consumption and service record on a computer could turn out to be more of a nuisance than an aid because the computer is not available in the car, where most of the questions about its state will probably be asked. It would be better to stick to a note book and calculator.

Do we need a computer?

However, given that a computerised solution is required, it is necessary at this stage to set up the parameters within which the solution must work. Must the solution be fast? Are answers required on a terminal? Must results be stored on disk as well? In fact, is all the necessary equipment available? For example, if we need to print a graph of a function, it will make quite a difference to the solution whether we have a graph plotter connected, or whether we have to simulate plotting by printing dots on a printer.

What sort of computer?

At this stage, too, one should be thinking of past solutions. Has this problem been solved before, or even something very like it? Time can be saved by reusing tried and tested methods, rather than starting from scratch. If the problem is in a particular domain, such as mathematics or biology, we should make sure that we have all the essential equations and methods worked out, and be aware of any constraints that apply to the numbers and arithmetic involved. As we shall see later on, computers have bounds on their arithmetic capabilities, and as a result errors can creep in.

Can we use an existing solution?

Algorithms

It is at the algorithm stage that the logical thought-processes must start, and the outline of a solution be worked out into a step-by-step method. Algorithms have been around since long before computers were first thought of and are visible in many walks of life. For example, in cooking, one might find the following recipe for meringues:

> Beat the egg whites until stiff. You will know that
> they have been beaten enough if they don't fall out
> when the bowl is turned over.

This is an unhelpful algorithm, since the test for completion will not allow the process to continue!

In general, algorithms in computer programming must have certain properties, if they are to be used as starting points for a program. These properties all relate to preciseness and are: unambiguous, finite, brief, self-checking and deterministic. An algorithm for summing positive and negative numbers together and separately would be:

The 'Summing three ways' algorithm.

Summing three ways

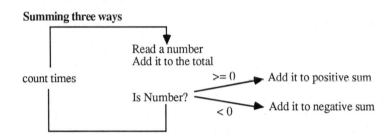

How to achieve good algorithms, and how to write them down, is looked at more closely in Section 1.5. Moreover, this whole book is a case study in algorithm development: there are over 60 worked examples where a problem is taken through a draft solution to an algorithm, and from there to a program which is tested on the computer.

1.4 Programming

Popular computer languages.

Now we have to write the algorithm down in a programming language. There are many, many such languages in use throughout the world, but relatively few that are available on all kinds of computers. These are known as the **high-level languages**, and include Pascal, Ada, Fortran, COBOL, BASIC, C, Lisp, Prolog and Modula-2. These languages are also **general purpose** in that they can, by and large, be used to solve a wide range of problems. They do have their special areas of application, though, with COBOL being business-oriented, Fortran being for scientific use, and Prolog being very good for artificial intelligence.

Named after Blaise Pascal (1623–1662) the French mathematician and philosopher.

The choice of which language to use for a particular application will depend on what is available, and whether it has any specific features that give it an edge over others. For learning to program, educators usually choose a language that is **modern, easy to understand** and has **good protection against mistakes**. Pascal fulfils all these goals. It was devised in 1970 by a Swiss professor, Niklaus Wirth, and is now used throughout the world in universities and colleges as a first teaching language. The particular version of Pascal used in this book is Turbo Pascal (a product of Borland International). As well as providing the Pascal language, Turbo Pascal includes a number of extensions which assist in developing programs.

Part of a Pascal program that implements the algorithm depicted above is:

A 'Summing three ways' program.

```
PROCEDURE Summation3;
  VAR
    number :real;
    i         : 1..10000; {say}
  BEGIN
    Total := 0;
    PosTotal := 0;
    NegTotal := 0;
    FOR i := 1 to count do begin
      read (number);
      Total := Total + number;
      if number > 0 then PosTotal := PosTotal + number
                        else NegTotal := NegTotal + number;
    END {for};
    readln;
  END; {Summation3}
```

The program is written in a stylised, yet fairly readable, English. Each step in the program is written on a new line, and the lines are indented to achieve certain effects. For example, the lines between the FOR and END {for} constitute a loop, and this is emphasised by the indentation.

High-level languages are **machine-independent** in that they can be run on any computer for which a compiler is available. Every computer also has its own specific **machine language** which it can execute directly. Programming is not usually done at this level, though sometimes it is necessary to use a symbolic form of the machine language, known as **assembly language** or just **assembler**.

Programming languages fulfil many of the properties of algorithms discussed above, but there are good and bad ways of using them, just as there are good and bad ways of using English. One of the goals of this course is to teach the correct way of using a programming language, so that the resulting program is both efficiently executable by the computer and easily understandable by humans.

Testing

Once a program has been written down in a programming language, it has to be submitted to the computer in some way, **compiled** into that computer's machine language and then executed. On the way, things may go wrong, and steps may need to be repeated. This is all summed up in Figure 1.3.

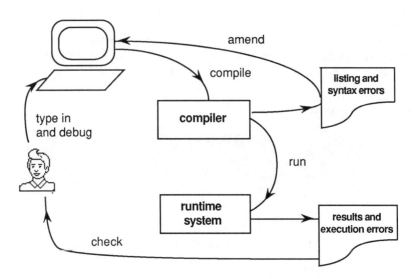

Figure 1.3   Life cycle of a program

From source code to object code.

The programmer takes the sheets of paper to a terminal and types the program in. The program, often known as **source code**, is sent to the compiler, which checks it for correct grammar or **syntax**. If anything is wrong, a list of **compilation** errors will be produced, or the errors could be indicated as they occur. The errors must be attended to by changing the program, and then the source is resubmitted to the compiler.

This process continues until there are no more compilation errors. The program is then translated by the compiler into a machine executable form, called **object code**. The object code can then be **run** on the computer, by a run-time system which is either part of Pascal or part of the computer's **operating system**. The program will produce results, and it may also produce **execution errors**. In either case, the results must be carefully scrutinized, a process which is usually better done away from the computer in peace and quiet. If the program is not executing correctly, then the necessary changes must be made, and the process begun again. Unfortunately, it is sometimes unclear what is causing an error, in which case, more information must be gained by putting additional instructions in the program. This process is known as **debugging**. Once a program runs without errors and produces the correct results, it can be released for production use. In the case of student programs, this usually implies handing it in for marking.

Documentation

When a program is running, it can provide instructions to the user as to what *An essential* it expects in the way of data or other responses. However, it is not always *part of a good* possible to provide all information about the operation of a program in this *program.* way, and it is then necessary to write a **product manual** or **user's guide** to go with it. Such a document should be written primarily in the terminology of the problem domain, not in computer terms.

On the other hand, there is also a need for a **system manual** or **implementor's guide** which does go into the technical details of the program, and can be used particularly by people who may need to modify the program later.

With modern environments such as Turbo Pascal, it is usual to find that *On-line help.* the documentation is **on-line** and available on the screen while the program is running. It is also possible to write one's own programs with this sort of facility built in.

Maintenance

Finally, the program is up and running, and like any piece of equipment, it *Don't forget this* needs to be maintained. It is not that parts of the program might 'wear out', *part.* but that the environment might change, such as a new kind of disk being added, or even a new processor. It is also true that **requirements** change over time, and because programs are so adaptable, people have come to expect an instant reaction to any desire for change. Thus programs are modified, expanded, speeded up or otherwise altered all the time, and this **maintenance** is a large part of any company's software budget.

As a student, you will be involved in relatively little maintenance, because once a program works, you move on to the next assignment. Nevertheless, it is worth remembering that the care that is put into writing clear programs and documentation to go with them will reduce the effort required to maintain such programs in the future.

1.5 Algorithm development

The development of a good algorithm is central to the process of transforming a problem into a computer program which solves it. Unfortunately, there is no science of algorithms that can be studied formally: much has to be learnt by experience and practice. Nevertheless, there are a few key techniques which we can follow, and which will guide us in the early stages of setting down methods in an orderly way.

We shall illustrate these techniques by considering the example of summing the first 20 positive numbers in a list.

Notations

The first issue we must settle is the notation for writing down an algorithm. There are many notations, some proprietary, some informal and some more suited for business data processing. Commonly used notations are **flow charts** and **pseudo-code**.

Consider the example of summing the first 20 numbers in a list. A flow chart to do this is shown in Figure 1.4. Flow charts have found their way into everyday life, and by their familiarity are reasonably easy to read. Their disadvantages, though, are numerous. They are complicated to draw, and almost impossible to amend; they tend to encourage too much detail immediately, and, most of all, they do not foster the algorithm techniques which good programming practice now promotes.

Flow chart for 'Summing 20 positive numbers'.

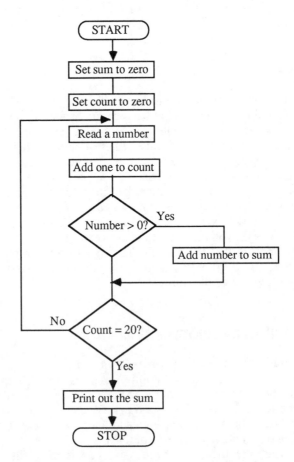

Figure 1.4 A flow chart for summing 20 positive numbers

The flow chart is already more detailed than the corresponding Pascal program would be.

The other popular alternative is pseudo-code, which is a stylised English more akin to modern programming. The same example in a pseudo-code would be:

(1) Set sum to zero
(2) Do 20 times
     (2.1) Read a number
     (2.2) If it is positive, add it to sum
(3) Print the sum

Pseudo-code
for 'Summing
20 positive
numbers'.

Pseudo-code treats algorithms at a higher level than flow charts. It employs indented levels to indicate structure and grouping, and enables us to see the algorithm at different levels of detail. The disadvantage of pseudo-code is that it loses the visual impact that lines and boxes convey.

Pseudo-code charts

In this book, we have chosen to use both charts and pseudo-code in an informal notation called **pseudo-code charts**. The form of pseudo-code charts is as simple as possible, making them easy to draw on paper, freehand.

The chart starts off with a **title** which indicates the overall intention of the algorithm. Thereafter, instructions are given in plain, though abbreviated, English, and lines are used to show alternative and repetitive paths. A pseudo-code chart for summing is given in Figure 1.5.

The box indicates that the instructions must be repeated: the action is given on the right hand side, and the information about how many times it must be done, on the left hand side. The question 'Is it positive?' is followed by an arrow that indicates what should be done in this case. After this choice has been taken, we proceed on and around the chart.

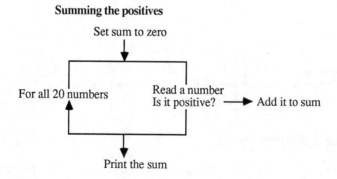

Pseudo-code
chart for
'Summing 20
positive
numbers'.

Figure 1.5 A pseudo-code chart for summing 20 positive numbers

The advantage of an informal notation such as this is that an algorithm can be expressed in greater or lesser detail: we are not restricted to the kinds of instructions that we write down. Some may be at a very high level, such as 'Solve the first equation for x', whereas others are almost atomic actions, such as 'Set sum to zero'. In all other ways, the charts combine the advantages of the other two methods with few of the disadvantages.

Top-down development

Having settled on a notation, we can now discuss some of the algorithm development techniques we shall need in the chapters that follow. The first is as old as the hills – or at least as old as Caesar's invasion of Gaul – and is termed **top-down development**. It involves viewing a problem in its entirety, and then breaking it up into **subproblems**. We then solve the subproblems in the same way, just by breaking them up, until such time as we reach a sub-problem that can be solved by an existing technique, or by a simple sequence of instructions. (Caesar called this **divide-and-conquer**.)

So, if we were taking our previous example from the top down, we would start off thus:

Top level algorithm for summing.

Summing the positives
 Set sum to zero
 Read and add the positive numbers
 Print the sum

The first and last instructions are already as simple as we can make them, but the middle one can be tackled further, giving:

Expanded algorithm for summing.

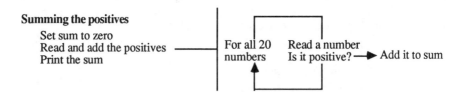

Summing the positives
 Set sum to zero
 Read and add the positives
 Print the sum

For all 20 numbers Read a number Is it positive? ➤ Add it to sum

The line-and-bar notation indicates a refinement of the instruction 'Read and add the positives'. Since we do the refinement step by step, this process is also known as **step-wise refinement**.

Structured programming

Within the field of computer programming, there was a revolution in the 1970s, as computer scientists sought to convert people from programming according to flow charts into something less error-prone. The key to the new methodology, which was known as **structured programming** was the use of a restricted set of constructs, which in themselves were simple, safe, and yet powerful. The three constructs are called:

- sequencing,

- selection,

- repetition.

Sequencing acknowledges that computers follow instructions in an ordered sequence, so that in the absence of any other information, sequencing prevails. Pascal features that support sequencing are the assignment (Section 3.2), input/output (Sections 2.2, 3.3, 5.2, 5.3) and the begin-end statements (Section 3.4).

Selection enables choices to be made, based either on some **condition** or on a **key value**. The idea is that the actions associated with a choice form a closed sequence in themselves, and when they are completed, control returns automatically to after the choice. This is why in our pseudo-code chart we show the following:

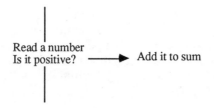

and do not bother to draw a line from 'Add it to sum' back to the main stream. Pascal statements which implement selection are the if-then-else (Section 3.4) and the case-statement (Section 5.4).

Repetition involves doing a sequence of actions several times, with either a count or a condition governing the number of the repetitions. Once again, the important point is that the sequence to be repeated forms a whole, and may not be split up, except by another of the structured constructs. We saw this even in our small example. Within the repeated read-add cycle, there are two paths: one has a read and a question, the other has a read, question and add. The distinction between the two is based on a selection construct in a proper way. Pascal features that implement repetition are the for-loop (Section 2.3), the while and repeat-loops (Section 4.4) and recursion (Section 8.3).

Modular decomposition

Techniques of algorithm development are intimately entwined with good programming practice. Where structured programming helps in the lower levels of programming, a technique called **modular decomposition** assists in the higher levels.

Controlling large projects.

Suppose we have a large, complex problem to solve, and in fact several people – maybe twenty or even a hundred – involved in the project. We would start by dividing up the tasks – but where do we draw the boundaries? How do we decide which subproblems go together, and which depend on the results from others? A complex problem may well not devolve into a simple hierarchical structure as explained in the discussion under top-down development.

Interfaces are the key.

The key here is to decompose the problem into modules based on **interfaces**, whilst keeping the interaction between the modules to a minimum. We start with the different sorts of data in the solution and consider the operations that will be needed to manipulate them. For each sort of data, we parcel it up with its operations into a **module**. The module then decides on which parts of the data and operations it will export to the rest of the program, and reserves for itself those that it does not deem to be of public concern.

In this way, we keep interfaces to a minimum, and lessen the chances of confusion and errors. Even in our little summing example, we can see the benefits of modular decomposition. Suppose this algorithm forms part of a very much larger system. We would set the interface up to be only that data that was necessary to be seen outside – the **black box** approach. Thus the interface could be defined as:

```
PROCEDURE PositiveSums (var sum : integer);
```

The program that used this black box would therefore only be concerned with the data in the sum: it would not have to know anything about number or count, which remain private to the workings of the algorithm.

Pascal features that support modular decomposition are procedures (Sections 2.2, 8.2–4), functions (Section 6.2) and parameters (Sections 2.4, 6.1). Turbo Pascal has added to these with the unit facility (Section 7.4) and object-oriented programming (Section 9.4).

Generalisation

An essential technique for launching an algorithm into the wide world of a programming project is to ensure that it is sufficiently general to be used in all the necessary cases. Take our example. We stipulated that 20 numbers would be read: what if there were 10 instead, or 400? Looking at the algorithm, it is clear that it will not change if there are more or fewer numbers. Thus we can generalise it to handle n numbers, making this part of the interface:

```
PROCEDURE PositiveSums (n : integer;  var sum : integer);
```

Generalisation is supported in Pascal by means of parameters (Sections 2.4, 6.1) and virtual methods in objects (Section 9.4).

Bottom-up and reusable programming

It would be incorrect to believe that top-down is the only way to develop algorithms. We can also start at the opposite end and look for the small problems that can be easily solved. These can form building blocks for the problems higher up. It is all a question of scale: we developed the 'Summing 20 positive numbers' algorithm from the top down, but within a wider picture, it could be part of a bottom-up process to develop tools for later use. In practice, a little bit of both is required – top-down and bottom-up.

The important spin-off from bottom-up development is that algorithms can be reused in many different projects. This is certainly a theme of this book. Many of the algorithms developed in the early chapters form essential tools for more complex problems later on. In all cases, we have taken care to express the algorithms with clear interfaces so that they are self-contained, and can be reused as is. Turbo Pascal also has a considerable library of reusable components, and many of these will be explored in this book.

Software components can be reused.

Data abstraction

Modern thinking is that proper attention to the structure of data in a program is as important as attention to the control constructs. Indeed, we have seen above that the vital technique of modular decomposition depends on the way in which the data is viewed in a program. Knowledge of data structuring techniques is an essential part of any programmer's repertoire. Pascal has a rich choice of such techniques, and these are covered in Chapters 7, 8 and 9.

1.6   Introducing Turbo Pascal

Turbo Pascal is one of the most widely used Pascal systems, world-wide. Version 2, available in the early 1980s, was immediately successful for two reasons: it provided a fast and efficient compilation environment, and it also extended the Pascal language to take account of modern programming trends and advances in the hardware.

Developed by Borland International in California.

These two objectives have continued to guide further revisions of the system, with version 3 in 1985, version 4 in 1986, version 5 in 1988, version 5.5 in 1989, and the latest version 6.0 available since 1990. In terms of what we have learnt in this chapter, Turbo Pascal provides nearly all the software components needed for developing programs – the editor, compiler, debugger, on-line documentation and efficient access to the filing system. The user interface is menu driven, with dialogue boxes, buttons and other pictorial features totally eclipsing the command-line interface associated with operating systems such as DOS. Examples of the interface are shown in the colour plates. Because the interface is so interactive, the best way to learn it is by trying it out. The later versions of Turbo Pascal have many demonstration programs and guided tours that a newcomer can explore.

Turbo vs standard Pascal

For a long time, programmers felt that programs should be written in a standard form of a language, so that they could be moved from one machine to another. However, sticking to a standard meant foregoing any advances in software techniques. Now that it is over 20 years since Pascal was first defined, the benefits of using all the power that is available have come to outweigh the disadvantage of non-portability. A widely distributed system such as Turbo Pascal has become a *de facto* standard, with its own portability base, albeit on a single make of hardware. Figure 1.6 shows a schematic of its main components.

The differences between Turbo Pascal and standard Pascal fall into four groups. These are:

- **Changes**. Some statements (such as case and read) operate slightly differently in Turbo.

- **Omissions**. Turbo has left out some Pascal features, such as conformant array parameters, get and put procedures, and procedural parameters.

- **Additions**. Turbo has added in to the language several new types and has extended the operations available on existing types. In particular, strings, files, procedures and objects have received attention, and some of these additions make up for the omissions.

- **Libraries**. A vital part of Turbo's power is provided by libraries of routines, which give access to graphics, memory management, and the operating system from within a Pascal program.

In addition, the Turbo environment provides its own on-line manuals, known as **help**. At any stage of development, the user can select a term or feature and summon up helpful information about it. Sample help screens are shown in the colour plates.

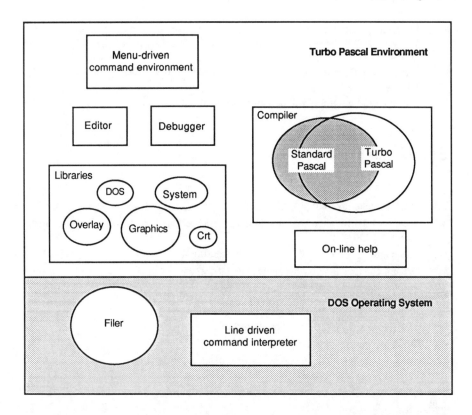

Figure 1.6   A schematic view of Turbo Pascal and DOS

Summary 1

1.   The functions of a **computer** are provided by **programs** and are constrained by the available hardware, software and devices.

2.   Different classes of computers have different **capabilities**, operate at different **speeds**, and are suitable for different **applications**.

3.   The **hardware** of a simple computer comprises a processor, memory, disk drives, screen, keyboard, printer and mouse.

4.   Typical **software** for program development includes a filer, editor, compiler, libraries and debugger.

5.   **Problem solving** involves several well-defined steps, and leads to a solution which can be phrased as a program in a **language** such as Pascal.

6.   Programs need to be carefully designed, written, tested, documented and maintained.

7.   A good notation for **algorithms** will promote structured programming.

8.   Modern algorithm **development** makes use of modular decomposition, generalisation, top-down, bottom-up and reusable programming, and data abstraction.

9.   The **Turbo Pascal** language has both omissions from and additions to standard Pascal.

10.   Turbo Pascal programs will be powerful, but not **portable**.

Self-check quiz 1

1.   What limits the capabilities of a particular computer?

2.   What is meant by multiprogramming?

3.   Explain the difference between the terms microcomputer , microprocessor, personal computer and chip.

4.   In what units is the speed of computers measured?

5.   What is the difference between RAM and ROM?

6.   What is the function of a compiler?

7.   What utilities does the Turbo Pascal environment provide?

8.   List five desirable properties of algorithms.

9.   What is a machine language?

10.   What is meant by a compilation error? By an execution error?

Problems 1

1.   List the input devices and output devices for the computer you are familiar with.

2.   What is the clock speed of the computer you are using?

3.   How much memory does your computer have?

4.   What is the capacity of the disks you are using?

5.   Would this textbook (including all the spaces) fit on your disk, assuming one printed character per byte of memory?

6.   List all the software that you encountered when getting your first Pascal program running on your computer.

7.   List all the computer applications that you come into contact with in the course of an ordinary week.

8.   What algorithms do you come into contact with in an ordinary day? Do they match up to the criteria listed in this chapter?

9.   Have you ever been on the wrong end of a computer error? If so, could you tell whether the mistake was in the program or in the data that was fed in?

10.   Turbo Pascal (version 5.5 and later) comes with a guided tour of the Turbo environment (the command is **tour**). Try it.

2

Beginning with Pascal

Our first introduction to Pascal emphasises the constructs for organising a program in a structured way, and for obtaining satisfying amounts of output with a few simple statements. It includes a look at Turbo Pascal's screen and window facilities.

2.1   Programs and output

A Pascal program consists of:

- **declarations** which describe the objects of a program – its constants, types, variables, functions and procedures;

- **statements** which provide the step-by-step algorithm, making use of the objects.

The **objects** in a program are associated with the data that the program is intended to manipulate. Objects need **identifiers** by which the statements can refer to them. In keeping with the properties of algorithms, the statements are executed in sequence, one after the other. Some statements are specifically designed to alter this sequence, and are sometimes known as **control statements**, because they alter the flow of control of the program.

A program that is solving a real problem will also usually require input and produce output:

- **input** is the actual data that the program will process;
- **output** forms the results of the program's endeavours.

The data and results are considered to be in **files**. Files are held on a device such as a disk, and the particular files required by a program can be specified for each run of the program.

The form of a program

These elements are combined in the program in the following form:

Program

PROGRAM *name (files)*;
    declarations
    BEGIN
        statements
    END.

The plain words such as PROGRAM, BEGIN and END are Pascal **keywords** which indicate the structure of the program. The words in italics describe parts of the program that must be supplied by the programmer. The program name is compulsory, but the files, declarations and statements are optional. Thus the following is a valid Pascal program which does nothing:

```
PROGRAM  DoNothing;
   BEGIN
   END.
```

There are many kinds of declarations and many kinds of statements. Throughout this book we shall be introducing the various declarations and statements in easy stages, until the whole language is covered. We start in this chapter by looking at statements for writing, then we look at the declaration and use of procedures, the statement for a counting loop, and finally a means of generalising procedures. By the end of the chapter, enough will be known about Pascal to perform simple, repetitive, printing tasks in the best possible programming style.

Output of strings

The forms for the Pascal statements to print a piece of text are:

Output statements

write (*list of items*);
writeln (*list of items*);
writeln;

---

where the list of items in parentheses consists of values to be printed, and the items are separated by commas. For the time being, we shall only consider items which are strings.

A **string** is any sequence of characters enclosed in apostrophes, for example:

     'London'   'USA'   '$5.95 per lot'   'User''s Guide'

To include an apostrophe itself in a string, it is given twice, as in the last example.
   A **writeln statement** prints out the list of items and ends the line of print. Thus the statements:

```
writeln('Mr John Smith');
writeln('33 Westridge Road');
writeln('Greenwood');
```

will cause the following to be written out:

Mr John Smith
33 Westridge Road
Greenwood

   The **write statement** works in a similar way except that it does not end the line of print, so that a subsequent write or writeln will continue to print on the same line from the last point reached.
   The list of items is optional for a writeln statement. If it appears on its own, it will finish off the current line. This can be used to obtain a blank line, as in:

```
writeln('Mr John Smith');
writeln;
writeln('33 Westridge Road');
writeln('Greenwood');
```

which would give as output:

Mr John Smith

33 Westridge Road
Greenwood

To include an apostrophe itself in a string, it is given twice.

Pascal statements are given in plain type, and the corresponding output is shown in bold.

Example 2.1 Printing a label

Our first program writes out a name and address for a label. The program is:

```
PROGRAM AddressLabel(output);
  BEGIN
    writeln  ('-----------------------------');
    writeln  ('|                           |');
    writeln  ('|  Mr John Smith            |');
    writeln  ('|  33 Westridge Road        |');
    writeln  ('|  Greenwood                |');
    writeln  ('|                           |');
    writeln  ('-----------------------------');
  END.
```

The program name clearly indicates what the program is to do. The word *output* after the program name indicates that the program is going to make use of an output file to do some writing. The keyword BEGIN indicates the start of the statements. After the keyword END, there is a full stop. The output produced by this program would be:

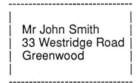

Notice that we can use dashes, bars and other such symbols for effect, in the same way as one would on a typewriter. There are many such printing tricks, and computers are particularly good at them. Further examples in this chapter illustrate some more.

Layout

How the program is written down, in terms of lines and spaces, does not have an effect on how the output appears. Only what is inside the apostrophes is actually written out. When writing strings, there is no gap caused by splitting them up into different items or into different write statements, nor do blank lines in the program have any effect. Therefore the following statements will cause Mr Smith's name and address to be printed as before:

```
writeln ('Mr ', 'John Smith');

write ('33 ');
```

```
writeln  ('Westri',
              'dge Road,');
write('Green');              write('woo'); writeln('d.');
```

The point is that the instructions given to the computer do not have to be in any special layout. We usually write them neatly one underneath each other, and we shall also use **indenting** to make groups of statements stand out, but there is no formal rule that says this should be so. Other points about the form of the program which we can make right now are:

Layout is important for humans.

- more than one statement can be written on a line;
- statements can be split over several lines;
- statements are separated by semicolons.

The effect of this last point is that a semicolon is placed at the end of virtually every statement.

Running the first program

Start Turbo Pascal on your computer (typically by entering the command **turbo**). You should be presented with a screen similar to Figure 2.1 (Turbo 5), or to one of the screens in the colour plates (Turbo 6).

This is the Turbo Pascal environment screen. Across the top is a menu of operations; across the bottom, a key to some function operations (Turbo 5 only). Most common operations can be selected either using a menu choice or a function key operation. The menu selections list the equivalent function codes.

Use the <esc> key or the **Edit** menu selection to enter the Edit window. Once there, type in the program *AddressLabel* above, correcting any errors by use of the arrow keys to move around, and the <del> or backspace keys to erase any errors. Now go back to the menu by using the <F10> function key and select the **Run** menu (either use arrow keys and <return> or the letter **R**). From the Run menu select the Run command. All being well, the output will be written to the screen. With Turbo 6.0 and later, you will be given an opportunity to view your results before pressing return to get back to the Turbo environment. With earlier versions of Turbo, the screen should flash as the output is written to the screen and then <return> directly to the Turbo Pascal environment. To see the output in these versions, select the **User screen** option from the Run menu, or use <alt><F5>.

Editing in Turbo Pascal.

Any Pascal errors will result in an error message on the Edit window, and place the cursor on the offending line. If you get such an error, compare your typing with the example, and correct any discrepancies.

You may save your program, using the **Save** option on the **File** menu or <F2>. You will be asked to rename the file from the default *NONAME*. Enter the new name. Notice that allowable names are up to eight characters long plus *.PAS* (you need not enter the *.PAS* part – the system will add it

About file names.

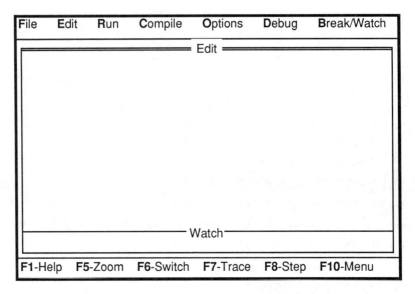

Figure 2.1 Turbo 5 Environment screen

automatically). The **New** option allows you to start a new program. The **Change dir** option allows the use of directories to store your programs. Later, you can use the **Load** or **Pick** (which shows the most recently used files) options on the File menu to retrieve the program again.

Now consider how to tackle a real problem, using the steps outlined in Chapter 1.

Example 2.2   Printing shapes

Problem We wish to have outlines of a little house and a tree.

Solution A solution would be to use a computer to print them, as we have been doing. (Another solution would be to use pencil and paper, but that would spoil this as a programming example!)

Algorithm First of all, we look to see if there are any existing algorithms or bits of program that we can use. So far, we have a program that prints a label: if we exclude the name inside, we would have the effect of printing a rectangle. Similarly, we could devise statements to print a triangle such as:

Using a bit of imagination and adapting the size of the label to be a square, we can construct a house and a tree from these components.

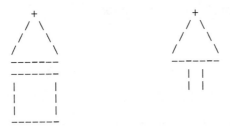

In order to describe the creation of these shapes, we use a notation which consists of a mixture of English and lines. The lines point to refinements of a particular action. Printing a box can be described thus:

Box ———— | Print line
          | Print side bars 3 times
          | Print line

and the house works out as:

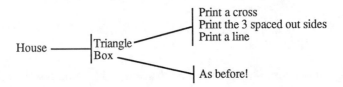

The box bit is not expanded, because how to print a box is already known. Finally there is the tree:

Tree ———— | Triangle
          | Print a double bar
          | Print a double bar

There is a lot of repetition here, which is especially noticeable with the bigger pieces – the box and the triangle. What we now need is a means of packaging up statements to print the individual components, and then a way of using these packages repeatedly in different circumstances, without writing out all the statements again.

2.2   Structuring with procedures

A **procedure** is a group of declarations and statements which is given a name and may be called upon by this name to perform a particular action. A procedure is therefore just like a program – it could in fact be called a **sub-program**. The simple form of a procedure declaration is:

Procedures =
declarations +
statements.

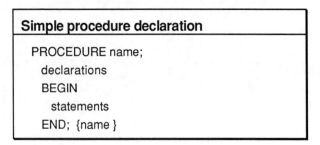

The difference between this form and that for a program is essentially in the last line, where the END is followed by a semicolon, not a full stop, and the name of the procedure is repeated in curly brackets after it. (The name at the end is optional, but conventional, and is used consistently throughout this book.) An example of a procedure would therefore be:

```
PROCEDURE box;
  BEGIN
    writeln('————');
    writeln('|        |');
    writeln('|        |');
    writeln('|        |');
    writeln('————');
  END; {box}
```

Creating a procedure like this is a **declaration**. The name *box* is declared to be the action of performing the given statements.

Having been declared in the declaration part of a program, a procedure can be **called** by mentioning its name thus:

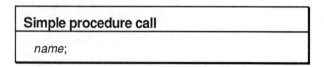

So for example, to print a box, all we need to say is:

```
box;
```

This constitutes a **statement**. When a call statement is executed, the procedure is entered and its statements are performed until its END is reached, whereupon execution passes back to the statement after the call.

Defining procedures in this way will enable us to cut down on repetition, but it also provides a means of creating a structure for a program, and the name of a procedure can be carefully chosen to reflect the action it performs, thus enhancing the readability of the program. With procedures in hand, we can turn again to the problem of the house and tree.

Example 2.3   Shape printing revisited

| Problem | We wish to print a little house and a tree. |

| Solution | Use the algorithm already developed above, together with procedures, to produce a program to print them. |

| Program |

```
PROGRAM Shapes (output);

   PROCEDURE box;
      BEGIN
         writeln('————');
         writeln('|        |');
         writeln('|        |');
         writeln('|        |');
         writeln('————');
      END; {box}

   PROCEDURE triangle;
      BEGIN
         writeln('    +    ');
         writeln('   / \   ');
         writeln('  /   \  ');
         writeln(' /     \ ');
         writeln('————');
      END; {triangle}

   BEGIN
      writeln('****** Printing shapes ******');
      writeln;

      writeln('A house');
      writeln;
      triangle;
      box;
      writeln;

      writeln('A tree');
```

```
            writeln;
            triangle;
            writeln('  ||   ');
            writeln('  ||   ');
        END.
```

There are a few points to note about this fairly substantial program. The procedures come first because they are declarations. Then the program itself begins by printing out an introductory string. This is a good idea, because the appearance of such a message will confirm that the program has begun to run. Then each shape has been given a name, and a few blank lines have been added between shapes.

 The program can be run, and it will produce the following output, as expected.

****** **Printing shapes** ******

A house

```
        +
       / \
      /   \
     /     \
     - - - - - -
     - - - - - -
     |       |
     |       |
     |       |
     - - - - - -
```

A tree

```
        +
       / \
      /   \
     /     \
     - - - - - -
       |  |
       |  |
```

Advantages of procedures

Procedures are vital to the problem solving process. The most important advantage of procedures is their ability to assist in the problem solving process. A solution becomes more manageable when it is divided up into smaller pieces. Each of these can be viewed as a procedure, with a name which reflects its function. Then the work of each procedure can be further broken down, with another layer of procedures to solve the subproblems. A program that is written in this way gives more information to the reader as to its function and its operation than one that consists of a single long sequence of statements.

There are other tangible advantages to procedures. If a procedure is carefully written, it may well be feasible to copy it for use in another program that requires the same functionality. Such a procedure is called **reusable**. Within a single program, procedures can also reduce repetition, thus making a program more compact. The smaller the program, the less memory it uses, and in certain circumstances memory may be at a premium. Thus procedures contribute to the efficiency of a program in terms of **space**. Shorter programs, provided they are neatly laid out, are generally easier to read than longer ones, and procedures contribute substantially to the **readability** of a program.

Procedures make for smaller, more general programs.

2.3   Repetition with counting loops

Computers, like all machines, are very good at doing the same thing over and over again. In a program, such repetition can be formulated as a **loop**. There are two kinds of loops possible in Pascal – **counting** loops and **conditional** loops. In this section we look at how counting loops are achieved; the conditional ones are introduced in Chapter 4.

In order to get on with programming quickly, this section adopts a 'just do it this way' approach for the declarations that have to be associated with loops. The full discussion of how and why these work is given at the start of the next chapter.

The form of a counting loop

A counting loop is specified in two parts, the loop variable declaration and the corresponding for-statement.

More about loops in Chapter 3.

```
Loop variable declaration

    VAR loop variable  :  lower.. upper,
```

```
For statement

    FOR loopvariable := lower to upper DO BEGIN
        statements
    END;
```

As before, the plain words form the template, and the ones in italics have to be appropriately filled in for an actual loop. The VAR declaration introduces a **loop variable** which is intended to operate between the values specified for *lower* and *upper*. These values may be numbers, or characters enclosed in single quotes; for example, the following would be valid loop declarations:

```
VAR
   i      : 1..10;
   letter : 'a' .. 'z';
```

Additional possibilities for loop variables in Chapter 5.

The keyword FOR introduces the loop and states that the loop variable will start at *lower* and finish at *upper*. The keywords DO BEGIN introduce the **loop body** which consists of statements finishing off with the keyword END. Notice that the END is aligned with the FOR and the statements in the body are indented. As some variation on the position of the other keywords is possible, some textbooks place the BEGIN on a separate line underneath the FOR. The present formulation is, however, a neat one and is used throughout this book. Too many capital letters in a program make it hard to read. Usually we only capitalise the first keyword on a line. Because of the introductory keyword, these loops are also known as **for-loops**.

Loop layout is a matter of taste.

The action of the loop is to repeat the statements for each successive value of the loop variable. As a first example, the following declaration and statement will cause five boxes to be printed, each followed by two blank lines. We assume the existence of the *box* procedure as defined earlier:

```
VAR counter : 1..5;

FOR counter := 1 to 5 do begin
   box;
   writeln;
   writeln;
END;
```

Simpler loops

If there is only one statement in the loop body then the keywords BEGIN and END can be omitted. For example, consider how to compress the writing out of the three lines comprising the vertical sides of a box. Using a loop, we could have:

```
VAR  line : 1..3;

FOR line := 1 to 3 do
   writeln('|           |');
```

The effect of this would be to start the loop variable *line* at 1, write the string, go around the loop, set *line* to 2, write the string again, go around, set *line* to

3, and write the string a third time. At this point the values indicated for *line* have been exhausted, and the loop ends.

Using the loop variable

The loop variable serves to record the current iteration of a loop and its values can be used in various ways:

- in a write statement;
- in simple arithmetic;
- as part of the bounds of another loop.

Arithmetic for integers is fully discussed in Chapter 4, but for the time being we note that simple expressions can be formed using addition (+), subtraction (−) and multiplication (*) together with parentheses. The usual rules of precedence apply, so that in the absence of parentheses, multiplication is done before addition or subtraction. *About simple expressions.*

Together, these facilities make looping much more interesting. In order to focus on the looping operations themselves, we shall explore a few examples of loops of this sort. The examples are given as fragments of a Pascal program: it is assumed that the declarations and statements will slot into the appropriate parts of a full program.

Printing sequences

To print out the first ten even numbers, we can have a loop going from one to ten, and then write out double the loop variable, as in:

```
VAR number : 1..10;

FOR number := 1 to 10 do
   write(number * 2);
writeln;
```

which will produce:

2   4   6   8   10   12   14   16   18   20

To print the odd numbers requires a bit of thought. If *number * 2* is an even number, then *number * 2 + 1* or *number * 2 − 1* is an odd number. Choosing one of these expressions, we have:

```
VAR number : 0..9;

FOR number := 0 to 9 do
   write(number * 2 + 1);
writeln;
```

which will produce:

1   3   5   7   9   11   13   15   17   19

A loop variable over characters can be used to print the alphabet, as in:

Loops for
characters.

```
VAR  letter : 'A' .. 'Z';

FOR letter := 'A' to 'Z' do
    write(letter);
writeln;
```

which would produce:

ABCDEFGHIJKLMNOPQRSTUVWXYZ

Nested loops

Since a loop is itself a statement, it can form part of the body of another loop, giving the concept of **nested loops**. For example, we could print a solid block of numbers such as:

```
12345
23456
34567
45678
56789
```

using:

```
VAR i, j : 1..5;

    FOR i := 1 to 5 do begin
    for j := i to i+4 do
        write(j);
    writeln;
    END;
```

An important consideration in nested loops is that the loop variables must be different. If we write:

A trap for the
unwary.

```
for i := ...
    for i := ...
```

havoc will result, as the outer loop variable's value will be altered unexpectedly by the inner loop.

Example 2.4   Landscape features

Problem   We wish to depict a landscape which includes mountains as well as houses and trees. A mountain can be represented by a filled-in shape as in:

```
          **
         ****
        ******
       ********
      **********
     ************
```

Solution   The shape consists of rows, where each row has the number of stars corresponding to its vertical position. Row 1 has 2 stars, row 2 has 4, row 3 has 6 and so on. In order to position the stars in the correct place, we note that the rest of a rectangle drawn around the mountain is spaces, so that in any one row, there is a corresponding number of spaces.

Algorithm   If we were to print only the right side of the mountain, that is:

Breaking a problem into smaller sub-problems.

```
*
**
***
****
*****
******
```

we could use nested loops, as described by the following algorithm.

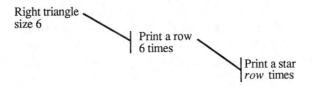

Program   This translates into the following procedure.

```
PROCEDURE RightTriangle;
VAR
   row, star : 1..6;

BEGIN
   FOR row := 1 to 6 do begin
      FOR star := 1 to row do
         write('*');
      writeln;
   END;
END; {RightTriangle}
```

Now consider the full mountain. On each row, there is one less space than the row number, that is, in row 1 there are 5, in row 2 there are 4, and so on. Once we have reached the correct place to start the stars, we print double the number, to get both sides of the mountain. Thus the loops to print the full mountain are:

```
PROCEDURE Mountain;
  VAR
    row, piece : 1..6;

  BEGIN
    FOR row := 1 to 6 do begin
      FOR piece := row + 1 to 6  do
        write (' ');
      FOR piece :=  1 to row do
        write('**');
      writeln;
    END;
  END {Mountain};
```

Skipping the body of a loop

Loop bodies can be skipped. When loop bounds consist of expressions, it may happen that when evaluated, the lower bound may already exceed the upper one. In this case, the loop body is not executed at all. In the *Mountain* procedure, the second nested loop:

```
FOR piece := row + 1 to 6 do . . .
```

will be in this situation when *row* is 6. No dashes are written for this row, which is exactly what was intended.

Counting backwards

Pascal has a further looping option, that of counting backwards. This is seldom needed and is indicated by replacing the *to* in the for-statement by the keyword *downto.* Thus to print the sequence:

10 9 8 7 6 5 4 3 2 1 0 –1 –2 –3 –4 –5 –6

we could say:

```
FOR n := 10 downto –6 do
  write(n);
```

A nice example of counting backwards is found in the song 'One man went to mow', which is discussed in the answers to Problem 2.3 at the end of the chapter.

2.4   Generalising with parameters

Procedures can be made more powerful by allowing the effect to differ slightly each time the procedure is called. For example, we have a procedure that prints a 6 by 6 mountain, and it would be useful to have it be able to print a 10 by 10 mountain, or a 45 by 45 mountain, or whatever. We may even wish to vary the character used to form the mountain – making it a dot or a plus, or whatever.

In other words, the action of printing a mountain by means of write and writeln statements should appear to be independent of the number of writelns that are actually needed. This is called **generalising** or **parameterising** a procedure and the variables that are going to be different are known as **parameters**. What we are aiming at is a means of being able to write:

```
mountain(5, '+');
mountain(10, '/');
mountain(12, '$');
```
A powerful facility.

This is achieved by declaring the procedure with parameters that are given names, like variables, and receive their values at the time the procedure is called. For the mountain, the declaration would become:

```
PROCEDURE mountain(size: integer; symbol : char);
```

There are actually three kinds of parameters in Pascal, but we shall just mention the simplest one – **value parameters** – at this stage. The others are covered in Chapters 6 and 8.

More on parameters in Chapters 6 and 8.

The form of a value parameter list

The parts of the procedure that are to be generalised are listed in the declaration, straight after the procedure name, together with their types. There are many different types in Pascal that we shall be discovering as we go along, but for now, we shall assume the existence of two:

- **integer**, which has values that are whole numbers, both positive and negative, in some large range;
- **char**, which has values that include the letters, digits and special symbols such as those commonly found on a keyboard.

Given this, the form for a procedure declaration with parameters is:

Procedure declaration

PROCEDURE *name* (*list of parameter declarations*);
  declarations
  BEGIN
    statements
  END; {*name*}

The list of parameter declarations looks very much like a list of loop variable declarations, except that we cannot specify the range of the values, and must only give the type, which at this stage we would regard as being integer or char. Each declaration for value parameters has the form:

Value parameter declaration

list of parameters : *type*;

Then somewhere in the body of the program, we would call the procedure with an appropriate list of parameter values for the particular version of the procedure that we want. The form of the call is:

Procedure call with value parameters

name (*list of parameter values*);

For the time being, we shall consider only simple numbers and characters as parameter values: the full power of parameters will be developed in later chapters.

Example 2.5   Assorted mountains

Problem   Set up a procedure to display a mountain of any size, with any character.

Solution   Set up a procedure with two parameters, *size* and *symbol*. Draw the mountain using write and writeln statements in nested counting loops.

| Examples | Examples of mountains produced by the procedure could be: |

Size	Character	mountain
3	$	$$
		$$$$
		$$$$$$
5	*	**
		****
		******
		********
		**********

| Algorithm | The nested loops are familiar from the previous section, so we   Using nested
go straight on to the programming stage. In this case, only a   loops.
procedure is required.

| Procedure |

```
PROCEDURE Mountain (size : integer;  symbol : char);
    VAR row, piece : 1..20;
    BEGIN
      FOR row := 1 to size do begin
        FOR piece := row + 1 to 6 do
          write(' ');
        FOR piece := 1 to row do
          write(symbol, symbol);
        writeln;
      END;
    END; {Mountain}
```

| Testing | Testing a procedure involves trying it out with various actual
parameters. Calling ours in a program with:

Mountain (3, '$');   will give $$
                                            $$$$
                                          $$$$$$

while:

Mountain (5, '*');   will give   **
                                              ****
                                            ******
                                          ****
                                        ****

as in our original examples. If we wanted to draw a mountain of zeros, we must be careful about using the *character* zero for the second parameter, not the number:

Mountain (4, '0'); gives	**00**
	0000
	000000
	00000000

2.5 Turbo Pascal and the screen

Since this text is specifically concerned with the dialect of Pascal known as Turbo Pascal, we shall introduce its features from the beginning. The most exciting addition to Pascal made by systems like Turbo is access to the graphics and colour capabilities of modern computer screens. In the examples that follow, we shall show how these can be used to draw very much more pleasing pictures than those obtainable with write and writeln. At the same time, we shall be exercising the features of Pascal already introduced in this chapter.

Standard procedures and units

Many operations need to be done so often that the procedures to do them are **standard** (built in) and supplied with the Pascal compiler. This includes such procedures as *write* and *writeln*. A list of the available standard procedures will be found in the Turbo Pascal Manuals, and there is a summary of them in Appendix B.

Introducing the Crt unit.
Turbo Pascal also provides a number of extensions to standard Pascal. Many of these are provided as **units.** (You can also, as we'll see later in Chapter 8, write your own units.). One such unit is the **Crt** unit which allows the use of simple character-based graphics. We shall investigate how to compose a pleasing landscape, using procedures from the Crt unit.

Other units which we shall investigate in this book are the Graph unit for good quality graphics (Sections 4.6, 5.6, 6.5, 7.5 and 9.5) and the DOS unit for interfacing with the PC's operating system (Section 8.6).

Defining the screen

The Crt unit views the screen as an (x,y) coordinate system, with the x-axis running across the screen and the y-axis running down.

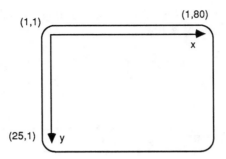

Windows

The most important feature of the Crt in modern programming is the ability to create **windows**. A window is a subarea of the screen, defined by minimum and maximum *x* and *y* coordinates. Once a window has been defined, all output from write and writeln statements goes exclusively to that subarea. We shall demonstrate two of the main uses of windows:

- positioning shapes and text at different places on the screen, without changing the original procedures;

Using windows for effect.

- using different portions of the screen for different aspects of the output and interface with the user.

We shall look at the first point here and the second one in Chapter 3.

The term 'windows' is unfortunately rather overused now. In addition to windows in the Crt unit, Turbo Pascal provides windows in the Graph unit (which we shall learn about later) – also called **viewports**. Moreover, operating systems are now coming out with their own windowing facilities, which Turbo Pascal exploits via 'Turbo for Windows' and more specialised units. The concept is the same in each case: it is the level of sophistication which changes. The Crt can be said to provide plain glass windows, whereas 'Turbo for Windows' provides everything that opens and shuts!

There are windows and windows.

Defining a Crt window

To define a Crt window, we call the *Window* procedure from the Crt unit, which is defined as:

```
PROCEDURE Window (xmin, ymin, xmax, ymax : byte);
```

The type of the parameters is given as *byte*, which holds a small integer value. Thus to declare a window 10x10 large, roughly in the centre of the screen, we would call:

```
window (35, 6, 44, 15);
```

Because we are no longer scrolling the output, it is important to first clear the screen, and this is done by calling:

PROCEDURE ClrScr;

also from the Crt.

Example 2.6   Composing a picture

Problem   We would like to draw a picture of a house, trees and mountains, something like this:

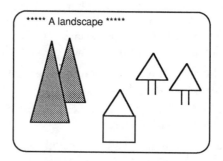

Solution   We can achieve an approximate effect by using the Crt. First we summarise all the bits and pieces that we already have for drawing shapes, and that we can reuse in the solution. These are:

- procedures to print a box and a triangle (from Example 2.2);

- examples of how to compose these into a house and a tree (also Example 2.2);

- a procedure to print a mountain of any size (from Example 2.5).

We want to be able to call the existing procedures, interspersed with the necessary positioning information. For this we can use windows.

Algorithm   Layout is an important part of this program, and we can, if we like, work out the position of each shape by trial and error. Let us take the house as an example. It is more or less in the bottom centre of the screen, and we know that it occupies about 10 characters across and 10 down. There is no harm in creating fairly roomy windows, since the unused parts of overlapping windows do not interfere with each other. We shall choose a 12x12 window for the house as follows:

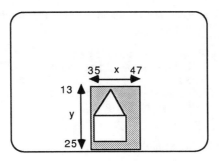

So to draw this part of the picture, we would say:

```
window (35, 13, 47, 25);
triangle;
box;
```

Because we have defined the window, each time there is a writeln statement, the next line starts on the left edge of the window, not on the left edge of the screen. Drawing the rest of the shapes follows a similar process.

| Program | The program makes use of the existing components. The main adaptation is the creation of a special *Tree* procedure, which calls the *triangle* procedure and then writes out the stem. Since trees are written twice, it makes sense to formalise the process in this way. | Procedures containing procedures. |

```
PROGRAM Landscape (input, output);
  USES Crt;

  PROCEDURE box;
    BEGIN
      writeln('————————');
      writeln('|          |');
      writeln('|          |');
      writeln('|          |');
      writeln('————————');
  END; {box}

  PROCEDURE triangle;
    BEGIN
      writeln('     +     ');
      writeln('    / \    ');
      writeln('   /   \   ');
      writeln('  /     \  ');
      writeln('————————');
  END; {triangle}
```

```
PROCEDURE Mountain (size : integer;  symbol : char);
  VAR row, piece : 1..20;
  BEGIN
    FOR row := 1 to size do begin
      FOR piece := row+1 to size do
        write(' ');
      FOR piece := 1 to row do
        write(symbol, symbol);
      writeln;
    END;
  END; {Mountain}

PROCEDURE Tree;
  BEGIN
    triangle;
    writeln('      | |');
    writeln('      | |');
  END; {Tree}

BEGIN
  ClrScr;
  writeln('***** A Landscape *****');
  window (35, 13, 47, 25);
  triangle;
  box;

  window(50, 5, 66, 14);
  Tree;
  window(60, 8, 76, 18);
  Tree;

  window (15,6,36,20);
  Mountain (8, '@' );
  window (1,7,42,23);
  Mountain (10,'*');
END.
```

Testing	Running the program should produce output similar to that proposed above.

Shading and colour

The Crt unit also provides facilities for altering the intensity of the output on the screen, using one of:

If you do not have colour.

```
PROCEDURE HighVideo;
PROCEDURE LowVideo;
PROCEDURE NormVideo;
```

Thus we could draw the mountains in different shades of the same symbol as follows:

```
LowVideo;
    window (15,6,36,20);
    Mountain (8, '*' );
Highvideo;
    window (1,7,42,23);
    Mountain (10,'*');
NormVideo;
```

If the computer you are using has a colour monitor, then you can also select the different colours for the background and the printing, using:

```
PROCEDURE TextBackground (color : byte);
PROCEDURE TextColor (color : byte);
```

where the color (note the American spelling) can be any one of the following:

0	Black
1	Blue
2	Green
3	Cyan
4	Red
5	Magenta
6	Brown
7	LightGray
8	DarkGray
9	LightBlue
10	LightGreen
11	LightCyan
12	LightRed
13	LightMagenta
14	Yellow
15	White

The numbers can be used in place of the words, and this is shown to advantage in the next and final example for this chapter.

Example 2.7   Goodbye

Problem We would like to print colourful goodbyes on the screen.

Solution We shall print four rows of four goodbyes each in the centre of the screen, and change the colour for each goodbye.

Algorithm This is obviously going to be a useful and reusable idea, so we shall conceive it as a procedure from the start. If we set up the window exactly correctly, we can simply write out the 16 goodbyes, using the loop variable to stipulate the text colour each time. The window should allow exactly 4 goodbyes per line, that is the *x*-width should be 4x7=28. On the other hand, the *y*-length must be one larger than 4, to avoid the scrolling effect when the last character in the window is filled.

Windows need extra space.

| Program | The procedure is:

See the colours in the plates.

```
PROCEDURE Goodbye;
   VAR c : 0..15;
   BEGIN
     window (22,10,49,15);
     for c := 0 to 15 do begin
       TextColor(c);
       write('Goodbye');
     end;
   END; {Goodbye}
```

| Testing | The procedure can be tested by putting it in any of the programs so far, and calling it at the end. Remember to include the Crt unit by means of a *USES Crt* statement, if it is not already there. You will notice that this window simply overwrites anything that was there before: this may be disconcerting, as one might wish to consider the output carefully, before seeing the goodbye message. Ways of making a program wait until the user is ready to continue are discussed in Section 4.2.

What lies ahead

We have taken a very quick tour through programs which incorporate write statements, simple procedures and counting loops, and looked at how Turbo Pascal makes displaying these on the screen very effective. The next chapter looks more closely at Pascal syntax and semantics, and introduces more of the basic concepts of programming. As more about Pascal is learnt, so can more exciting examples be investigated, illustrating that computers can be really useful tools.

Summary 2

1.   Programs consist of **declarations** and **statements**.

2.   **Output** is performed through the write and writeln statements.

3.   **Layout** of statements is important for readability.

4.   **Procedures** are groups of statements that serve a common purpose and can be called upon from other places in the program.

5.   Statements can be repeated by grouping them in a **counting loop**. Counting loops consist of a loop variable declaration and a FOR statement.

6.   The **loop variable** can be printed out from inside the loop, used in simple arithmetic or used to draw pictures.

7.   The loop variable should always specify the **range** of the corresponding loop. If the lower bound of a loop exceeds the upper, then the body of the loop is not performed at all. Loop variables can be used to count backwards if DOWNTO is specified.

8.   Procedures can be made more general by giving them **parameters**. Parameters are declared with their types, but not with ranges.

9.   Turbo Pascal enables the program to control the position of writing on the screen through the **window** facility, supplied by the **Crt** unit.

10.   The **intensity** and **colour** of writing on the screen can be altered through procedures in Turbo's Crt unit.

Self-check quiz 2

1.   What is the difference between a write statement and a writeln statement?

2.   Can a program have two loop variables of the same name?

3.   Give the for-statements and write statements that will print the sequence **0 10 20 30 40** ...

4.   Spot the errors in the following program.

```
PROGRAM Messy (input, output)

VARIABLE loop : 1..5;

PROCEDURE Tops;
   writeln('Tops');
END; {Tops}

BEGIN
   FOR loop = 1 .. 10 do begin
      write('Programming is ');
      Tops;
      writeln(!);
   end;
END;
```

5.   Which would appear first in a program listing – the declaration of a procedure or the call of it?

6.   The following procedure is meant to print out the five times table. What will it actually print out? Correct it in two different ways.

```
PROCEDURE Fivetimes;
   VAR multiple : 1..12;
   BEGIN
      for multiple := 1 to 12 do
         write('5 times ');
         write(multiple);
         write('is');
         writeln(5*multiple);
   END; {Fivetimes}
```

7.   How many stars would be printed by:

FOR star := 10 downto 5 do write('*');

8.   Write a for-loop to print the sequence **–13 –5 3 11 19 27 35** .

9.   What will the following statements and calls to the Crt unit produce?

```
window (1,1,1,25);
writeln('Hello');
```

10.   Devise statements and procedure calls to the Crt which will print Hello in yellow in the centre of the screen.

Problems 2

Answers are provided for problems marked with a §.

2.1§ **Printing names** Write procedures to print out the letters of the alphabet that form your name, in a large format using asterisks. Each letter is formed on a 9 by 7 grid. For example, some of the letters might look like this:

Then write a program to call the procedures in the right order to print your name. You will need to use windows to get each letter in the right place on the screen.

2.2§ **Mystery output** Given the following program, what output does it produce?

```
PROGRAM Mystery (output);
VAR i : 1..2;

PROCEDURE splodge;
VAR line : 1..4;
BEGIN
  FOR line := 1 to 4 do
    writeln('********');
END; {splodge}

BEGIN
  FOR i := 1 to 2 do begin
    splodge;
    writeln('   | |');
    writeln('   | |');
    writeln('   | |');
    splodge;
    writeln;
  END;
END.
```

2.3§ **One man went to mow** Write a program which uses loops to print out the song 'One man went to mow'. Use digits rather than words for the numbers, as in:

```
1 man went to mow, went to mow a meadow,
1 man and his dog, went to mow a meadow.
```

2 men went to mow, went to mow a meadow,
2 men, 1 man and his dog, went to mow a meadow.

3 men went to mow, went to mow a meadow,
3 men, 2 men, 1 man and his dog, went to mow a meadow.

2.4§ **Times tables** In the olden days, exercise books used to have multiplication tables printed neatly on the back. These would be arranged 3 across and 4 down, with each row being of the form:

```
 4 times table        5 times table        6 times table
 1 x   4 =    4        1 x   5 =    5        1 x   6 =    6
 2 x   4 =    8        2 x   5 =   10        2 x   6 =   12
 3 x   4 =   12        3 x   5 =   15        3 x   6 =   18
 4 x   4 =   16        4 x   5 =   20        4 x   6 =   24
 5 x   4 =   20        5 x   5 =   25        5 x   6 =   30
 6 x   4 =   24        6 x   5 =   30        6 x   6 =   36
 7 x   4 =   28        7 x   5 =   35        7 x   6 =   42
 8 x   4 =   32        8 x   5 =   40        8 x   6 =   48
 9 x   4 =   36        9 x   5 =   45        9 x   6 =   54
10 x   4 =   40       10 x   5 =   50       10 x   6 =   60
11 x   4 =   44       11 x   5 =   55       11 x   6 =   66
12 x   4 =   48       12 x   5 =   60       12 x   6 =   72
```

Write a program which makes good use of procedures and parameters to print out a complete set of all the 12 multiplication tables.

2.5   **Chequer board** A chequers (or draughts) board consists of alternating squares of black and white, eight across and eight down. Investigate ways of drawing such a board on the screen. Two suggested approaches are:

- print a row of the screen at a time, carefully organising an inner loop to swap the colours;

- use windows to print a square at a time, using an outer loop to swap the colours, and inner loops to govern the coordinates of the squares.

2.6§ **Number triangle** Write a program which uses for-statements and write statements to produce the following triangle:

```
1
2  2
3  3  3
4  4  4  4
5  5  5  5  5
```

Adapt the program in the previous problem to print the triangle so that the numbers are centred, as below. Adapt it again to print the triangle upside down.

```
      1
   2  2
  3  3  3
 4  4  4  4
```

3

Changing and choosing

In this chapter, the ideas of syntax and semantics are introduced, the declarations section is fleshed out, and three new statements are added – for assigning, reading and selecting alternative paths. The chapter introduces the first case study of a program to calculate income tax. It concludes with a look at random numbers and how they can be used to help test programs.

3.1 Basic syntax

Like any natural language (such as English or Spanish), Pascal has rules determining what is correct and what is not correct. The difference is that computer languages are more fixed, having relatively few permitted words and few ways of composing them into statements. This actually makes learning the language easier, and one expects to be able to master the rudiments of a computer language in a matter of weeks, whereas mastering a natural language may take years.

Keywords, identifiers and comments have their own simple rules, which will be discussed below. The punctuation allowed in Pascal is a mixture of ordinary marks such as comma, semicolon and parentheses, and arithmetic symbols such as + and /. These are introduced as needed in the next few chapters.

Spaces and blank lines are important in aiding the readability of a Pascal program, and should be used freely. One word of caution – if a program has many blank lines, or has statements spread out over several lines, then the amount of information that can be displayed on a screen is limited, and it may be hard to understand a program that is presented in small fragments. In this book, we tend to use blank lines between procedures, and to keep statements fairly compact. Other books use other conventions, such as always putting BEGIN on a new line. The resulting spread over several pages of what could be a short program does not really aid readability.

Pascal programs are usually typed in small letters or **lower case** but free use can be made of capital letters (known as **upper case**) for emphasis. Some Pascal systems have built into them **pretty printers** which will reformat your program into a fixed style of indenting and mixture of cases, while some systems insist on lower-case letters only. We shall assume that you can control how your programs are written, and we shall adopt a neat, consistent style for laying them out.

Keywords

There are 48 words in Turbo Pascal which have special meanings and are reserved for use as **keywords**. Some of these are:

PROGRAM	PROCEDURE
BEGIN	to
USES	do
FOR	VAR
IF	then

Keywords can be written in small letters or in capitals, depending upon which looks better at the time. The convention we use is that the first keyword on a line, such as PROCEDURE or FOR, is written in capitals, while other less important words such as *to* and *of* can stay in small letters. Other text books have different conventions, sometimes putting all keywords in capitals, or using bold or italics for this effect. The point is that Pascal doesn't care about case, so that all the following are valid versions of a keyword:

PROCEDURE	Procedure
pRoCeDuRe	**procedure**
procedure	

Two of Pascal's keywords – CONST and VAR – are abbreviations. They introduce the constant and variable sections of the declarations, and must be used in this abbreviated form. However, other keywords cannot be abbreviated. For example, PROC cannot be used for PROCEDURE.

Identifiers

The terms 'name', 'word' and 'identifier' have been used rather loosely up to now to describe sequences of letters. The proper Pascal term is **identifier**, and there is a precise definition of what constitutes an identifier:

> An **identifier** is a sequence of letters and digits that
> * starts with a letter,
> * treats the lower- and upper-case letters as equivalent,
> * does not have the same spelling as any keyword.

Although standard Pascal does not, many versions of Pascal, including Turbo Pascal, allow the use of the underscore character as if it were a letter, to improve readability. Identifiers may not include spaces. This restriction becomes important when identifiers are formed from phrases rather than from single nouns or verbs. A convention often used is to employ the second property and put a capital letter at the start of each English word, thus serving to break up an otherwise confusing jumble of letters. For example, we could write:

Pascal identifiers may not include spaces.

	ReduceToOne
or	*reduce_to_one*
rather than	*reducetoone*

Bearing all this in mind, which of the following are valid identifiers?

Capitals are useful for breaking up long identifiers.

ReduceToOne	LastLimit
t	rectangles
FirstValue	second_value
1stvalue	Hello!
X	MI5
Maxsides	end
water-level	Number of lines

The following ones are invalid, for the reasons given:

1stvalue	cannot start with a digit
Hello!	! is not a letter or digit
end	END (and hence end) is a keyword
water-level	- is not a letter or digit
Number of lines	spaces are not letters or digits

Mistakes in the formation of identifiers are detected by the compiler. Turbo Pascal normally shows the offending word and prints a message such as:

without any explanation as to what exactly is wrong. The most common mistakes are using a keyword or starting an identifier with a digit. However, after a few weeks of programming, the rules become second nature.

Predefined identifiers

Pascal has certain identifiers which are predefined for all programs, but are not keywords. Some we have seen are:

Integer and
writeln should
not be in
capitals.

```
integer
write
writeln
```

and others will be introduced later. The point about these identifiers is that they should be regarded as keywords from the point of view of not defining them as something else. If we declared the word *write* as a loop variable, say, then the original meaning of *write* would be lost, and trying to use it for writing would fail. Once again, conforming to this restriction should become natural after a while.

Comments

Although Pascal is a precise language, parts of programs can sometimes be a bit cryptic. To make these parts easier to understand, comments can be added.

> A **comment** is any text enclosed in { }, except curly brackets themselves.

(Most systems, including Turbo Pascal, permit (* and *) to stand for curly brackets.) Apart from explaining what is going on, comments are also used to amplify the bare syntax of Pascal in various ways. One such example is the practice of following the end of a procedure with its name, as in:

```
PROCEDURE Mountain (size : integer; symbol : char);
    ...
END; {Mountain}
```

Other occasions for comments will be introduced later, but we note here that comments should only be used to amplify the Pascal, not to duplicate it.

Syntax

In Chapter 2, we introduced the *form* of various parts of a program with three such forms being given – for the program itself, for a procedure and for a counting loop. To recall, the forms for procedure declarations and counting loops are:

Simple procedure declaration

```
PROCEDURE name;
   declarations
   BEGIN
      statements
   END; {name }
```

Loop variable declaration

```
VAR loopid : lower.. upper;
```

For-statement

```
FOR loopid := lower to upper do begin
   statements
END;
```

These forms are ways of describing the **syntax** of Pascal. The syntax defines exactly which words are needed in what order to achieve a desired effect. In the notation we have used for the syntax, the plain words are those that *have* to be there, forming a **template**, while the words in italics represent syntactical elements that are filled in each time.

There are other more formal ways of representing syntax, one of which uses so-called bubble diagrams. In this notation, the counting loop would be described as in Figure 3.1. Such diagrams are useful when writing a compiler or resolving difficult syntactical points, but for the purposes of learning the language, the template approach is adequate. Nevertheless, the complete diagrams for Turbo Pascal are given in Appendix G.

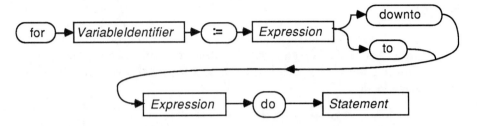

Figure 3.1 Syntax diagram for a for-loop

Semantics

Whereas syntax gives the form of the Pascal construct, the semantics tell us how it works, or what it means. In most cases, it is sufficient to describe the semantics in clear English. Consider, for example, the description of the for-statement from Section 2.3:

Semantics of a
for-statement.

> The action of the loop is to repeat the statements for each successive value of the loop variable within its given range.

This is followed by examples and further details of the special cases that may occur. In keeping with the tutorial style followed in this book, the semantics are discussed in the text and summarised at the end of each chapter. For a more succinct description of semantics, one should consult the Pascal Standard.

3.2 Variables, constants and assignment

A Pascal program, as we saw before, consists of:

- declarations, and
- statements.

The purpose of the declarations is to associate identifiers with the objects that are going to be used in the statements. There are six kinds of declaration, each of which is introduced by a special keyword, viz:

CONST	PROCEDURE
TYPE	FUNCTION
VAR	USES

The first three introduce constant, type and variable declarations. The next two define procedures and functions, and the last one is a special Turbo Pascal keyword which announces any units used and must come before the others.

In standard Pascal, there is a strict ordering of these sections, and the first three can occur only once each. Turbo Pascal has relaxed this rule, and declaration sections can be intermingled and repeated as necessary. However, the discipline of declaring in the standard order has its advantages, and we have followed it for the most part in this book.

Ordering of sections is optional.

In this section we look at constant and variable declarations; type declarations are covered in Chapters 6 and 7 and there are more details about procedures and functions in Chapters 6 and 8. Units are discussed in full in Chapter 7.

Variables

The Pascal programs in Chapter 2 were fairly rudimentary in that they did certain things without much change. Changes did come about through adding for-loops, the provision of parameters and in setting different windows. All of these rely on **declarations**. The loop variable acquired different values as the loop progressed, and these values could actually be used to alter the effect of other statements. The parameter could acquire a different value each time the procedure was called. This idea of different values being represented by the same identifier at different stages in the execution of a program is generalised in the concept of a variable:

> A **variable** denotes a value that may change during execution. Every variable has associated with it an identifier and a type. The type determines the range of values of the variable and governs how the variable may be used.

Variables record the changing state of a program.

Variables are declared in var-declarations. After the keyword VAR, any number of variables may be declared, with their associated types, as in:

Variable declaration

VAR
    identifiers : *type*;
    identifiers : *type*;

    . . .

    identifiers : *type*;

If there is more than one identifier for a type, then they are separated by commas. The type may be one of the six main predefined types, which are:

integer	real	boolean
char	text	string

or one of the special Turbo types (included in Appendix A) or a user-defined type, as described in Chapters 6 and 7.

If the type is integer or char (for character), then we can indicate the actual range of values needed instead, using a **subrange** as follows:

Subranges make variable declarations more specific.

Subrange type

---

lower .. upper

Thus instead of specifying:

    VAR height : integer;

we try to be specific, as in:

    VAR
       height : 0 .. 5; {metres}

It is a good idea to use a comment to give any other useful information such as physical units, currencies and so on.

For this chapter, we shall only deal with integers and characters. Within this limitation, examples of declarations are:

Line up the types.

```
VAR
   side          : 1..3;
   grade         : 'A' .. 'F';
   line          : 1..10;
   temperature : -50..60;  {in degrees Celsius}
   initial       : char;
   myweight,
   yourweight   : 0..250;   {in kilograms}
   x, y, z       : integer;  {unknowns}
```

It is worthwhile keeping declarations neat and tidy, with the identifiers and types lined up.

Assignment

Having declared a variable, we can now use an assignment to give it a value. The assignment statement has the form:

> ### Assignment statement
>
> *variable := expression;*

An expression consists of variables, constants, literals, functions and operators combined together in a way consistent with the type of identifier on the left hand side. For integers, simple expressions can be formed using the operators for plus (+), minus (–), multiplication (*) and division (**div**) as well as parentheses. The div operator performs integer division, discarding the remainder. A full discussion of expressions is given when the properties of each type are explored.

Short introduction to expressions.

> The effect of an **assignment statement** is to evaluate the expression and to assign the resulting value to the variable indicated by the identifier.

The symbol which indicates the assignment is read 'becomes'. Thus we can write:

    temperature := 24;

and read it '*temperature* becomes 24'. The value of the expression is 24, and this is assigned to the variable *temperature*. In the next sequence:

    myweight := 65;
    yourweight := myweight + 5;

myweight is assigned the value 65, and this is then used to calculate the value for the variable *yourweight* which is 70.
To test that you understand this, what will be the values of *p, q* and *r* at the end of the following sequence of assignments?

    p := 8;
    q := 5;
    r := q;
    q := q + 1;
    p := p + q – 2 * r;

Tracing the action of a program.

It is always useful in these cases to examine what is going on by simulating what the computer would do, keeping track of the values of variables as each statement is executed. We can construct such a 'trace' for the above statements by recording each variable's values in a column, using ~ to mean that a value has not yet been assigned.

statement	p	q	r
	~	~	~
p := 8;	8	~	~
q := 5;	8	5	~
r := q;	8	5	5
q := q + 1;	8	6	5
p := p + q − 2 * r;	4	6	5

Thus the answers are 4, 6 and 5 respectively for *p*, *q* and *r*.

Some points about variables

The variables in a program together hold a record of the **state** of the program at any one instant. Reasoning about state, and its correctness, is difficult, so it is generally good practice to keep the number of variables to a minimum. However, variables are required when a state needs to be remembered for later use, or for transmitting values between statements. One way of keeping the number of variables to manageable proportions is to ensure that they are declared specifically in the procedures that need them, rather than all together at the start of a program.

Two problems which illustrate the use of variables rather well are now discussed.

Example 3.1   Swapping

| Problem | The values in two variables need to be interchanged. |

| Solution | Write some assignment statements. |

| Algorithm | Suppose the variables are called *x* and *y*. A first stab at an answer might be: |

```
x := y;
y := x;
```

What happens here? If *x* has the value 5 and *y* has the value 9, then a trace reveals:

statement	x	y
	5	9
x := y;	9	9
y := x;	9	9

The result is incorrect. The problem occurs in the first statement, when the value of *y* is put in *x* causing the original value of *x* to be lost. In order for the swap to work correctly, the value of *x* must first be copied, so that it can subsequently be used for setting up *y*. To do this, an additional variable is needed. Since it is only of temporary use, it will be called *temp*. The correct sequence of statements is:

Swapping needs a temporary resting place.

```
temp := x;
x := y;
y := temp;
```

and the trace would be:

statement	x	y	temp
	5	9	~
temp:= x;	5	9	5
x := y;	9	9	5
y := temp;	9	5	5

~ means not yet defined.

Example 3.2 The Fibonacci sequence

Problem A Fibonacci sequence consists of a series of numbers in which each number is the sum of the two preceding ones. Print the first ten numbers in such a sequence.

Example The first ten Fibonacci numbers are:

1 1 2 3 5 8 13 21 34 55

Solution The Fibonacci numbers are defined by an algorithm in which each number is calculated from its two predecessors. The first two Fibonacci numbers are 1 and 1. A loop can be used to calculate each number in turn from its predecessors.

Algorithm As a first try, consider a loop consisting of:

Print the sum of the two numbers
Make the first number the second
Make the second number the sum of the two numbers

This won't work for a similar reason to the previous example: a value has been overwritten by the time it is needed. In this case, on the last line, the sum is needed, but by this time, the first number has already been changed. So we need to remember the sum at the time of printing it, and use this for the new second value. The algorithm should be:

A Fibonacci
algorithm.

Calculate the sum of the two values
Print the sum
Make the first number the second
Make the second number the sum (as calculated earlier)

The program follows easily.

| Program |

```
PROGRAM Fibonacci (output);
VAR
    first,
    second,
    sum : 1..100; {say}
    i    : 3..10;  {say}
BEGIN
    writeln('****** First 10 Fibonacci numbers ******');
    first := 1;
    second := 1;
    write(first, ' ', second);
    for i := 3 to 10 do begin
      sum := first + second;
      write (' ', sum);
      first := second;
      second := sum;
    end;
    writeln;
END.
```

Literals and constants

The type integer has associated with it a notation for **literals** that is particular to it and which produces the usual form of numbers 0, 1, 2 and so on. Other types that we shall encounter will have less obvious forms for literals, so it is worth noting and remembering the concept.

Disadvantages
of literals.

Literals can be freely used in a program, but doing so has two disadvantages:

- there is no information given as to what the literal stands for;

- changing a literal that appears several times in a program can be error-prone.

Both these factors can be overcome by declaring a **constant** with a name and a value. Thereafter the named constant can be used wherever the literal is required. The name should convey more information than a plain number, and if the value has to change, then the change need only be made once – in the declaration.

Constants are declared in the CONST section which has the form:

> **Constant declaration**
>
> CONST
>   *identifier = value*;
>
>   . . .
>
>   *identifier = value*;

and there can be several declarations under one heading as follows:

```
CONST
     max          = 10;
     speedlimit   = 90;    {kph}
     gramsperkilo = 1000;
     grams        = 'g';
     Kilo         = 'K';
     Firstname    = 'John';
     Surname      = 'Williams';
     space        = ' ';
```

If, for example, *max* were to be raised to 50, say, then only this one declaration would need to be altered, not all occurrences of 10. Since there may be occurrences of the literal 10 which are not related to *max,* confusion is also avoided. Advantages of named constants.

In Turbo Pascal, the value of a constant may be specified by a constant expression – an expression containing no variables, so that its value will be fixed. This is useful when we wish to have the value of one constant depend on the value of another, previously defined, constant. Furthermore, in Turbo Pascal, addition can apply to strings, which can be very useful. The following constants are based on the previous list. Turbo Pascal allows constant expressions.

```
CONST
     bigmax     = max * 10;
     urbanlimit = speedlimit − 40;
     fullname   = firstname + space + surname;
```

Initialising

When variables are declared, no value is specified for them. Thus variables must always be initialised by the program before being used. This point is illustrated by the traces in Section 3.2 above, where variables which had not been touched had tildes (~) to indicate that they were undefined. The importance of remembering this property is brought out in the next example.

Global and local variables

Side effects are
bad.

The variables that are declared at the program level are termed **global** and are available for use by all procedures within the program. If a global variable is changed by some procedure by mistake – perhaps because different people were writing different procedures – then errors will occur that will be difficult to trace. A procedure that changes a global variable is said to have a **side effect**, and side effects are generally a bad thing. Thus we would like to keep our procedures **self-contained** and limit, if not entirely avoid, side effects.

At present we have not learnt enough about Pascal to eliminate side effects, but we can keep them to a minimum by declaring variables specifically in the procedures that need them, rather than all together at the start of a program. These variables are called **local** variables, and one can rely upon them being altered only by the statements within the procedure itself.

Using parameters does not in itself reduce the need for global variables, since one still needs to send a value into the procedure, and this could be in a variable. However, defining procedures with parameters makes them more self-contained and less reliant on globals.

3.3 Input with read and readln

A program will most often need to acquire values for its variables from the outside world. Such values form the **data** for the program and could consist of tables stored on disk, replies to questions or just lists of values to be typed in. Values for variables are acquired by means of the read and readln statements.

The form of read and readln statements

The three general forms of these statements are:

Input statements

read (*list of variables*);
readln (*list of variables*);
readln;

The list of variables consists of identifiers separated by commas, as in:

    read(myweight, yourweight, temperature);

Data must be supplied which conforms with the types required. Thus for this statement, suitable data would be:

    65 70 23

The read statement picks off values to put into each variable in its list, and is quite happy to skip over spaces and blank lines when looking for a number. It will not usually skip over anything else, so that, using the ordinary read statement, we cannot put other information between numbers, such as:

    65kgs   70kgs   23degrees C

The readln statement works just like the read statement except that when it has filled up all its variables, it looks for the end of line, skipping everything in its path.

Numbers should be separated by, or ended with, a space or the end of a line.

Example 3.3   Summing a list of numbers

Problem   There is a list of numbers that needs to be summed.

Solution   It is quite straightforward to read the numbers into the computer, adding each one in turn to a total. The problem is how to know when the end of the numbers has been reached. There are actually four ways:

- **state in advance** how many numbers there must be and keep a running count;
- **precede the data by a count** of how many numbers there actually are, and keep a running count;
- put a **special terminating value** at the end of the numbers, such as zero or 999;
- make use of an **end-of-file property** to mark the end of the numbers.

The first two methods are applicable to counting loops, since they rely on the number of numbers being known before reading starts. In the next two methods the number of numbers is not relevant, rather the reading stops when a certain condition is achieved. These two are applicable to conditional loops, and are discussed in Sections 4.4 and 5.3 respectively.

Of the two methods for counting loops, the second is more general, since the same program will be able to read in 10 numbers, or 55, or 1800, with just the data being changed.

| Algorithm |

Summing a list of numbers
Read in the count
Set the total to zero

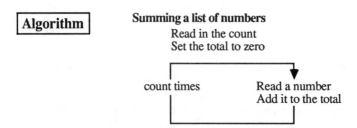

count times   Read a number
                     Add it to the total

The algorithm is fairly simple, but has one important feature: the total must be initialised to zero before adding commences.

| Program | In the program header, the parentheses now include *input* as well as *output*, since the program is going to be reading and writing.

```
PROGRAM Summation1 (input, output);
  CONST
    max = 10000;
  VAR
    count ,
    i         : 1..max;
    total,
    number : integer; {anything}
  BEGIN
    writeln('****** Summing numbers ******');
    read(count);
    total := 0;
    FOR i := 1 to count do begin
      read(number);
      total := total + number;
    END;
    writeln;
    writeln('The total is ', total);
  END.
```

| Testing | If this program was run, and we knew how to put in the data, then the screen might have the following on it:

****** Summing numbers ******
7 85 65 43 90 12 55 50
The total is 407

The plain type indicates the values that are typed in; bold type indicates output from the program. The problem is that not all users of a program will know how the data has to be entered, and therefore the program should give some guidance. Let's examine this issue in full.

Interactive programs

An **interactive program** is one that is run with the user sitting in front of a terminal and entering data as necessary. This is how most programs are run these days, and even large programs will start off with a bit of dialogue before starting on their computations. In interactive mode, it is the computer program, rather than the user, that is in control all the time. The program decides what needs to be read, and what will be written. The only way the user can alter the course of the program is by responding to set questions. In particular, the user can't just ask the program 'What should I do next?' or 'How do you want your data?'. It is the responsibility of the programmer to provide all the necessary information to guide the user and to anticipate any problems. As we learn more about Turbo Pascal, so this issue will be taken up again and again. Meanwhile, we can look at some basic techniques of dialogue and amend the summation program accordingly.

Promoting user-friendly programming.

Dialogue

Dialogue with a user via a terminal should be precise, but friendly. Instructions should be quite clear, yet should not take up too much space. The reason for this is that it is not helpful if the instructions disappear off the top of the screen before the user has had time to respond to them. There are many ways of issuing instructions and choice depends on personal taste, but the following list of guidelines is a good start:

1. **Introduction.** A program should introduce itself, so that the user knows it has started running. If there are different versions of a program, the version name or number should appear in the introduction. Examples are:

    Six hints for good dialogue.

    ****** Summing numbers ******
    ****** Summing numbers (Version 2 – with dialogue) ******

    The title of the program should remain on the screen throughout its lifetime, so that using the bottom few lines in a window is attractive for this purpose. We would say:

    ```
    window (1, 22, 80, 25);
    writeln('***** Summing numbers *****);
    ```

2. **Prompts**. Data can be requested by a prompt being written out on the screen first. If the answer expected is a single item, then a *write-readln* sequence enables the answer to be written on the same line as the prompt. The user enters the reply ending up with a return. As an example:

    ```
    write('How many numbers (1..10000)? ');
    readln(count);
    ```

would produce:

How many numbers (1..10000)? 7

The return has two functions: it serves to terminate the number (a space would too) and it preserves the neatness of the dialogue. To coordinate the statements with the intended data format therefore, we recommend a *readln* rather than a *read* at this point.

3. **Limits**. If a limit applies on the value to be read, then this should be made quite plain, as in the above example. It is equally helpful if the fact that there is no limit is also communicated, as in the next example.

4. **Avoid 'screen creep'**. Bulk data should not be subject to individual requests. Thus if a list of items is required, there need not be a prompt for each item, just one for the list. Further, to free the user from counting them, a *writeln* can be issued after the list, rather than the program waiting for a *readln*. So, reading numbers could go like this:

```
writeln('Type in ', count, ' numbers (any size).');

FOR i := 1 to count do begin
  read(number);
      ...etc....
END;

writeln; {To stop the typing}
writeln('That''s enough, thanks.');
```

which would run as:

Type in 7 numbers (any size).
65 34 −22 90 19 87 −15
That's enough, thanks.

5. **Keeping track**. It may sometimes be more helpful to indicate which number is being read in, with a prompt inside the loop:

```
writeln('Type in ', count, ' numbers (any size).');
FOR i := 1 to count do begin
  write(i,': ');  readln(number);
      . . . etc . . .
END;
writeln('That''s enough, thanks.');
```

which would run as:

Type in 7 numbers (any size).
```
   1: 65
   2: 34
   3: -22
   4: 90
   5: 19
   6: 87
   7: -15
```
That's enough, thanks.

6.   **Windows**. Dialogue can usually be confined to a special area of the screen – say the last four lines. Questions that are to be repeated can appear on the same line each time, giving the user more confidence, and keeping the interface neat and tidy. To do this effectively, we need more Crt functions.

Snappy dialogue

To achieve really 'snappy' dialogue, we need four more Crt routines. These are:

```
PROCEDURE GotoXY (x, y : integer);
PROCEDURE ClrEol;
FUNCTION WhereX : byte;
FUNCTION WhereY : byte;
```

GotoXY positions the cursor at the given (x, y) coordinates. *ClrEol* (clear to end of line) clears all the characters from the cursor to the end of the line. We can use this to ask a question repeatedly at the same place, but removing the previous answer first. For example:

GotoXY is pronounced 'Go to x y'.

```
gotoxy (1,10);
write('What is the next request? ');
ClrEol;
readln(ch);
```

WhereX and *WhereY* provide the current cursor positions to the program. They can be used in a variety of ways to make the program less dependent on fixed places on the screen. For example, in the above sequence, having read the request, we could go back and acknowledge it on the same line as follows:

```
write('What is the next request? ');
ClrEol;
readln(ch);
gotoxy (1, wherey - 1);
write('Request ',ch, ' will be processed.');
```

Use of ClrEol in dialogue.

Example 3.4 Summation revisited

| Problem | Provide better dialogue for the summation program.

| Solution | Given all the above advice, the summation program can be greatly improved. We start by designing a screen layout which distinguishes between the control of the program and the input of data. Since the latter will occupy more space, we give it most of the screen, and reserve five lines at the bottom for the control. What we are aiming at is something like the screen layout shown in Figure 3.2. The crucial point is the split between the two windows on the x-axis, shown by the line. This is at $y = 21$.

| Program | In order make the program more readable, we have introduced some procedures, including one to do the actual summing. Notice that we left i and *number* as local variables, but had to keep *total* global, because it is used elsewhere as well.

```
PROGRAM Summation2 (input, output);
USES Crt;

CONST
    max  = 10000;
    split = 20;
VAR
    sets, s  : 1..20;
    count    : 1..max;
    total    : integer;

PROCEDURE Introduction;
VAR
    i  : 1..80;
BEGIN
    ClrScr;
    window (1,split,80,25);
    for i := 1 to 75 do write('-'); writeln;
    writeln('****** Summing numbers ',
        '(Version 2 – with snappy dialogue)******');
    write ('How many sets of numbers (1 .. 20)? ');
    readln(sets);
END; {Introduction}

PROCEDURE Request;
BEGIN
    window (1,split,80,25);
    gotoxy(1,4);
    write ('How many numbers (1 .. ', max, ') for set ', s, '? ');
    ClrEol;
    readln(count);
    gotoxy(1,5);
```

Stating the
limits for input
data.

A split screen.

```
1: 65
2: 34
3: -22
4: 90
5: 19
6: 87
7: -15
8: 0
9: 100
10: 6
11: -1
12: 77
That's enough, thanks.




- - - - - - - - - - - - - - - - - - - - - - - - - - - - - - - - - - - - - - - - - - - - - - - - - - -
****** Summing numbers (Version 2 – with snappy dialogue) ******
How many sets of numbers (1 .. 20)? 5
Type in  the 12 numbers for set 1 (any size).
```

Figure 3.2 A sample split screen for results and dialogue

```
        ClrEol;
        writeln('Type in the ', count, ' numbers (any size)');
      END; {Request}

  PROCEDURE sum;
    VAR
      number : integer;  {anything}
      i : 1..max;
    BEGIN
      total := 0;
      FOR i := 1 to count do begin
        write(' ', i,': ');  read(number);
        total := total + number;
      end;
    END; {sum}

BEGIN
  Introduction;
  for s := 1 to sets do begin
      Request;
      window(1, 1, 80, split-1);
```

```
                            sum;
                            writeln('That''s enough, thanks.');
                            window (1,split,80,25);
                            gotoxy(1, 5);
                            writeln('The total for the ', count, ' numbers in set ',
                                s, ' is ', total);
                      end;
                END.
```

At the point when the last number for set 1 had been read in, the screen would look like that above. If there had been more than 22 numbers, the upper window would scroll, leaving the heading and instructions intact in the bottom section.

3.4 Selection with if-then-else

Two methods of changing the values of variables have been covered so far, assignment and reading in. We now consider how to check the values in variables, and choose alternative actions based on the result of the check. Pascal has two **selection** statements known as the **if-statement** and the **case-statement**. The first is covered here, and the second in Section 5.4.

Form of the if-statement

The general form of the if-statement is:

If-statement

IF *condition* THEN *statement*
    ELSE statement;

---

where a condition, in its simplest form, consists of a comparison between two items or expressions of the same type, using one of the following six operations:

=	equals
<>	not equals
<	less than
<=	less than or equals
>	greater than
>=	greater than or equals

Examples of simple conditions are:

```
speed > speedlimit
year = 1066
day <> 29
initial = 'J'
age <= 18
```

In the if-statement we refer to the statement following the *then* as the **then-part** and similarly to the statement following the *else* as the **else-part**. The whole if-statement is executed as follows. First, the condition is evaluated. If this result is true, then the then-part is executed, and the else-part is skipped. If the result is false the then-part is skipped and the else-part is executed. A simple example would be:

More about conditions in Section 4.3.

```
if number >= 0 then writeln('Positive')
            else writeln('Negative');
```

In the general form of the if-statement, the else-part is given in italics. This means that it is optional and the statement can be used in an *if-then* version. For example:

```
if day = 25 then writeln('Christmas, Hooray');
```

A consequence of this option is that if the else-part is present, the statement before the keyword ELSE must not have a semicolon at the end. The reason for this is to enable Pascal to distinguish between if-then and if-then-else statements.

No semicolon before an else-part.

Example 3.5 Summing three ways

Problem | A list of numbers needs to be summed, and separate sums kept of the positive and negative numbers as well.

Solution | Start with the summation program from the previous section. Add in two new totalling variables, and use an if-statement to enable values to be added to one or the other.

Algorithm

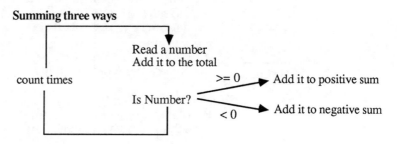

Summing three ways

Program	Because the program is now more complex than *Summation*, we shall break it up into procedures.

```
PROGRAM ThreeSums (input, output);
CONST
  max = 10000;
VAR
  i, count        : 1..max;
  Total, PosTotal,
  NegTotal        : integer;
```

A very important procedure.

```
PROCEDURE Initialise;
  BEGIN
    writeln('******Three sums *****');
    write('How many numbers (1..', max, ')? ');
    readln(count);
    Total := 0;
    PosTotal := 0;
    NegTotal := 0;
  END; {Initialise}

PROCEDURE ReadandTotal;
  VAR number : integer;
  BEGIN
    write(i,': ');  read(number);
    Total := Total + number;
    if number > 0 then PosTotal := PosTotal + number
                       else NegTotal := NegTotal + number;
  END;  {ReadandTotal}

PROCEDURE Finalise;
  BEGIN
    writeln('That''s enough, thanks.');
    writeln('The total is ', Total);
    writeln('The positive total is ', PosTotal, ' and ',
                    'the negative total is ', NegTotal);
  END;  {Finalise}

BEGIN
  Initialise;
  FOR i:= 1 to count do
    ReadandTotal;
  Finalise;
END.
```

Testing	A complete run would look like this:

***** Three sums *****
How many numbers (1..10000)? 5
Type in the 5 numbers (any size)

1 : 65
2 : 34
3 : –22
4 : 90
5 : 19
That's enough, thanks.
The total is 186
The positive total is 208 and the negative total is –22.

Compound statements

There may be times when several statements are needed in the then- or else-parts of an if-statement. These must be enclosed in *begin-end*, as was done with for-loops. Such a group of statements enclosed in *begin-end* is called a **compound statement**, and may be used in place of a statement. The form of a compound statement is therefore:

> The general grouping construct.

```
Compound statement

  BEGIN
      statements
  END;
```

Suppose that in the *Threesums* program, it is also required to know how many positive and negative numbers were read. Then two more counters are needed, and, to each part of the if-statement, an extra statement is added to do the counting. Thus the if-statement would become:

```
if number >= 0 then  begin
    PosTotal := PosTotal + number;
    PosCount := PosCount + 1;
end
else begin
    NegTotal := NegTotal + number;
    NegCount := NegCount + 1;
end;
```

Successive else-ifs

Sometimes, there are more than two possibilities that need to be considered. One way in which this is done is by **successive else-ifs**. The condition of the first if-statement eliminates one case, leaving the rest to the else-part. The else-part in its turn introduces another if-statement which selects out another condition and leaves the rest to its else-part, and so on. This is illustrated nicely in an example that prints out a class of pass for various ranges of marks, thus:

```
if marks >= 75 then writeln('First') else
if marks >= 70 then writeln('Upper second') else
if marks >= 60 then writeln('Lower second') else
if marks >= 50 then writeln('Third') else
                    writeln('Fail');
```

Notice a few points about this statement:

- The conditions are carefully ordered, so that each eliminates a certain range of marks. Thus the line that writes out a third class for anything over 50 will only be reached when it has already been established that the mark is under 60.

- The last class, fail, is given for all the rest of the marks, and does not need a condition.

- Layout of successive if-statements is important, and should try to reflect the pattern of conditions as much as possible.

A secondary consideration is that the most frequently occurring conditions should be checked first. If it is more likely that people will fail, then it will be marginally more efficient to arrange the order of the conditions thus:

Careful layout of control constructs aids readability.

```
if mark < 50 then writeln('Fail') else
if mark < 60 then writeln('Third') else
if mark < 70 then writeln('Lower second') else
if mark < 75 then writeln('Upper second') else
                    writeln('First');
```

Example 3.6   The highest number

Problem   Find the largest in a sequence of numbers.

Solution   A program can read in the numbers one at a time, remembering the highest so far, and updating this if necessary. We note that negative numbers should be catered for as well.

Algorithm   This is a very interesting algorithm, because it is based on induction. We start by assuming that we have found the highest of n numbers. Then the $n+1$th number is read. To find the highest of the $n+1$ numbers, all that needs to be done is to compare the new number to the highest so far, and if it is higher, to replace the highest. This process can then be repeated for as long as required.

The question is, how does the process start? Well, the highest number of a sequence that is one long must be just that number. So we start by reading in one number, make it the highest and proceed from there. The algorithm is:

Algorithm development by induction.

Find the highest number

Read a value for the highest, to start

for all the numbers | Read a number
More than highest? ──────▶ Replace highest

| **Program** |

```
PROGRAM Highestvalue (input,output);
VAR
  highest,
  number : integer;
  i, n      : integer;
BEGIN
  writeln('*****  Finding the highest number *****');
  write('How many numbers (1 or more)? ');
  readln (n);
  writeln('Type them in');
  read(highest);
  for i := 2 to n do begin
    read(number);
    if number > highest then highest := number;
  end;
  writeln;  writeln('That''s enough, thanks');
  writeln('The highest number was ', highest);
END.
```

| **Testing** | A typical run would produce:

***** Finding the highest number *****
How many numbers (1 or more) ? 8
Type them in
67 -34 56 12 3 9 101 44
That's enough, thanks
The highest number was 101

It is a good idea to test such an algorithm with the first number being the highest, then with the last, and then with one in the middle, or to have all the numbers except one equal. More testing is left up to the reader.

3.5 Case study 1: Tax collecting

There are several case studies in this book, their purpose being to bring together new features in a single program. The problems that are posed are more complicated in their formulation than the explanatory examples used with each feature, and the resulting solution could develop into a fairly long program. The case studies are also intended to attack problems for which a computer is really useful: that is, those that would be quite difficult to solve by hand. During the development of these case studies, you should come to realise that:

- the specification of a problem is often unclear, and can change with time;
- there are different ways of solving a problem;
- there are always more features that can be added.

Problem

Tax rules in Zanyland.

Tax in Zanyland, where the currency is a dolly (D), is calculated according to the following rules. The taxable amount of a person's income is obtained by subtracting from the actual income the abatements that apply. Abatements are as follows: D1600 for a single person, D3000 for a married person and an additional D1000 for the first child, D1200 for the second child and D1400 for each subsequent child up to a maximum of six. The abatement is reduced by one dolly for every five dollies that the income is over D15 000, but it cannot be negative. Tax is then calculated at a flat rate of 25% on the taxable amount. We want to use the computer to calculate tax for several people.

Solution

A wordy specification has to be reduced to an itemized form in order for it to become clear how the calculation proceeds. The important words should be highlighted, because they will eventually be the variables in the program. At the same time, we should try to decide which of these will be input values and which will be results. A rework of the problem specification is:

- Abatements are:

single person	D1600
married person	D3000
first child	D1000

second child   D1200

third to sixth child   D1400

- For **excess income** over D15 000, the abatement is reduced by 20% of the excess.

- The **taxable amount** is **income** less abatements.

- **Tax** is calculated as 25% of the taxable amount.

The input values must be the **income** and then the **marital status** and lastly, the **number of children**. From these three, the abatements, the reduction because of excess and the taxable amount can be calculated. Lastly, the **tax** can be arrived at. The tax is the one essential result, but it would also be helpful for people to see the others involved in the calculation.

Examples

From this, a preliminary input and output scheme can be designed, and some examples tried out. One problem is how to indicate the status, since so far only the reading and writing of integers have been mentioned. For the time being, we can use 1 for single and 2 for married.

Income	Status	Children	Abatements	Reduction	Amount	Tax
D15000	1	0	D1600	0	D13400	D3350
D15000	2	0	D3000	0	D12000	D3000
D15000	2	1	D4000	0	D11000	D2750
D20000	2	1	D4000	D1000	D17000	D4250

Algorithm

The algorithm to perform this calculation could get messy, and one way of keeping it tidy is to think in terms of procedures from the start. Thus we identify the top level of operations and give each a name. The calculation can then be expressed as:

```
Read the income, status and children
Calculate the abatements
Allow for excess
Calculate taxable amount and tax
```

Now each operation is developed in turn. The first one is simple, consisting of a single read statement. The next operation is the most complicated. Because it illustrates several different ways of using the if-statement, we'll look at it in detail.

The first calculation concerns the abatement for marital status. It is assumed that a person is either married or single – there are no other options. Therefore a straight two-way selection is appropriate as in:

Abatements
based on marital
status.

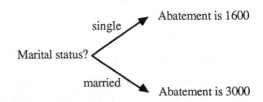

For the children, things are not as simple. The key point is that the child abatements are cumulative, so that having applied one, the option still exists to apply further ones. One way of expressing this is to work out exactly the abatements for different family sizes, and then use successive else-ifs, as depicted by:

Abatements for
children.

Children	Abatement
0	0
1	1000
2	2200
3	3600
4	5000
5	6400
6	7800
more	7800

However, this diminishes the advantage of using the computer in the first place, and also means that changes to the abatement amounts will be harder to incorporate. It is better to let the computer do the calculations.

A second approach is to check the different possibilities in turn, accumulating the amounts as specified. The first two work out as:

One child (or more)?———▶ Add on 1000

Two children (or more)?———▶ Add on 1400

The question is how to do the three to six children case. Having four similar statements seems too repetitive. Another way would be to multiply the abatement (D1400) by the number of children over two. To do this means checking if there are that many, giving:

More than two children?   ⟶   Multiply 1400 by (children − 2) and
add it to the abatement

However, this is not correct because it will grant abatements for any number
of children, not just the first six. It is necessary to add in another condition
and to adjust the number of children down to six, maximum, giving:

More than two children?⟶ More than six children?   ⟶   Set children to 6
Multiply 1400 by (children − 2) and
add it to the abatement

There is a very strong argument against adjusting a data value in this way. If
the number of children were to be used again later in the program, the
adjustment might not apply. It is therefore safer and clearer to declare a new
variable to hold the effective number of children. This is done in the
program.

Copy the original data before changing it.

Allowing for excess involves more selections but these are not expanded
on here. There is one problem, though, and that is that calculating 20% of an
amount may result in a value which is not an integer. Conversions to integers
are covered in full in Chapter 4, but meanwhile, assume that the following
will do the necessary:

integer variable := round(*non-integer expression*);

Program

Because the number of variables and constants is large, they are grouped
under headings consisting of comments. Notice that ranges for money,
children and people are carefully specified with the aid of constants from the
limits section.

The program also addresses the question of good layout of the input and
output. We have decided to let the user type in the three input values and
present the five output values on the same line. Notice that the input values
are read, and then rewritten in the correct place. In order to get these lined
up, we have to back-up using *WhereY*–1, and then *gotoxy*.

User interface issues.

```
PROGRAM Taxes (input, output);
  USES Crt;

  CONST
    {limits}
```

```
                    maxchildren  = 20;      {surely no more!}
                    maxmoney     = maxint;
                    maxpeople    = maxint;

                    {abatements}
                       formarried    = 3000;
                       forsingle     = 1600;
                       firstchild    = 1000;
                       second        = 1200;
                       further       = 1400;
                       qualify       = 6; {number of children that can count}

                    {rates}
                       ceiling       = 15000;  {above which excess applies}
                       excessrate    = 0.20;   {i.e. 20%}
                       taxrate       = 0.25;   {i.e. 25%}

                    {status codes}
                       married   = 2;
                       single    = 1;

                 VAR
                    {Input values}
                       status     : 1..2;
                       children   : 0..maxchildren;
                       income     : 0..maxmoney;      {the sky's the limit}

                    {calculated values}
                       abatements,
                       taxable,
                       tax                  : 0..maxmoney;
                       effectivechildren  : 0..maxchildren;

                    {loop variables}
                       i,n   : 1..maxpeople;

                 PROCEDURE PrintInstructions;
                 BEGIN
                    writeln;
                    writeln('Type in the three data values for each person');
                    writeln('The calculated values will be printed on',
                                   ' the same line.');
                    writeln('Income    Status    Children  Abatements',
                          '   Reduction    Amount       Tax');
                    writeln('    (D)    (1 or 2)');
                 END;  {PrintInstructions}

                 PROCEDURE ReadAndAdjust ;
                 BEGIN
                    readln(income, status, children);
                    gotoxy(1,wherey − 1);
                    clreol;
```

Setting out
variables in
groups aids
readability.

```pascal
        write('D',income:5, status:8, children:8);
        if children > qualify
          then effectivechildren := qualify
          else effectivechildren := children;
      END; {ReadAndAdjust}

  PROCEDURE CalculateAbatements;
      BEGIN
        if status = single then abatements := forsingle
        else abatements := formarried;
        if effectivechildren >= 1 {For the first child, if any}
            then abatements := abatements+firstchild;
        if effectivechildren >= 2 {For the second child, if any}
            then abatements := abatements+second;
        if effectivechildren >= 3 {For the rest, if any}
            then abatements := abatements +
              further * (effectivechildren - 2);
      END;  {CalculateAbatements}

  PROCEDURE AllowforExcess;
      VAR reduction : integer;
      BEGIN
        reduction := 0;
        if income > ceiling then begin
          reduction := round ((income - ceiling) * excessrate);
          if reduction > abatements
            then abatements := 0
            else abatements := abatements - reduction;
        end;
        write(abatements:12, reduction:12);
      END; {AllowforExcess}

  PROCEDURE CalculateTax;
      BEGIN
        taxable := income - abatements;
        tax := round(taxable * taxrate);
        writeln(taxable:12, tax:12);
      END; {CalculateTax}

  BEGIN
    ClrScr;
    writeln('****** Zanyland tax record ******');
    write('How many people (0..any number)? ');
    readln(n);
    PrintInstructions;
    FOR i := 1 to n do begin
      ReadAndAdjust;
      CalculateAbatements;
      AllowforExcess;
      CalculateTax;
    END;
  END.
```

Testing

Choice of test data is as important in programming as choice of meaningful identifier names. It is no good just throwing any old numbers at the program. Data should be carefully chosen so that:

- it is reasonably easy to check the answers;
- errors on the boundaries will be shown up;
- all checks built into the program are tested.

The way to achieve these goals for this problem is to choose nice round numbers for the income values, and to change one of the three input values at a time. In this way the effect on the output values can be checked. The boundary conditions are things like no reduction, or a reduction exceeding the abatement, or having more than six children. In all these cases, special checks apply and must be tested.

Reasoning about the program's correctness.

Some sample data was given under the examples above. The income started out at D15 000, with only the status and number of children changing. Then the income became larger, so that reductions would start appearing. The next step would be to have a much larger income and no children, so that the reduction would exceed the abatements, as in:

Income	Status	Children	Abatements	Reduction	Amount	Tax
30000	1	0	1600	3000	30000	7500

Now consider the following case of a poorly paid person with one child:

3600	2	1	4200	0	−400	−100

This is incorrect, since the taxable amount can't logically be negative, nor can the tax itself. What happened was the abatements exceeded the actual income. This possibility was not mentioned in the specification of the problem, but it is nevertheless something that, when noticed, needs correction. The fix will be made in the *CalculateTax* procedure, which becomes:

```
PROCEDURE CalculateTax;
BEGIN
   if income <= abatements
      then taxable := 0
      else taxable := income − abatements;
   tax := round(taxable * taxrate);
   writeln(taxable, tax);
END; {CalculateTax}
```

More testing is necessary, and is left up to the reader.

3.6 Turbo Pascal and random numbers

Having learnt how to read in data, we can now write programs that deal directly with the real world. However, a problem is that in order to test such programs, we do need to provide a substantial amount of data. Typing in the data every time, especially when a program is not quite working correctly, can be tedious. There are two alternative approaches to testing programs interactively. These are:

1. Keep the data in a file, as described in Chapter 5.
2. Generate the data randomly.

Random numbers

Random generation of data is an interesting idea. In many cases, we are interested in a uniform distribution of values within a given range, that is, every value in the range has an equal chance of occurring. Turbo Pascal provides a facility for doing this with the following routine:

```
FUNCTION Random (range : word);
```

Random will return a value x such that $0 \leq x < range$. *Random* can be used as part of an expression, or wherever a value would be appropriate. For example, to simulate the throwing of two dice with values between 1 and 6, we would declare:

> Random integers up to a limit.

```
VAR
  dice1, dice2 : 1..6;

  dice1 := Random (6) + 1;
  dice2 := Random (6) + 1;
  writeln (' Throw is ', dice1:1, ' and ', dice2:1);
```

Remember that *Random* generates numbers from 0 up to, **but not including**, the range. So *Random* (6) gives values between 0 and 5, and we add 1 to get the correct dice values.

An alternative version of *Random* does not have a range parameter and generates a real number between 0 and 1.

> Random real numbers between 0 and 1.

Example 3.7 A screen filling program

| **Problem** | We would like to have a program which creates a pretty abstract design on the screen. |
| **Solution** | Such programs are called screen filling programs, and are used to cover the screen when the computer is not in use. A simple |

version could display 30 randomly sized and coloured triangles.

Algorithm We can use the mountain procedure from Example 2.6. We need to decide on the variation we would like for the size: probably between 3 and 12 will be reasonable. To get such random numbers, we would use:

size := Random (10) + 3;

The position of the triangle can then vary accordingly. The right hand side of the window must allow for *size* characters in both the *x* and *y* directions. Colour, of course, varies between 0 and 15. We could write:

Program

```
PROGRAM ScreenSaver (output);
USES Crt;

CONST
  xmax = 80;
  ymax = 24;
VAR
  x        : 0..xmax;
  y        : 0..ymax;
  i        : 1..100;
  colour : 0..15;
  size     : 0..ymax;

PROCEDURE Mountain (size : integer; symbol:char);
VAR row, piece : integer;
BEGIN
  for row := 1 to size do begin
    gotoxy(size – row + 1, wherey);
    for piece := 1 to row do
      write(symbol, symbol);
    writeln;
  end;
END; {Mountain}

BEGIN
  ClrScr;
  for i := 1 to 30 do begin
    size := random(10) + 3;
    x := random (xmax – size*2 – 1) + 1;
    y := random (ymax – size – 1) + 1;
    Textcolor(random (16));
    window (x, y, x + size * 2 + 1, y + size + 1);
    Mountain (size, '*');
  end;
END.
```

Testing Running the program should produce very pleasing results. If you do not have a colour screen, then you can alter the colour part to generate a 0, 1 or 2, and use these to switch to low, high or normal video.

Random numbers for testing

Now consider how random numbers can be used to aid testing. In the case study in the previous section, three values were read in for each person. This was done in the procedure *ReadandAdjust* with the statement:

```
read (income, status, children);
```

where the variables were declared as:

```
VAR
    income   : 0..maxmoney;
    status   : 1..2;
    children : 0..maxchildren;
```

We can replace the read statement by the following calls to *Random*.

```
income := random(maxmoney);
status:= random(1) + 1;
children := random(maxchildren+1);
```

In addition to *Random*, we can also use the Turbo Pascal procedure *Randomize* which initialises the random number generator with a random value. However, when testing a program, we would prefer the data to be the same each time, so that we can predict and check the answers.

Randomize changes the random sequence.

Summary 3

1. **Identifiers** consist of a sequence of letters and digits which starts with a letter and does not contain spaces. Pascal does not distinguish between upper and lower case letters.

2. Turbo Pascal has 48 **keywords**, such as BEGIN and FOR.

3. There are several **predefined identifiers** (such as *integer* and *writeln*) which have special meanings and must not be redeclared as identifiers.

4. **Comments** are enclosed in { } and can serve to amplify and explain parts of the program.

5. A **variable** denotes a value which may change during execution of the program. Each variable has a type which governs the values it may hold.

6. An **assignment statement** gives a variable a (new) value.

7. Using named **constants** rather than implicit literals makes a program more readable and maintainable. Turbo Pascal permits simple expressions in constant declarations.

8. When reading numbers, the **read statement** will skip spaces before a number and

insists on a space or line end to finish a number.

9. It is important to maintain a good **dialogue** with the user of a program, through careful use of read and write statements.

10. The current position of the **cursor** can be obtained from *WhereX* and *WhereY*.

11. The **if-then-else statement** serves as a two-way selection mechanism, or as a single selection mechanism in the form of if-then, or as a multi-way selection mechanism with successive else-ifs.

12. Then- and else-parts that consist of more than one statement must be grouped with BEGIN-END, forming a **compound statement**.

13. Turbo Pascal provides a facility for generating uniform **random numbers** with the *Random* routine.

14. The random number generator can be **reset** by calling *Randomize*.

Self-check quiz 3

1. Given the following declarations, which ones would cause the compiler to report errors and why?

```
CONST
   max       = 10;
   K         = 1,000;
   initials  = 'JFK'
   Prize     = D50;
   2ndPrize  = D25;

VAR
   maximum   : 0..max;
   i, j, k   : integer;
   start, end : char;
```

2. Can a comment extend over more than one line?

3. What are the six main predefined types?

4. What does the Crt's *ClrEol* procedure do?

5. State four ways of controlling a variable number of data items.

6. Given the following statements and data, what will be printed out?

```
VAR                          Data:
   i, j, k : integer;        67   56
BEGIN                        98   91
   read (i);                 11   33
   readln;
   read(j);
   readln(k);
   writeln(i,j,k);
END;
```

7. The following set of statements is very inefficient. Why is this so? Rewrite them more efficiently.

```
if pre = 'm' then write('milli');
if pre = 'c' then write('centi');
```

```
         if pre = 'K' then write('kilo');
```

8.   The following piece of program is meant to swap the values in x and y if it is necessary, so that x lands up with the lower one. What will actually happen? Correct the program.

```
         if x > y then
            temp := x;
            x := y;
            y := temp;
```

9.   What are the advantages of using named constants in a program?

10.   Write an expression to generate random numbers between -32 and 212.

Problems 3

Answers are provided for the problems marked §.

3.1§ **Large class symbols** The classes of pass at Zanyland College have names and abbreviations that correspond as follows:

I	First	III	Third
II-1	Upper second	F	Fail
II-2	Lower second		

Assume that there are five procedures called *eye, one, two, dash* and *eff*, which respectively print out the symbols I, 1, 2, – and F in large format as described in Problem 2.1. Now write a successive else-if sequence which uses these procedures to print out in large format the symbol for a given mark.

3.2§ **Rainfall figures** The rainfall figures in millimetres are available for each day of the past four weeks. We want to know:

- the total rainfall for each week;
- the wettest day of the 28;
- the driest week of the 4.

Write a program which will read in several sets of 28 rainfall figures and print out the three bits of information required. Sample data and results would be:

```
Sample data   Sample results
3 0 0 7 8 21 0   39mm
0 1 1 0 0 0 4    6mm
9 6 7 0 0 0 0    24mm
0 0 0 0 0 0 1    1mm
The wettest day was day 6.
The driest week was week 4.
```

3.3§ **Golf scores** The Zanyland Golf Course has nine holes. At each hole, a player is expected to be able to sink the ball in the hole in 1 to 5 shots. This gives a course average or **par** of 30. A player's score for the course is the sum of the numbers of shots for each hole. Depending on his past performance, a player is granted a **handicap** which is subtracted from his score to give his actual result for a game. Players are also interested in knowing whether they have scored under par or not. When players play together, the winner is the one with the lowest score. If the scoring of a golf game were computerised, sample input and output might be:

Player	Handicap	Shots per hole	Total	Result	Under Par?
1	6	1 3 6 2 1 4 3 2 4	26	20	yes
2	3	2 2 2 2 4 4 4 2 2	24	21	yes
3	2	4 5 4 3 4 1 3 5 4	33	31	no

The winner is player 1 with a handicapped result of 20

Write a program which:

- reads in the shots per hole for several players;
- calculates each total score, handicapped score and par decision;
- determines the winning player and the winning score.

3.4 **Parking meters** The Zanyland Traffic Department wants to decide whether or not to mount a campaign against illegal parking. A number of traffic inspectors are sent to different zones in the city where parking time is restricted. The different zones have different time restrictions. Each of the traffic officers has to monitor any ten cars in their zone and record the actual time the vehicle was parked in the time-restricted zone. If 50% or more of the cars were parked for a longer period than allowed, the traffic department will decide to launch a massive campaign. Write a program which:

- reads in the number of zones;
- reads the time limit and actual parking time for ten vehicles for each of the zones;
- determines the number of cars exceeding the time limit in each of the zones;
- decides whether a campaign should be mounted or not;
- identifies the zone where the situation is the worst.

Sample input and output might be:

Please enter the number of zones: 3

Area	Limit	Parking times	Over limit
1	60	20 40 70 35 45 78 34 56 73 5	3
2	45	62 47 68 40 53 62 120 8 15 72	7
3	30	66 32 41 89 7 25 29 33 54 17	6

A campaign must be mounted.
Concentrate on area 2

3.5 **Price cutters** Various Zanyland supermarkets are having a price war on bread, milk and eggs. Write a program which will read in prices for these products for five supermarkets and calculate:

- the total cost of the three items at each supermarket;
- the lowest price for each item and the number of the supermarket where it can be obtained;
- the lowest total price and the number of the corresponding supermarket.

Design output similar to that in Problems 3.3 and 3.4.

3.6 **Testing** Adapt the programs of Examples 3.3, 3.4 and 3.5 to use random data.

3.7 **Flickering squares** Define two windows on the screen and write a program to fill them with stars, by generating random x-y coordinates, and a random choice of which square gets a star.

Types and looping

This chapter considers two important issues: the properties of the data types integer, boolean and real, and the formulation of conditional loops. It ends with a discussion of Turbo Pascal's Graph unit, and shows how it can be used to display graphs and fractal images.

4.1 Types

Variables, constants, expressions and functions all have **types** in Pascal, and the type governs exactly how they can be used.

Predefined types

Turbo Pascal has six main **predefined** types which are:

- integer,
- boolean,
- character,
- real,

- text,
- string.

Every type has five properties, which completely define the type's values, what they look like and how they operate. These properties are:

- range of values,
- notation for constants,
- input and output capabilities,
- operators,
- predefined functions.

In the next few chapters, we shall introduce each of the predefined types by defining all of its properties.

User-defined types

Pascal also enables us to construct our own types, often called **user-defined** types, by means of one of the following six methods:

- **enumerating** a list of values,
- restricting values to a **subrange**,
- collecting several items of different types into a **record**,
- collecting several items of the same type to form an **array**,
- forming a **set** of items of a certain type,
- collecting items of the same type into a **sequential file**,
- **pointing** to a dynamically created variable.

When we create new types, we give them names, and can then use these names in our programs as easily as we use integer or any of the other predefined type names. These user-defined types are discussed in Chapters 6, 7, 8 and 9.

4.2 Integers

Integers are used for counting – one of the computer's most common tasks. The integer type in Pascal is applicable to all those items that are inherently whole numbers such as a year, number of children, and counters of all sorts. What follows is a full discussion of the properties of the type.

Range of values

In mathematical terms, the integer numbers extend infinitely on either side of zero; on a computer, they are bounded by the storage allocated to hold them. The Turbo Pascal *integer* type has a range of:

-32768   to   +32767

This may be restrictive. Turbo Pascal provides additional integer types not available in standard Pascal, that is:

Type	From	To
byte	0	+255
shortint	-128	+127
integer	-32768	+32767
word	0	+65535
longint	-2147483648	+2147483647

Whatever the range that is available, Pascal provides a predefined constant called *maxint* which gives the value of the largest integer. Thus on any machine, one can discover the range by simply printing out *maxint*, as in:

writeln('Maxint is ', maxint);

Notation for literals

Literals are the symbols used to express the values of a given type. For integers, the literals are formed from digits optionally preceded by a sign of plus or minus. Pascal is, however, strict about how numbers are written, and in particular, there cannot be spaces or commas in them to separate the thousands. The following are all valid Pascal integers:

10000   -16567   80

whereas the following are not:

10,000   -16 567   80c

Turbo Pascal also has a notation for hexadecimal (base 16) numbers. Preceding a literal (which can include the letters A to F) with a $ causes it to be interpreted as a hexadecimal number, so $1E has the value 30.

Margin notes:

Don't assume that integers are large enough.

Invalid integers.

Hexadecimal values.

Input and output

Integer values can be read and written using the usual four input/output statements: *read*, *readln*, *write* and *writeln*.

For input, the number supplied as data must conform to the notation for literals and therefore may not contain commas, full stops or spaces. The read and readln statements will skip any leading spaces, including blank lines, before the integer begins. However, they will not skip over any other characters. Standard Pascal permits any non-digit to end a number but this flexibility is not usual in other languages. Turbo Pascal and some other Pascal systems don't implement it. It is best to restrict data design to numbers that are always terminated by spaces or ends-of-line. Thus for example, the following statement:

```
read (age, weight);
```

would accept data such as:

```
36   75
```

but would not in Turbo Pascal accept:

```
36 years 75kg
```

Numbers are left-justified by default.

An integer is written as one would expect, so that:

```
d := 30;
writeln('The month of June has ', d, ' days');
```

gives:

The month of June has 30 days

with the number following the string, and occupying just as much space as needed. Notice that it looks neat to leave a space at an end of a string that is to appear before or after a number.

In order to line up numbers of different sizes, Pascal provides a **field-width indicator**. The indicator consists of a colon and a value or expression and may be included after any item to be written. The effect of the indicator is to place the value to be written in a **field** of the stipulated number of spaces. The number is right-justified in the field so that spaces may remain on the left.

Suppose we wish to tabulate the negations and squares of five numbers. The numbers are known to be less than one hundred thousand, so a field width of 6 will be adequate for the number and its negation. For the square, a field of 10 will do. In order to obtain a gap between the numbers we add 3 to each width giving:

```
PROGRAM Table (output);
  VAR
   i  : 1..5;
   n  : longint; { numbers may exceed 32767 }
  BEGIN
   FOR i := 1 to 5 do begin
     read(n);
     writeln(n:9, −n:9,  n*n:13);
   END;
  END.
```

For data such as:

    4 1000 −5 0 144

the output will be:

Tables need right-justification.

```
        4        −4            16
     1000     −1000       1000000
       −5         5            25
        0         0             0
      144      −144         20736
```

If a field width is too small, the field is expanded and the numbers will always be printed with their correct values, even if the lining up may go awry.

Finally, note that the field width may be any integer expression. There is a good example of this feature under the discussion of real type properties at the end of Section 4.5.

Field widths may be expressions.

Operators

Integer literals, constants, variables and functions can be formed into integer expressions using the three operators: + (plus), − (minus) and * (multiply). There are also two more that permit integer division, giving the quotient and remainder respectively. These are:

    x div y   divide x by y and discard the remainder
    x mod y   remainder after x is divided by y

Mod is not defined if *y* is negative and, of course, both *mod* and *div* are undefined if *y* is zero. Some examples will clarify this.

```
17 div 6  = 2       17 mod 6  = 5
 6 div 17 = 0        6 mod 17 = 6
18 div 6  = 3       18 mod 6  = 0
−13 div 2 = −6      13 mod −3 = undefined
```

The relational operators such as = and < (introduced in Section 3.4) can also be used between integers.

Functions

There are four predefined functions which operate on integers and return integers as their values. They are:

abs(n)	the absolute value of n
sqr(n)	the square of n i.e. $n * n$
succ(n)	the successor of n i.e. $n + 1$
pred(n)	the predecessor of n i.e. $n - 1$

Examples of these functions are given in the problem that follows. In Turbo Pascal, there are also two procedures which take a string and produce its numeric value, and vice versa. They are:

val(s, n, code)	the numeric value of s (plus error code)
str(n, s)	the string value of n

A call to the *Str* procedure can also specify field indicators for the number.

/ always yields a
real number.

Although only the +, – and * are defined between integers to produce integer results, a division operator / can be used between integers and it will produce a real result. Real numbers are covered in detail in Section 4.5, but in some of the examples that follow, the use of real division is necessary. In order to convert the result to an integer, so that it can be used within the context of Pascal so far, there are two functions:

trunc (x)	truncates x to the next integer nearest zero
round(x)	rounds x to the nearest integer

These two functions take a real expression and produce an integer. Thus we have:

trunc (6.3)	6	round (6.3)	6
trunc (6.8)	6	round (6.8)	7

Example 4.1 Tabulating functions

Problem   Tabulate on the screen the values of the four integer functions between two given limits, but ensure that the table does not whizz past if it is longer than a screenful.

Drawbacks of
scrolling.

Solution   The tabulation part is straightforward, involving a for-loop around a writeln. The second part is harder, and it refers to the fact that many computer terminals scroll in a simple-minded way. Making a program print in bursts involves:

detection and *reaction*.

We must detect when the screen is full – when a count reaches 20, say – and we must react by stopping the program and waiting for a command to continue.

Algorithm   Detecting when a count reaches a certain value can be done in two ways. The first is to check it, and if it has reached the value, reset it back to 1 for the next batch. This would be phrased as:

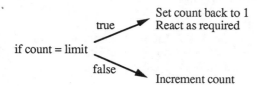

```
                                        Set count back to 1
                            true        React as required
    if count = limit
                            false
                                        Increment count
```

Notice that *count* is set to 1, not 0, because that arm of the if-statement excludes the incrementing. The algorithm could be rephrased as:

```
    If count = limit  ──────▶  Set count back to 0
                               React as required

    Increment count
```

Both versions are perfectly correct.

The other approach to detecting a limit is to let the counter run on indefinitely and to use the *mod* operator to detect every time it hits a multiple of the limit. This would be phrased as:

```
    If (count mod limit) = 0 ──────▶ React as required
    Increment count
```

For example, if the limit is some small number like 5, then *count mod limit* will be 0 when *count* is 0, 5, 10, 15, and so on. Since this approach uses some of the new integer operators, we shall use it in the ensuing program.

Finally, the reacting is done by requesting input from the keyboard. This effectively stops the program until the person running it wishes to continue. A simple technique is to ask the user to press the return key, and within the program to detect this by means of a readln.

Program

```
PROGRAM Tabulating (input, output);

CONST screenlength = 20;

VAR
  lower, upper, n  : -100 .. 100;  {say}
  linecount        : 1 .. 440;

PROCEDURE wait;
  BEGIN
    write('Press the return key to continue.');
    readln;
  END; {wait}

BEGIN
  writeln('****** Table of integer functions ******');
  write('Lower and upper bounds between −100 and 100 :');
  readln(lower, upper);
  writeln; writeln('   N     ABS       SQR      SUCC     PRED');
  linecount := 1;
  FOR n := lower to upper do begin
    writeln(n:5, abs(n):8, sqr(n):12, succ(n):8, pred(n):8);
    if (linecount mod screenlength) = 0 then wait;
    linecount := linecount + 1;
  END;
END.
```

Example 4.2   Timetables in the 24h clock

Problem   A delivery firm has acquired a new fleet of vehicles which are
able to travel 15% faster than the old vehicles (while still
staying within the speed limit). They would like to print out new timetables
automatically for their deliveries, based exactly on the old ones.

Solution   Below is a typical timetable. There is no pattern to the times,
so the only way of making the conversion will be to read in
each number in turn and print out the new time as 85% of the old. The
question is how to do arithmetic on times.

Departs	Zone 1	Zone 2	Zone 3	Zone 4
0600	0610	0622	0654	0712
0630	0640	0752	0824	0844
0700	0711	0735		
0730	0742	0756		
0745	0800		etc.	
0800				
0810				

| Algorithm | Times consist of two parts – hours and minutes. The only way to do multiplication on a time is to convert it to minutes or hours first, perform the calculation, then convert it back. The overall algorithm is:

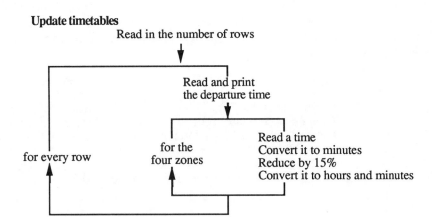

Update timetables

Read in the number of rows

Read and print the departure time

for every row

for the four zones

Read a time
Convert it to minutes
Reduce by 15%
Convert it to hours and minutes

Notice that we don't convert the departure times, only the arrivals!

The first conversion involves splitting an integer into two parts, which we can do with the mod and div operators. The algorithm is:

Convert to minutes	**Example 0715**
Find hours from time div 100	7
Find minutes from time mod 100	15
Set minutes to hours * 60 + minutes	435

Converting back is similar. The algorithm is:

Convert to hours and minutes	**Example 435**
Set hours to minutes div 60	7
Set minutes minutes mod 60	15
Set time to hours*100+minutes	715

| Program | Developing a program like this can best be done with procedures. We start with the 'top-level' as follows, using comments and procedure calls to indicate bits that need to be filled in later.

```
PROGRAM NewTimetable (input, output);

  {***Declarations here***}

BEGIN
  Initialise; {Print headings etc.}
  Getsizeoftable; {No. of rows}
  FOR r := 1 to noofrows do begin
    read (time);
```

Top-down development.

```
        CvtToMinutes;
        minutes := (minutes*newpercent) div 100;
        CvtToHoursandMins;
        write(time);
      END;
    END.
```

Then we expand each of the procedures and at the same time, set up declarations. For example,

```
PROCEDURE CvtToMinutes;                    Declarations
  BEGIN
    hours := time div 100;                 time      : 0..2359;
    minutes := time mod 100;               minutes   : integer;
    minutes := hours*60 + minutes;         hours     : 0..23;
  END; {CvtToMinutes}
```

The development of the rest of the program is left to the reader.

4.3 Booleans

Booleans are named after the mathematician George Boole (1815–1864).

Conditions govern the decisions made in programs as to alternative paths to follow. A condition yields a value **true** or **false**. Another name for a condition is a **boolean expression** and the result of such an expression can be stored in a **boolean variable**. For example, given the declarations:

```
VAR
    minor, pensioner  : boolean;
    age               : 0 .. 140;
```

we can store various facts about the age of someone as:

```
minor := age < 18;
pensioner := age >=65;
```

and then use these later to make decisions such as:

```
if minor then writeln('No driver''s licence for you!');
if pensioner then writeln('You need not pay on the bus.');
```

It could be argued that the boolean variables are unnecessary because the statements:

```
if age < 18 then writeln('No driver''s licence for you!');
if age >= 65 then writeln('You need not pay on the bus.');
```

will achieve the same effect. However, this would not be the case if the value of *age* had been changed before the if-statement is executed. Thus boolean variables, like any variables, are really useful when the value of a condition must be remembered after other things have happened. This is illustrated in the following example.

Example 4.3 Counterfeit cheques

| Problem | Counterfeit cheques are in circulation and the banks have discovered that they all have the same distinctive properties. In the 10 digit cheque number, if there are:

- three or more zeros in succession,

- and/or four or more non-zeros in succession,

then the cheque could be counterfeit. We would like the computer to assist in warning of a possible counterfeit.

| Solution | When the cheques are handled by the banks' computers, the first thing that is read is the number. For the purposes of this example, we could write a program to read in cheque numbers and to analyse them for the above properties. The analysis could detect the occurrence of either of the runs described above and if either is found then the cheque can be marked as suspect.

| Algorithm | The algorithm for analysing a number involves reading it in, digit by digit, and counting the number of zeros and non-zeros. However, these have to occur in runs, so once a run is 'broken', the relevant count will be reset. It will therefore be necessary to remember that a critical count was reached at some stage: this is best done with a boolean variable. The algorithm looks like this:

Read a digit

Is it

= 0 → Increment count of zeros
Reset count of non-zeros
If 3 zeros, set counterfeit

<> 0 → Increment count of non-zeros
Reset count of zeros
If 4 non-zeros, set counterfeit

Storing boolean state information.

| Program | The program follows the algorithm closely, making use of procedures for clarity. The digits of the cheque have to be entered with spaces following, so that they can be read as integers using the read statement.

```pascal
PROGRAM CheckaCheque (input, output);
  {For the occurrence of >=3 zeros or >=4 non-zeros in a row}
  USES Crt;

  CONST
    NoofDigits = 10;
  VAR
    counterfeit          : boolean;
    CountofZeros,
    CountofNonZeros  : 0 ..10;
    digit                : 0 .. 9;
    i,j, n               : 1 ..  10000;        {maximum in a batch}

  PROCEDURE RecordZero;
    BEGIN
      CountofZeros := CountofZeros + 1;
      CountofNonzeros := 0;
      if CountofZeros = 3 then counterfeit := true;
    END; {RecordZero}

  PROCEDURE RecordNonzero;
    BEGIN
      CountofNonzeros := CountofNonzeros + 1;
      CountofZeros := 0;
      if CountofNonzeros = 4 then counterfeit := true;
    END; {RecordNonzero}

  BEGIN
    Clrscr;
    writeln('****** Checking for counterfeits ******');
    writeln('How many cheques are there? ');
    readln(n);
    writeln('Enter each cheque number with digits separated ',
        'by a space');
    FOR i := 1 to n do begin
      counterfeit := false;
      CountofZeros := 0;
      CountofNonzeros := 0;
      FOR j := 1 to NoofDigits do begin
        read (digit);
        if digit = 0 then RecordZero
        else RecordNonzero;
      END;
      gotoxy(30,wherey-1);
      if counterfeit then writeln('COUNTERFEIT')
      else writeln('OKAY');
    END;
  END.
```

Testing

Cheque numbers should be chosen so as to test the special cases. For example, sample input and output might be:

```
****** Checking for counterfeits ******
How many cheques are there? 5
Enter each cheque number with digits separated by a space
0 0 0 3 3 0 0 4 4 0        COUNTERFEIT
0 0 3 3 3 0 0 3 3 3        OKAY
0 0 3 3 3 0 3 0 0 0        COUNTERFEIT
4 4 4 4 0 0 5 5 0 0        COUNTERFEIT
6 6 6 6 6 6 0 0 0 0        COUNTERFEIT
```

Once again, we used the cursor control routines to get the answers on the same line as the input.

Properties of the type boolean

Values and notation

There are only two boolean values – false and true – and they are known by these identifiers. This is in contrast to integers, which have a numeric notation, and to characters and strings, which also have a special notation, as we shall see later. The fact that boolean literals are identifiers means that care must be taken not to redefine them. If we had a declaration such as:

> VAR true : integer;

implying that we were going to count or compute something in the variable called *true*, then this would hide the boolean meaning of the identifier *true*, and we would not be able to use it.

Operators

There are four boolean operators namely *and, or, xor* and *not* which can be explained by means of tables:

not			and	false	true
false	true		false	false	false
true	false		true	false	true

or	false	true		xor	false	true
false	false	true		false	false	true
true	true	true		true	true	false

For the expression *x and y* to be true, both *x* and *y* must be true; for the expression *x or y* to be true, either *x* or *y* or both can be true. There is also a precedence between the operators, in that in the absense of parentheses, *not* and *and* will always be evaluated before *or* and *xor*.

Referring back to the earlier example with the minor and pensioner conditions, suppose the variable *employed* contains the information whether the person is working or not. Then further facts can be deduced as follows:

```
youngworker := minor and employed;
voter := not minor;
taxpayer := voter or employed;
```

Boolean operators can be combined to express more complex conditions. For example, if both minors and pensioners can go free on the buses provided they are not working, then we have:

```
freebus := (pensioner or minor) and not employed;
```

Boolean operators are very useful in conjunction with the relational operators in establishing detailed conditions. For example, to test whether a number falls between two limits, *min* and *max*, we can say:

```
if (number >= min) and (number <= max) then . . .
```

In Pascal, the precedence between the relational operators and the boolean ones is such that the boolean operators will always be executed first (that is, they have higher precedence). This is why the parentheses are needed in the above example. If they are omitted, the compiler would first try to group *min and number,* which is not what was intended.

Another example is an expression for deciding whether school should be cancelled because it is too cold or too hot, that is:

```
gohome := (temperature > 40) or (temperature < 0);
```

It is necessary to mention the variable being tested for each test, that is, it is incorrect to say:

temperature > 40 or < 0

It is worth noting that expressions with *and* operators can be converted into equivalent expressions using *not* and *or* operators, such as:

```
not a and not b    =>    not (a or b)
not a or not b     =>    not (a and b)
```

In programming, it is best to choose one style or the other and stick to it, so as not to get confused. Note finally that when using *not*, the brackets are important, in that *not a or b* is very different to *not(a or b)*.

A boolean can be used as the loop variable in a for-statement, though of course the loop will never be more than two iterations long.

Functions

There is one useful function which takes an integer and returns a boolean value, that is:

odd (n) returns true if *n* is odd, false if it is even

An example of the use of this function would be in deciding whether one is allowed to water the garden, which in times of drought may only be permitted for even numbered houses on even days (Monday is 1), and odd numbered houses on odd days, or on Sunday (the seventh day). Given the declarations:

```
VAR
    housenumber : 1..500;
    day           : 1 .. 7;  {Monday is 1}
```

and appropriate values in the variables, we could say:

```
AllowedtoWater :=
    (odd(housenumber) and odd(day))  or
    (not odd(housenumber) and not odd(day)) or (day = 7);
```

If instructions could be left that watering was to be done whenever possible, then an if-statement would be appropriate, as in:

```
if (odd(housenumber) and odd(day)) or
      (not odd(housenumber) and not odd(day)) or (day = 7)
then WatertheGarden;
```

In addition to the *odd* function, *ord, succ* and *pred* can be applied to boolean values, but their use is fairly limited. Two other functions return boolean values. These are *eoln* and *eof,* which are discussed in the next chapter along with files.

Input and output

Boolean values cannot be read but they can be written, producing the values *TRUE* and *FALSE*. The space taken on output is 4 and 5 characters respectively but can be increased by using a width indicator.

An example of booleans in for-statements is the printing of truth tables:

```
PROGRAM Truthtables (output);
  VAR b, c : boolean;
  BEGIN
    writeln('****** Truth tables ******');
    writeln('not |      and | false true   or | false true');
```

```
writeln('==============   ====================== ',
       '=====================');
FOR b := false to true do begin
  write(b:6, not b:7,b:10);
  FOR c := false to true do write(b and c:7);
  write(b:10);
  FOR c := false to true do write(b or c:7);
  writeln;
end;
END.
```

4.4 Conditional loops with while and repeat

This text started off by introducing loops in order to emphasise the power of programming in handling repetitive tasks in a simple way. The loops that have been used up to now have all had a common property – their duration was explicit. By looking at the starting and finishing values of the for-statement, the number of times the loop would execute could be calculated. However, not all solutions can be formulated in such precise terms. For example, when reading data, it is not always possible to know in advance how much data there will be, or when the person supplying the data will wish to stop. Thus we need the concept of a **conditional loop** – one that will stop according to some conditions. Specifically, these conditions need not necessarily be defined in terms of a fixed number of iterations.

The form of conditional loops

Conditional loops are phrased in terms of while or repeat statements. A general form of a loop using the while statement is:

While statement

Initialise the conditions
WHILE *conditions* DO BEGIN
   Statements to perform the loop
    and change the conditions
END;

While-loops check the condition at the beginning.

After statements to initialise variables involved in the conditions, the loop itself starts by checking the conditions. If they evaluate to true, the body of the while-statement is entered and executed. When the END is reached, control goes around again to the WHILE and the conditions are checked again. This process is repeated until the test of the conditions evaluates to false, at which point the looping stops, and control is passed to the statement following the END.

The general form of the repeat statement is similar:

Repeat statement

Initialise the conditions
REPEAT
    Statements to perform the loop
        and change the conditions
UNTIL *conditions;*

The repeat loop starts off by going through its body at least once before checking the conditions. This can sometimes be a desirable property, but in general the while-statement is more useful.

Repeat loops check the condition at the end.

Notice that the repeat statement is the only one in Pascal that does not need a BEGIN-END around a group of statements. Putting them in would not invalidate the statement, but it would look peculiar to experienced Pascal programmers, and is therefore not a good idea.

The two very important points about conditional loops are that:

Remember these.

- the conditions must be initialised; and

- the conditions must change during the loop.

If the conditions are not initialised, then the loop will be working on incorrect or even undefined information. If they are not altered during the loop, then there will be no chance of them changing and causing the loop to end.

Simpler forms

The general form of a while loop can be simplified in two ways. If only one statement forms the body of the loop, then the BEGIN-END can (but doesn't have to) be omitted. It is unusual for both processing and changing to be possible in a single statement, but we shall see examples of it later. Most conditional loops will consist of several statements and will need the BEGIN-END.

The other simplification is more common, in that only a single condition may apply to the loop, not several as implied in the general form. A condition is expressed as a boolean expression and this may be as simple as a single variable. Very often the conditions start with *not*, as we shall see.

Example 4.4   Highest common factor

Problem	We wish to find the highest common factor (HCF) of two numbers.

Solution	One possible solution would be to find all the factors of each number and then compare both lists for the highest one.

Fortunately, there is a quicker way!

Suppose a and b are the numbers, a is larger than b and their HCF is f. Then $a - b$ and b will also have an HCF of f. If we use this fact, repeatedly replacing the larger of the two numbers by their difference, until the two numbers are the same, then this figure will be the HCF, even if it is 1.

A simple but elegant algorithm.

Algorith m	The above discussion can be be expressed in the following algorithm:

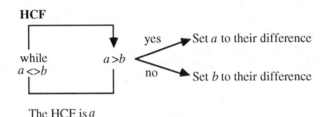

HCF

while
$a <> b$ $a > b$ yes → Set a to their difference
             no → Set b to their difference

The HCF is a

Examples

a	b	$|a - b|$
65	39	26
26	39	13
26	13	13
13	13 HCF	

a	b	$|a - b|$
99	66	33
33	66	33
33	33 HCF	

Program

```
PROGRAM  HCF (input, output);
VAR
  a, b : 0 .. maxint;
BEGIN
  writeln('****** Finding the HCF ******');
```

```
write('What are the two numbers? ');
readln(a, b);
WHILE a <> b do
  if a > b then a := a – b
            else b := b – a;
  writeln('The HCF is ', a);
END.
```

Developing a conditional loop

Before going on to the next problem, consider some small illustrative examples of conditional loops, bearing in mind the importance of formulating them correctly. In order to convey the sense of the looping process, some of the examples make use of procedures, which do as their names suggest.

The first example simulates trying to find a pair from a drawerful of mixed coloured socks:

```
PickaSock;
PickAnotherSock;
WHILE not  aPair DO BEGIN
  DiscardaSock;
  PickAnotherSock;
END;
```

The loop is initialised by having two socks in hand: this is essential so that the check for a pair can be correctly performed. The loop is correctly formulated in that the condition will change each time round, as a new sock is selected. There are, however, two crucial flaws in the loop. *How to formulate a loop correctly.*

Suppose a pair is never found. The condition is not met so the loop continues, but the operation *PickAnotherSock* will eventually fail, and the whole operation will crash. The other problem is similar – suppose there were no socks in the drawer to start with. In this case, neither of the initialising statements can be performed, and the program as it stands will not be able to execute. These two situations can be summed up as:

• guard against not being able to begin;

• guard against never ending.

The remedy is to provide additional conditions as the guards. In this case, we need to know if sufficient socks (that is, at least two) exist to be able to test for a pair, and then we need to know when the drawer becomes empty. Both conditions are based on the number of socks in the drawer, and we assume that this figure can be provided in some way. The corrected version of the loop then becomes:

```
IF NumberofSocksinDrawer >= 2 then begin
   PickaSock;
   PickAnotherSock;
END;

WHILE (NumberofSocksinDrawer > 0) and not aPair  DO BEGIN
   DiscardaSock;
   PickAnotherSock;
END;
```

{At this point, a pair may or may not have been found}

Follow-up actions. There is one final consideration with any conditional loop. If there is more than one part to the condition governing the loop, it may be necessary to know at the end which part caused the loop to stop. In the example, it seems sensible to be able to decide whether the search was successful or not. This is called a **follow-up action**, and is performed by rechecking some of the conditions, as in:

```
IF aPair then writeln('Got a pair of socks')
          else writeln('Bad luck, no pair found.');
```

Notice that when conditions are connected (as they often are), one must be careful as to which is tested. In this case, it would not have been correct to test for empty as in:

```
IF empty then writeln ('Bad luck, no pair found.')
          else writeln ('Got a pair of socks');
```

since the pair could have been found on the very last time round the loop. The drawer would also be empty, but that is irrelevant for this purpose.

As an exercise, write the necessary if-then-else statements to report on whether a pair was found or not, whether the drawer was empty initially, or whether it became empty during the search.

Conditional loops and input data

The next example deals with input data: we wish to read numbers until a certain target number is found, and then stop. The loop is:

```
read(target);
read(number);
WHILE number <> target do
   read(number);
```

Here we have a case of a single statement in the loop body. Reading is special in that it involves processing data, and it also changes the value of variables. Thus a read performs the dual function of the body of a loop and changing the conditions.

Now consider the two guards mentioned above: the loop may not be able to start if no data exists, and it may never end if the target does not appear. Both of these relate to an **end of data** condition, which we shall assume for the moment is maintained in a boolean function called *endofdata*. Assuming that at least the target can be read, then the loop is rephrased as:

Protecting a
read statement.

```
read(target);
if not endofdata then read(number);
WHILE not endofdata and (target <> number) do
    read(number);
```

The lesson here is that read statements should always be protected, whether by conditions in if-statements or in while-statements.

If knowing the reason for stopping is important then the following statement would be reasonable:

```
IF number=target  then writeln('Found ',target:1)
                  else writeln(target:1, ' is not there.');
```

Reasonable, but not strictly correct: if there was no data at all, then nothing is ever read into *number*, and so this question cannot be asked. This indicates that the case of no data must be handled and got rid of quite separately from the normal case. The correct statements to do this are given next.

Trailer values

The condition for end of data could be formulated in several ways. One way would be to use the built-in functions, which are discussed in Section 5.3. Another way is to have a **terminator value** which is supplied by the user as the last item. To make things flexible, the trailer for that particular run of the program could also be read in. Thus the loop to search for a target number and end correctly could be formulated as:

```
read(trailer);
read(target);
read(number);
WHILE (number <> trailer) and (number <> target) do
    read(number);
if number = target then writeln('Found ',  target:1)
                    else writeln(target:1, ' not there);
```

Typical data for such a loop would be:

```
0  5
1  2  7  4  5  9  0
```

The trailer is 0 and the target 5, so the loop will read values until the 5 is reached, and then stop. Since the target was found, the message *Found 5* will be printed. Since there are values left in the data, it may be helpful to skip over them. The if-part of the loop could be extended to include a loop, thus:

```
if number = target
  then begin
    writeln('Found ',  target:1);
    repeat
      read(number);
    until number = trailer;
    end
else writeln(target:1, 'not there.');
```

As with counting loops, conditional loops can be nested, and both kinds of loops can be nested with each other as the application requires.

Example 4.5 Controlling an apparatus

| Problem | An engineering apparatus is controlled by numbers that may change, but must always be in descending order. As soon as the sequence is no longer descending, the machine stops. How would this aspect of its operation be programmed?

| Example | An example of an input sequence would be:

$$100 \quad 67 \quad 33 \quad 32 \quad 31 \quad 54$$

At this stage the machine must stop.

| Solution | We assume that the numbers will be read into a program, and that for the purposes of the investigation they can then be ignored. What is important is to get the algorithm for checking on the sequence correct.

On avoiding assumptions.

| Algorithm | To check that a number is in sequence, we have to have both it and the previous number in hand. Each time round the loop, we replace the previous number with the one read in. As far as starting off goes, we cannot make an assumption as to the value of the first number, so the remembered number cannot be preset to a special value. Instead, the first two numbers are read in separately, and then the while-loop starts, checking that even these are in sequence.

| Program | The relevant portions of the program would be:

```
VAR
  N, previous : integer;

  read(previous);
  read(N);
  while N < previous do begin
    previous := N;
    read(N);
  end;
```

Extension Since the program is feasible, the maker of the apparatus has asked that it be written, but with the following additional conditions:

- the first number must be positive;

- the numbers must not go below 0.

For each number, he asks that we print out that many dots on the same line.

Algorithm The condition on the while-statement will need two parts now: to check the new number against 0 and to check it against *previous*. In addition, an if-statement is needed at the beginning to check that the very first number is positive. Printing the dots is best done in a separate procedure. Since the reacting will be done with *previous* in the first case, and then with *n*, we give the procedure a parameter to make this easy to do.

Program

```
PROGRAM Controller (input, output);
  USES Crt;
  VAR
    previous : 0 .. maxint;
    N        : integer;

  PROCEDURE React (dotcount : integer);
    VAR dot : 1 .. maxint;
      BEGIN
        Gotoxy(4,wherey-1);
        FOR dot := 1 to dotcount do write('.');
        writeln;
      END; {React}

  BEGIN
    ClrScr;
    writeln('***** Controlling the apparatus *****');
    writeln('Type in the numbers');
    readln(previous);
    React(previous);
    readln(N);
    IF previous <= 0 then
      writeln('The machine cannot work on that.')
    ELSE begin
```

```
              WHILE (N >= 0 ) and (N < previous) do begin
                React(N);
                previous := N;
                readln(N);
              END; {while}
              writeln;
            END; {if}
            writeln('Machine shut down okay.');
          END. {controller}
```

| Testing |

Sample input and output for the program would be:

***** Controlling the apparatus *****
Type in the numbers
15 ....
12 ....
9 ....
7 ....
3 ...
−1
Machine shut down okay.

The testing should include the case where the data starts off negative.

Stopping from the keyboard

Introducing
keypressed.

Turbo Pascal offers a facility for stopping a program by pressing a key on the keyboard. The Crt unit has a function called *keypressed* which can be tested by a conditional loop and which becomes true as soon as a key is pressed. For example, the *GoodBye* procedure from Example 2.7 can be reworked to continue printing goodbye until the user stops it.

Interminable
goodbyes.

```
          PROCEDURE EndlessGoodbye;
            VAR c : 0..15;
            BEGIN
              window (22,10,49,14);
              while not keypressed do begin
                TextColor(random(16));
                write('Goodbye');
              end;
            END; {EndlessGoodbye}
```

4.5 Reals

Real numbers are those that may have fractional parts, and are used for quantities where this is appropriate, such as prices, weights and measures, and mathematical results. A real number does not have to have a fractional part, though, and the values of all the integer numbers are contained in the set of reals. We now discuss all the properties of the type *real*.

Notation for literals

There are two ways of writing real numbers. Fixed point is the usual way, with a decimal point (not comma) being used. Examples of fixed point reals are:

$$3.141593 \qquad 0.18 \qquad 5.0 \qquad 0.000004 \qquad 10000000$$

The second real form is one that splits the number into a **mantissa** and an **exponent.** This is known as **floating point** form. The purpose of the floating point is to be able to represent very large or very small numbers without having all the zeros. The exponent indicates a power of 10 by which the mantissa must be modified. Since the power can be positive or negative, and there is no rule about how the split must be made, there can be many ways of representing a single number in floating point form. For example, consider the number forty million. In fixed point form it is 40000000.0, which is rather hard to read. In floating point form it can be written as 4E7 or 40E6. Similarly, for a very small fraction such as 0.000001, the floating point form could be 0.1E–5 or 1.0E–6.

Floating point form = mantissa + exponent.

When dealing with physical values measured in kilometres or nanoseconds or megabytes for example, keeping exponents to multiples of three helps to reflect the prefix conventions of SI units. Thus we would have:

5085 kilometres	5.085E6 metres
7 nanoseconds	7.0E–9 seconds
10 megawatts	10E6 watts

Range of values

The range of values of a real number is very much larger than that of an integer. Since there are two parts to a real number – the mantissa and exponent – the range is expressed in terms of the number of significant digits that can be accommodated and the highest value of the exponent. As with the integers, the range depends on the number of bits allocated to each part. In Turbo Pascal, reals use 48 bits, giving the following range:

- 11 digits of accuracy;
- exponent from −38 to +38.

The effect of the limit on significant digits is that the following two numbers, if read in, would both be stored as the same value:

12345678.12345678
12345678.1234567812345

As with the integer type, Turbo Pascal supports additional real types which use different storage sizes and have different accuracies and exponent ranges, given approximately by:

Special Turbo real types.

Type	Accuracy	Exponent	Size
real	11 digits	-38 .. +38	48 bits
single	7 digits	-45 .. +38	32 bits
double	15 digits	-324 .. +308	64 bits
extended	19 digits	-4591 .. +4931	80 bits

Because they cannot be exactly expressed in decimal notation, real variables cannot have lower and upper bounds that can be checked by the compiler, as is the case with integers. However, such information is useful to readers of the program and it is good practice to indicate the expected accuracy and range of each variable as a comment. Examples of real constant and variable declarations are:

```
CONST
  VAT = 0.15;  {15%}
```

User-defined ranges for reals.

```
VAR
  second      : real;   {0.00 .. 59.99}
  percentage  : real;   {0.0 .. 100.0}
  share       : real;   {0.00 .. 0.99}
  cost        : real;   {0 .. 100E6}
  temperature : real;   {− 40 .. 50}
  x, y, z     : real;   {−1.000000E−15 .. 1.000000E15}
```

Operators and functions

There are four operators for reals: + − * / . The slash symbol is used for division. It is not applicable to integers in the sense that it does not produce an integer result. However, if / is applied to integers, Pascal will perform the division and produce a real result.

There are ten standard functions that operate on real numbers. They can be divided into the five mathematical functions:

abs (x)	$\lvert x \rvert$	absolute value
sqr(x)	x^2	square
sqrt(x)	$\sqrt{x}$	square root
ln(x)	$\log_e x$	natural logarithm
exp(x)	e^x	natural anti-logarithm

the three trigonometric functions, for angles in radians (not degrees):

REMEMBER: the trigonometric functions work in radians not degrees.

sin(x)	$\sin x$	sine in radians
cos(x)	$\cos x$	cosine in radians
arctan(x)	$\tan^{-1} x$	inverse tangent

and the two conversion functions:

trunc(x)	smallest integer less than x
round(x)	nearest integer to x

These last two functions were discussed in the section on integers. In addition, the Turbo *Random* function can be used to produce a number between 0 and 1:

Random   a real number x, such that $0 \le x < 1$

This is in contrast to the integer version of *Random* which has a parameter which dictates the upper bound.

Turbo also provides three more functions:

pi	the value of π, i.e. 3.1415926535897932385
int(x)	the integer part of x
frac(x)	the fractional part of x

Real numbers are used mainly for mathematical calculations and, because programs are written a line at a time, the formulae sometimes look quite different to the usual mathematical layout. The main difference is in the use of / for division, rather than a line underneath the numerator, and in the use of functions for square root and so on. These points are illustrated in the following examples of real expressions, with their mathematical equivalents:

sqr(x) * sin(sqr(x)) $x^2 \sin x^2$

sqrt(sqr(b) − 4 * a * c) $\sqrt{b^2 - 4ac}$

a / (b * c) $\dfrac{a}{bc}$

$$5 / 9 * (F - 32) \qquad\qquad \frac{5}{9}(F - 32)$$

Parentheses are often needed in order to ensure the correct precedence. The operators / and * have the same precedence and are evaluated left to right, so that:

$$a / b * c \quad \text{is} \quad \frac{ac}{b} \quad \text{not} \quad \frac{a}{bc}$$

Pascal does not have a built-in operator for raising something to a power. Exponentiation is achieved by using the *ln* and *exp* functions as follows:

$$x^y \;=\; e^{\,y\,\ln(x)} \;=\; \mathsf{exp}(y * \mathsf{ln}(x))$$

However, if y is a small known integer, then it may be easier to simply use multiplication, as in:

$$x^4 \;=\; x * x * x * x$$

Note that it is not permissible to raise a negative number to a fractional power using *exp* and *ln* directly.

Input and output

Real numbers of either form can be read in using read and readln, with the same convention as for integers that the number should end with a space or the end of a line. Real numbers can be written out in write and writeln statements, but in the absence of any formatting, they are written in floating point. Most of the time, though, numbers will be required to be output in fixed point, in which case, two field widths must be given for:

- the complete number,
- the decimal places.

If the number as stored in the computer has more decimal places than specified for printing, then it is rounded. The complete number is right-justified in the field given for it. If the integer part of the number needs more space than is given, then the number reverts to floating point form. The column for the sign can be used by the number itself if the number is positive. Finally, if the width for the decimals is missing or zero, floating point is used. These rules are illustrated in the following few examples, where ~ indicates a printed space:

```
CONST
    x   = -1024.83;
```

```
writeln (pi:5:3);          3.142
writeln (pi:10:7);         ~3.1415930
writeln (pi:12:1);         ~~~~~~~~~3.1
writeln (pi:7);            3.142E0
writeln (x:8:2);           −1024.83
writeln (x:6:2);           −1.02E3
```

Example 4.6 Plotting a graph

| Problem | We would like to print a sin graph going across the screen.

| Solution | It is very easy to print a sin graph going **down** the page, that is *A simple* with the x-axis going down, and the y-axis across. The known *solution.* variable, x, can increase linearly and an asterisk be printed at the appropriate place on each successive line. The simplest program to do this is:

```
PROGRAM GraphDown (output);
  CONST pi = 3.141592;
  VAR
    d : 0..95;
    y : real;
  BEGIN
    writeln('****** Sin Graph ******');
    writeln;
    d := 0;
    while d <= 90 do begin
      y := sin(d*pi/180)*30;
      if round(y) = 0
        then writeln('*')
        else writeln('*':round(y));
      d := d + 5;
    end;
  END.
```

The output for *GraphDown* is shown in Figure 4.1.

This program assumes that there is only one y value for each x, which is quite a restriction. Instead, we should regard the screen as an x-y space and for each value of x on the horizontal axis, calculate the correct value of y and move to a corresponding position on the screen, using *Gotoxy*.

| Algorithm | Armed with *Gotoxy*, we can turn the graph the correct way *A much better* round, and not worry about problems of linearity. We still *solution.* loop over the x-axis, but use the expression for y to take us into the screen's space, and there print the asterisk. In order to get the graph's origin in the centre of the screen, we must add about half the x- and y-axis lengths to each point. To make this more understandable, more constants and variables are declared in the program.

Figure 4.1 Simple graph of sin(x) down the page

| Program | This program shows the function for a full period from −180 to +180 degrees.

```
PROGRAM GraphAcross (output);

USES crt;

CONST
  start    = −180;
  finish   = 180;
  ycentre  = 10;
  yoffset  = 12;
  interval = 5;

VAR
  d, xoffset : integer;
  x, y       : real;

BEGIN
  clrscr;
  writeln('***** Sin graph across *****');
  writeln;
  d := start;
  xoffset := abs (finish − start + 1) div 2;
  while d <= finish do begin
    y := sin(d*pi/180) * ycentre + yoffset;
    x := (d + xoffset ) div interval;
    gotoxy (round(x), round(y));
    write('*');
```

```
        d := d + interval;
    end;
END.
```

| Testing | Run the program and see what happens. The output should be a full sin curve plotted across the screen with asterisks as
follows:

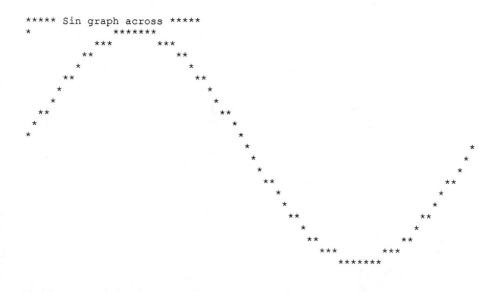

Arithmetic limits

Since computer arithmetic is done in fixed-sized words there has to be some
way of handling calculations that go outside the range of numbers provided.
There are two possibilities:

- an approximate value is used and calculation continues; or
- an error occurs and calculation is abandoned.

Two problems
with computer
numbers.

The first approach is used when there is a loss of precision in how the number
is stored, and the second is used when the number actually goes outside the
range. These two cases are now considered.

Loss of precision

The mantissa of a floating point number holds all the digits of precision
available. Sometimes an operation may produce a number which has more

digits than can be accommodated. Some digits will be lost, and this may affect subsequent calculations and the end result.

To illustrate this effect, assume that there is a little computer with reals stored with:

- 4 digits in the mantissa,
- 1 digit in the exponent.

First consider the problem of inexact division. The expression 10 / 3 * 3 should produce 10, but in fact may work out as:

Losing
precision.

$$10 / 3 * 3 \quad = \quad 3.333$$
$$*3$$
$$= \quad 9.999$$

Precision was irretrievably lost in the division. This is quite a common result and you should see if it happens on your computer. If the answer is printed in floating point form, the inaccuracy should be apparent; if printed in fixed point with a field width for the fraction smaller than the digits provided by the mantissa, then the number may be rounded and appear to be correct. Thus on the little computer with 4 digits in the mantissa:

writeln (10 / 3 * 3, 10 / 3 * 3 :8:1);

gives:

.999E0   10.0

This phenomenon is the same no matter how large the mantissa.

The second problem occurs in large multiplications. If two four-digit numbers are multiplied, the result will have seven or eight digits, but still, on our little computer, only four can be stored. For example:

Losing
accuracy.

$$60.08 * 4.134 = 248.3\overline{7072}$$

cannot be represented

$$= 248.4$$

Such effects become more noticeable with very large numbers. On this little computer with a 4-digit mantissa, we have:

largest number	0.9999 E 9 or 999 900 000
second largest number	0.9998 E 9 or 999 800 000

In between these, there is nothing, so that any of the 100 000 missing values have to be represented by one of these. For example:

999 934 628 is represented by 999 900 000
999 876 543 is represented by 999 900 000

When multiplying, see what happens:

$$73.56 * 1101 \ = \ 80\,989. \lfloor 56 \rfloor$$

cannot be represented

$$= 80\,990$$

Overflow and underflow

These are error conditions where a number itself, rather than just its precision, is too large or too small. They apply to integers and reals.

The largest integer value is given by the constant *maxint*. It is not possible to create or store an integer value larger than this. The computer should catch such attempts and signal an error. In Turbo Pascal, the checking of such errors may be switched on or off, using the Compiler selection in the Options menu. You should ensure that range checking is on for all program development. The following small program, which repeatedly doubles a number, will illustrate the result of range checking. Run it with the checking switched on and again with the checking off. With checking off, strange results occur when *maxint* (32 767) is exceeded:

```
PROGRAM Overflow (input, output);
  VAR
   i   : 1..20;
   x   : 1..10000;
  BEGIN
   x := 1;
   FOR i := 1 to 20 do begin
    x := x+x;
    writeln(x);
   END {for};
  END.
```

Testing the limits of integers.

More subtly, it is also not permissible to go out of range during a computation, even if the final result is within range. So, for example, the following expression cannot be evaluated:

```
maxint * 2 div 3
```

Overflow.

because twice the value of *maxint* cannot be represented, even as a temporary value. However, if the expression is rewritten in the following way, the evaluation becomes possible:

maxint div 3 * 2

Just switching to real division as in:

maxint * 2 / 3

would not help because Pascal remains in integer mode as long as possible. Thus it will still treat the multiplication as an integer operator, and only switch to real when encountering the /.

At the other end of the scale, for floating point we have for our little 4-digit computer:

smallest number   0.1000E– 9 or 0.0000000001

Any value less than half of this will be stored as zero. This fact must be remembered when performing computations with very small numbers. Multiplication is especially vulnerable, as shown in this expression:

Underflow. $a / (b * c)$ where $a = 0.0000004$ or 0.4E–6
                                            $b = 0.00001$ or 0.1E–4
                                            $c = 0.000\,004$ or 0.4E–5

$b * c$ produces 0.4E–10 which is smaller than the smallest real, and therefore is represented as 0. As a result, the division will fail. As often happens, reordering an expression enables it to be evaluated more accurately. In this case, the equivalent form of $a / b / c$ will work. a / b gives 0.04, and this divided by c gives the answer of 10 000.

Numerical computing

There is an area of computer science – called numerical analysis – which examines how to deal with boundary cases of finite number systems. For ordinary programming, it is sufficient just to be aware of the problems and to be able to recognise the effects when they occur. Remember that difficulties in integer arithmetic will not necessarily go away if the calculation is done in reals. It is always better to use integers if they are applicable, because the precision problems are avoided. Moreover, real variables cannot be used in several places where integers are acceptable, for example as loop variables in for-statements or as key-expressions in case-statements.

4.6 Turbo Pascal and the Graph unit

Turbo Pascal's Crt unit provides basic screen control at the character level. Many screens these days can be driven at a much finer grain, known as the pixel level, where a pixel is a tiny dot on the screen. The Graph unit in Turbo Pascal enables us to access and control the screen at this level.

Hardware details

The resolution that can be obtained on the screen, and hence the range of x and y values and colour range, depends on the graphics adapter installed in the computer. Turbo Pascal supports eight or more different adapters. One of the most common at present is the VGA adapter which has a screen of 640 x 480. Details of other possibilities can be found in the Turbo manual.

For each adapter, Turbo Pascal provides a graphics driver, called a BGI file (Borland Graphics Interface). This file must be accessible on the DOS path for programs to run correctly. For the VGA adapter, the file is called EGAVGA.BGI.

Basic graph facilities

The facilities provided by the graph unit are extensive, and we shall mention only a selection here. Appendix E gives a full list of what is available.

To perform basic movement, line drawing, writing and colour control, we need the following procedures:

```
PROCEDURE InitGraph (var Driver, Mode : integer; Path :string);

PROCEDURE CloseGraph;

PROCEDURE ClearDevice;

PROCEDURE MoveTo (x, y : integer);

PROCEDURE LineTo (x, y : integer);

PROCEDURE SetColor (Colour : Word);

PROCEDURE SetBkColor (Colour : Word);

PROCEDURE SetLineStyle (Style : Word; Pattern : Word; Thickness : Word);

PROCEDURE OutText (TextString : string);

PROCEDURE OutTextxy(x, y : integer; TextString : string);
```

It is necessary to call *InitGraph* before using any of the other graph facilities. The parameters supplied to *InitGraph* select one of the BGI files in the correct mode, in a given directory. In order to let programs run without knowing in advance what adapter is installed, we can use Graph's detect facility. *ClearDevice* does the same as *ClrScr*: it resets the screen. *InitGraph* does a reset by default. A simple startup of the graph unit entails:

```
USES Graph;

VAR
  Driver, Mode : Integer;

BEGIN
  Driver := Detect;
  InitGraph (Driver, Mode, 'C:\TP\BGI');
```

assuming that the drivers are located in the TP\BGI directory on the C drive. It is good practice to close the graph unit down with *CloseGraph* at the end of the program. If Graph cannot find the adapter or the driver, it will return an error message and stop: full details of what to do about this are given in the Turbo manuals.

Line drawing.
The *MoveTo* procedure is used to move to a given (x,y) coordinate, analogous to *gotoxy*. *LineTo* has a similar effect, except that a line is drawn on the way. To set the colour used for drawing lines, we use the procedure *SetColor* and we can change the background colour with *SetBkColor*.

Text writing.
Once in graphics mode, the program should avoid writing to the screen with writes or writelns: instead it should use *OutText* or *OutTextxy*. With the *x-y* coordinates, the string is written at the given position, otherwise it is written at the current position on the screen. To output numbers, we have to first convert them to strings, using the *Str* function. To mix strings and numbers, therefore, is a bit cumbersome, but can be done using the + operator. For example, to print a message at the top of the screen, we could use:

```
str(n,s);
OutTextxy (0, 0, 'Graph of sin from 0 to '+ str(n) + ' pi');
```

The Graph unit provides many variations of text styles and formats, as well as procedures for selecting and changing them. These are considered again in Chapter 5.

Plotting with Turbo Pascal

We can now consider how to plot proper graphs on the screen. In order to keep a program independent of the hardware, Turbo Pascal provides a means of ascertaining the maximum x and y coordinates that apply for the graphics adapter in place when the program runs. There are two functions:

GetMaxX   gives the maximum x coordinate (e.g. 640)
GetMaxY   gives the maximum y coordinate (e.g. 200)

and for reasons of efficiency, their values are usually copied into variables at the start of a program.

To plot a graph, we would want a coordinate system which goes from *xmin* to *xmax* and from *ymin* to *ymax*, as in:

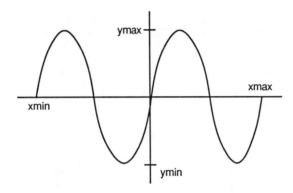

Then we can transform a point x in this system to one on the Turbo screen with the equations:

$$screen\text{-}x = (x - xmin) \,/\, range\text{-}of\text{-}x * screen\text{-}width$$

where:

$$range\text{-}of\text{-}x = (xmax - xmin)$$

and the screen width is given by *GetMaxX*. For y, we apply a similar transformation, except that we must 'flip' the value over on the screen, because the y-axis goes downwards, not upwards. This is done by subtracting *screen-y* from *GetMaxY*, as in the next example.

Example 4.7   Plotting a curve

Problem	Plot the graph of *a sin (bx)* between $m\pi$ and $n\pi$, where a, b, m and n are read in.

| Solution | The graph will consist of points which are joined together by lines. If we make the points close together, the line will actually look quite smooth. We can experiment with this by reading in the number of points required.

To establish the points on the graph, we loop through x values, calculate the y values and transform both to their corresponding screen values as shown above. We can keep the calculation of the x and y values quite distinct from their transformation to points on the screen. Notice that the formulae will produce real numbers, which will have to be rounded and converted to integers for use in the line drawing procedure.

| Algorithm | It is only the conversion of coordinates which is tricky. Given that, the plotting algorithm is straightforward.

Plot a curve
Read in data
Switch to graphics
Set x to xmin
Move to position (x, asin(bx)) ——————————— | Convert coordinates
                                              | Move to screen position

While x <= xmax
          Draw to position (x, asin(bx)) —— | Convert coordinates
          Increment x | Draw to screen position

Notice that we conduct the initial dialogue in normal mode, and then switch to graphics to draw the graph. This is a simple approach for now: reading in graphics mode is covered in the next chapter.

| Program |

```
PROGRAM CurvePlot (input,output);
USES Graph;

CONST
  nsteps = 200;
VAR
  x, y, dx        : real;
  a, b            : real;
  xmin, xmax,
  ymin, ymax      : real;
  xrange, yrange  : real;

PROCEDURE Startgraphics;
  VAR  driver, mode: integer;
  BEGIN
```

```
      driver := detect;
      InitGraph (driver, mode, ' ');
      ClearDevice;
    END; {SetUp}

PROCEDURE Initialise;
  VAR m, n : integer;
  BEGIN
    writeln('Graph of a sin bx between m pi and n pi');
    writeln('Type in values for a, b, m and n');
    readln(a,b,m,n);
    xmin := m * pi;
    xmax := n * pi;
    if (m > 0) and (n >= 0)
    then xrange := xmax-xmin
    else
    if (m <= 0) and (n < 0)
    then xrange := abs(xmax - xmin)
    else xrange := xmax + abs(xmin);
    ymin := -a;
    ymax := a;
    yrange := 2*a;
  END; {Initialise}

PROCEDURE PlotReal(x, y : real; drawline: boolean);
  VAR
    screenX, screenY: integer;
  BEGIN
    screenX := round((x-xmin)/xrange*GetmaxX);
    screenY := round((y-ymin)/yrange*GetMaxY);
    if drawline then  LineTo(screenX, screenY)
              else  MoveTo(screenX, screenY);
  END; {PlotReal}

BEGIN
  Initialise;
  StartGraphics;
  dx := xrange/nSteps;
  x := xmin;
  y := a * sin(b*x);
  PlotReal(x, y, false);
  WHILE x <= xmax do begin
    y := a * sin(b*x);
    PlotReal(x ,y, true);
    x := x + dx;
  END;

  readln;
  CloseGraph;
END.
```

> **Testing** The program can be run with different data values to produce different shaped curves. The curve below had $a = 2$, $b = 2$ and ran from $-\pi$ to π.

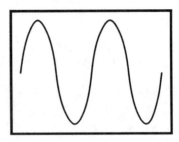

To test that the program correctly adapts to different screen sizes, it will have to be run on different computers.

Pixel graphics

Not all graphs are linear – some are planar, and must be plotted point by point. On a graphics screen, these points are called **pixels**. The procedure:

```
PROCEDURE PutPixel (x, y : integer; Colour : word);
```

draws a dot of the given colour at the given x,y coordinate. The following Turbo Pascal program uses only *PutPixel* and is surprisingly simple for the complex pictures it can produce.

Example 4.8 The Mandelbrot set

Named for the mathematician who discovered it, Benoit B Mandelbrot.

There is a mathematical formula which can generate an infinite variety of colourful pictures such as the one on the cover of this book. The Mandelbrot Set is generated by iterating a simple function on the points of the complex plane. Some of the points diverge in ever growing values, and these points lie outside the set. Other points cycle, and these lie within the set. Each point can be plotted on the screen, with black indicating that the point lies within the set, and a different colour indicating a different rate of divergence, and 'distance' from the set. A simple algorithm for the Mandelbrot set is:

```
For each pixel point (x, y) do
    iteration := 0
    z := complex(0.0, 0.0)
```

```
      while (iteration < 100) and ((mod z) < 4) do
         z := z*z + complex (x,y)
         iteration := iteration + 1
      end
   end;
```

A point will be plotted if the loop terminates before mod x reaches 4. The number of iterations taken is then used to establish the colour of the point.

Different parts of the set can be plotted by setting the ranges of x and y. For the full Mandelbrot set, we need $x : -1.5$ to 0.5 and $y : -1.2$ to 1.2. Other values can be chosen to blow up different areas of the image. Because this program involves a considerable amount of real computation, it may take quite a while to run, especially if the computer does not have a maths co-processor installed.

Warning: this program can take a long time to run.

```
PROGRAM Mandelbrot;

USES graph;

CONST
   xmin     = -1.5;
   xrange   = 2.0;
   ymin     = -1.2
   yrange   = 2.4;

VAR
   yaxis, xaxis   : integer;
   x, deltax,
   y, deltay      : real;
   driver, mode   : integer;
   MaxX, MaxY     : integer;

PROCEDURE plot (x, y : integer;  colour : integer);
   BEGIN
      if colour  > 0
         then putpixel (x, y, (colour mod 14) + 1)
         else putpixel (x, y, 0);
   END;

FUNCTION iterate (x, y : real) : integer;
   VAR
      n           : integer;
      i, r, zi, zr : real;
   BEGIN
      zr := x;  zi := y;
      n := 100;
      REPEAT
         n := n - 1;
         r := zr * zr - zi * zi + x;
         i := 2 * zr * zi + y;
         zr := r;
```

```
                        zi := i;
                        UNTIL (zr * zr + zi * zi > 4) or (n = 0);
                        iterate := n;
                      END;  {iterate}

                    BEGIN
                      mode := detect;
                      initgraph (driver, mode, ' ');
                      MaxX := GetMaxX;
                      MaxY := GetMaxY;
                      deltax := xrange / MaxX;
                      deltay := yrange / MaxY;
                      y := ymin + yrange;
                      for yaxis := 0 to MaxY do begin
                        x := xmin;
                        for xaxis := 0 to MaxX do begin
                          plot (round(xaxis), round(yaxis), iterate (x,y));
                          x := x + deltax;
                        end;
                        y := y – deltay;
                      end;
                      readln;
                    END.
```

| Testing | The output from the program is shown in the colour plates. |

Viewports

Windows in the Graph unit.
Analogous to windows in the Crt, the Graph unit provides **viewports**. All graphics output will appear in the current viewport, until a new viewport is declared. The procedure to declare a viewport is:

```
PROCEDURE SetViewPort (x1, y1, x2, y2 : integer; Clip : boolean);
```

The *Clip* parameter determines whether any output should be cut off at the viewport boundaries, if it tries to exceed them. There are two constants defined in Graph, *ClipOn* and *ClipOff*, and most of the time one would want to set a viewport with clipping on. However, when debugging a graphical display, it may be useful to set clipping off, to see where the output actually is going!

More to come

The graph unit also has a rich selection of routines for controlling input and for drawing shapes: these are discussed in the next two chapters.

Summary 4

1. Turbo Pascal's main **predefined types** are integer, boolean, real, character, string and text.

2. Turbo Pascal **integers** range from –32 768 to 32 767. For numbers outside this range, up to about ±2 thousand million, use longint.

3. Turbo Pascal **reals** have about eleven digits of accuracy with an exponent range of ±38. Longer reals are provided if the computer has a mathematics co-processor.

4. Numeric data can be **formatted** on output using field widths.

5. **Boolean** values are true and false. They can be written, but not read.

6. Real numbers use a **floating point** representation which gives flexibility on size and accuracy. This can cause problems with very large and very small numbers.

7. The following table summarises the operators and functions for the types discussed so far:

Type	Operators	Functions
Integer	+ – * div mod	abs, sqr, succ, pred, trunc, round, random, str
Boolean	not and or	odd, ord
Real	+ – * /	abs, sqr, sqrt, ln, exp, sin, cos, arctan, trunc, round, random
String	+	val

8. **Conditional loops** can be constructed using either while-statements or repeat-statements. The conditions must be initialised before the loop begins, and they must change during the loop.

9. **Trailer values** are a useful way of terminating a sequence of data of unknown length.

10. The Crt unit has a **keypressed** function for detecting user intervention from the keyboard.

12. The **Graph unit** in Turbo Pascal provides line, point and shape drawing facilities at the pixel level.

13. The size of the graphics **screen** can be ascertained by calling *GetMaxX* and *GetMaxY*.

14. The screen can be divided up into **viewports** and the program can switch between different viewports.

Self-check quiz 4

1. What are the five properties that define a type?

2. How would you write out the value of the smallest integer on your computer?

3. If *x* has the value 1948, what would be the output of:

```
write (x, x:10, x mod 2,ord(odd(x)));
```

4. Under what conditions are the *mod* operator and the *exp, ln* and *arctan* functions not defined?

5. Rewrite the following as a single assignment statement:

```
if (day = 29) and (month = 2)
  then possiblyleap := true
  else possiblyleap := false;
```

6. The following expression is meant to compute whether x is in the interval 1 to 10 inclusive. What is wrong with the expression? Rewrite it correctly.

```
(x >= 1) or (x <= 10)
```

7. The following loop reads and totals a temperature value every second. What is wrong with it?

```
for sec := 1 to 60 do begin
  write(sec);  read(temp);
  total := total + temp;
end;
```

8. The totalling has now to be done every tenth of a second. Could the for-loop be adapted? Rewrite the loop as a while-loop and then as a repeat-loop.

9. Given the following constant declaration and corresponding write statement what would the output be, if the computer being used has 11 decimal digits of precision? What would it be on a computer with 4 digits of precision?

```
CONST pi = 3.14159265;

writeln(pi : 10:6);
```

10. At the Zanyland Factory, the 24-hour day is divided into three shifts:

```
Shift 1      – from 00.00 to 07.59
Shift 2      – from 08.00 to 15.59
Shift 3      – from 16.00 to 23.59
```

Write an assignment statement which calculates from the time (which is given as a real number) the appropriate shift (which is an integer number).

Problems 4

Answers are given for problems marked with a §.

4.1§ **Examination marking** An examination paper has four questions in Section A and four in Section B. Each question is valued at 20 marks. Students must answer five questions in total, with at least two from Section A and two from Section B. If more questions than required are answered, then the first ones are counted and the latter ones disregarded. Unanswered questions are indicated by a zero mark.

Write a program to read in eight marks for each of several students and print out their final marks according to the rules. If rules are broken, print appropriate messages. Sample data and results are:

Sample Input		Sample Output	
Section A	Section B	Result	Comment
10 15 0 0	20 8 17 0	70	
10 9 7 20	0 0 0 10	36	Too many from A.
5 6 10 0	19 5 3 14	45	More than 5. Too many from B.

4.2§ **Rabbits!** A scientist needs to determine when she will run out of space to house her rabbits. She starts with two rabbits and it is known that a pair of adult rabbits (that is, those more than three months old) produce on average two rabbits every three months. The scientist has space to house 500 rabbits. Write a program which will determine how many months it will be before she runs out of space. Adapt the program to print out a table of the rabbit populations (adult, non-adult and total) every three months for 5 years.

4.3§ **Pattern making** A certain engineering apparatus is controlled by the input of successive numbers. If there is a run of the same number, the apparatus can optimize its performance. Hence we would like to arrange the data so as to indicate that a run is coming.

　　　Write a program which reads a sequence of numbers and prints out each run of numbers in the form *(n*m)* where *m* is the number to be repeated *n* times. These instructions are printed in brackets on a new line, to indicate that they are going to the apparatus. Note that a run could just consist of a single number. The numbers are terminated by a zero, which halts the apparatus. Sample input and output would be:

Sample input and output
```
20 20 20 20 20 20 20 20 20 20 50
(10*20)
50 50 50 50 60
(5*50)
60 60 60 60 20
(5*60)
30
(1*20)
30 30 30 90
(4*30)
0
(1*90)
(0)
```

4.4 **Graph printing** Improve the sin graph plotting program developed in Example 4.7, so that it adds simple axes, vertically along the left side of the graph and horizontally through the centre of the graph. Change the function being plotted, to try plots of simple quadratic functions.

4.5 **Graphing daily temperature changes** A weather station records the temperature every two hours, for 24 hours. The minimum and maximum temperatures ever recorded are −10 and 50 degrees Celsius respectively. We want a graph of the diurnal variation. Write a program to read in the twelve temperatures for a day and plot a suitable graph on screen, with a horizontal line drawn through the average temperature.

4.6 **Drawing a grid** Write a program which will draw a grid of 20 divisions down and 10 across, using the full screen. Have the program discover the size of the screen and divide it up accordingly.

4.7 **Real functions** Write a program similar to that in Section 4.2, this time tabulating the values for all the real functions, for values between two given limits. Experiment with the layout and field widths to obtain a reasonable looking table.

4.8 **Landscapes again** Redo Example 2.6 using the Graph unit and viewports.

4.9 **Averages** Adapt the summation program to print out the mean of the numbers.

4.10 **Hare and fox** A hare starts at a point (0,0) and runs due north at a constant speed *P*. A fox starts at some point (*x,y*) and gives chase at some speed *Q*, running directly towards the present position of the hare. Simulate the chase on the screen using graphics at whatever level you have available. Allow the user to experiment with different values of *x, y, P* and *Q*.

4.11§ **Conversion tables** Engineers in a plant have been trained to work in kilograms when measuring mass, but their clients and suppliers often wish to know quantities in pounds (lbs) and ounces (oz). The engineers would like to print out conversion tables to paste on little cards 20 lines deep. The output should be arranged in three columns to look like this:

kg	lbs oz	kg	lbs oz	kg	lbs oz
10.0	22 1	12.0	26 7	14.0	30 14
10.1	22 4	12.1	26 11	14.1	31 1
10.2	22 8	12.2	26 14	14.2	31 5
10.3	22 11	12.3	27 2	14.3	31 8

Write a program which reads in the starting kg value and prints out the appropriate card for 6 kg from there on. *Hint*: The conversion factor is 1 kg = 2.205 lbs.

4.12 **Birthdays** The probability of two people in a group of n having the same birthday is:

$$p(n) = 1 - \frac{365}{365} \times \frac{364}{365} \times \frac{363}{365} \cdots \frac{365 - n + 1}{365}$$

Write a program to evaluate and print this probability for groups of 2 to 60 people.

4.13 **Car tax** There is a special tax on cars in Zanyland which is presently at the following rate:

Net price	Rate
< D5000	15%
D5000 – D10000	D1000 (flat rate)
>D10000	10%

Write a program which prints out the net price, tax and gross price for cars with net prices between D2500 and D12500 in steps of D500.

4.14 **Powers** Raising to a power x^y can be done by a loop, provided y is an integer. Using nested loops with x and y, write a program to print out a table of x to the power y for y up to 5 and x up to as high as your computer will go in integers. Then convert x to a real number by multiplying by 1.0 and see how high you can go.

4.15 **Areas of shapes** A firm of engineers is interested in knowing the area of different shapes with the same basic measurement. Specifically, they would like to compare the area of a square, circle, equilateral triangle and rhombus (angle 45°) with the measurement r used as follows:

Write a program to print these values (in m²) for a range of values of r from 1 to 20 metres. *Hint*: the area of a circle is πr^2, of an equilateral triangle $\frac{\sqrt{3}}{4}r^2$, and of the rhombus $\frac{r^2}{\sqrt{2}}$.

4.16 **Summing a series** Write a program which prints out the first 10 terms in the series:

$$\sum \frac{1}{i^2} = 1 + \frac{1}{2^2} + \frac{1}{3^2} + \dots$$

Character processing

This chapter looks at characters, strings and text and considers ways in which they are processed. It introduces the last control statement – the case-statement – and pays a good deal of attention to user-interface issues. We end with a case study on exam mark calculations and a look at the input/output facilities of Turbo Pascal's Crt and Graph units.

5.1 Characters

So far we have dealt mainly with numeric values. Much of computing is concerned with numbers, but certainly not all of it. Computers are also **information** processing machines, and information consists mainly of text. Text itself is comprised of **characters**, and Turbo Pascal has features which enable characters to be handled particularly well.

Properties of the type *char*

The character type in Pascal is called *char*. We shall examine the properties of *char* as we did for integers and booleans.

Range of values

Turbo Pascal supports the ASCII character codes from 0 to 255. These include the letters, digits, punctuation symbols, arithmetic operators and various other special control and display characters. Only the characters that are represented on a typical keyboard can be typed in directly. This set includes:

A B C D ...
a b c d ...
0 1 2 3 ...
. , ; : ? ! % ( ) + – = / * @ $ ...

ASCII stands for American Standard Code for Information Interchange. The remainder of the 256 characters can be displayed by using their ASCII number in the function *chr*, or by prefacing the number with a #. For example, to ring the bell on a PC, we can:

```
write(chr(7));        or        write(#7);
```

For a full list of characters, see Appendix F.

Notation for literals

A character literal is written within single quotes (or apostrophes), for example, 'A' or '+'. A quote itself is written twice, within its own quotes, that is, ''''.

Input and output

Character input and output is straightforward. Characters can appear in read and write statements, interspersed with numbers and strings. If *ch* and *sign* are character variables and *amount* is an integer, then we can have statements such as:

```
read(ch);
writeln('The balance is ', sign, amount:1);
```

which would produce the output:

The balance is –300

The length of a character is one. If a field width is specified in the write statement, the character will be right-justified in the appropriate number of spaces. For example, we might have the statement and output:

```
writeln ('Jones', 'A':4);                    Jones    A
```

Operators

The six relational operators are defined for characters:

$$= \quad <> \quad < \quad > \quad <= \quad >=$$

The ordering achieved by the relational operators is based on the underlying character set, so we should not rely on any group of characters, say the letters, always coming before, say, the digits. However, we can assume that the letters themselves are in the correct alphabetic order and that the digits 0 to 9 are also in sequence.

A loop variable of a for-statement can be of type character, as can the key of a case-statement (see Section 5.4). For example, consider the excerpt: *Characters in loops.*

```
{Printing all characters between two that are given}
read(first, last);
if first < last
then
   for ch := first to last do write(ch)
else
   for ch := last to first do write(ch);
```

Given *OK* as data, it will write out **KLMNO**.

Finally, there is a special operator for set membership, *in*, which can be put to good use with characters. It is discussed at the end of the section.

Functions

There are five predefined functions for characters in Turbo Pascal, namely:

succ(ch)	the next characters after *ch* (c.f. +1 for integers)
pred(ch)	the character before *ch* (c.f. −1 for integers)
ord(ch)	the ordinal value of *ch* in the underlying character set
chr(n)	the character whose ordinal value is *n*.
UpCase(ch)	the upper case version of *ch*, if applicable.

Converting to capitals.

There are natural error conditions associated with these functions. If there are 256 possible characters with ordinal values from 0 to 255, then *pred(0)* and *succ(255)* are undefined, as is the *chr* of any number outside this range.

The *ord* and *chr* functions can be used to discover the ordering of the characters on a computer. Assuming that there are 256 characters, the following program will display them, together with their ordinal values.

```
PROGRAM CharacterSet (output);
  VAR i : 0 .. 255;
  BEGIN
    for i := 0 to 255 do write(i:4, chr(i):2);
  END.
```

Running this program, one notices that funny things happen on the screen at first – this is because special characters such as DEL, LF, BEL, and so on are being printed. To omit these characters, the loop can start at 32 or so.

Exercise
Alter the program to print out the characters in neat columns across the page.

Example 5.1   A window border

| Problem | Knowing that we shall be using several windows at a time in future programs, we would like to be able to create a nice border around each, as for example:

Knowing that we shall be using several windows at a time in future programs, we would like to be able to create a nice border around each, as for example:

| Solution | To display double lines like this, we could use the Graph unit and the drawline procedure. However, we may not have a suitable graphics adapter, and may wish to stick to the Crt unit. Fortunately, the ASCII set includes special characters from which such a box can be constructed. They are:

To display double lines like this, we could use the Graph unit and the drawline procedure. However, we may not have a suitable graphics adapter, and may wish to stick to the Crt unit. Fortunately, the ASCII set includes special characters from which such a box can be constructed. They are:

Special ASCII characters.

Each of these components occupies the space of one character. We must therefore decide that the border will be drawn just outside the given window coordinates, and of course we shall have to check that there is space to do this.

Note, however, that when we write in the last character of a window, scrolling occurs, which we would not want for our border, so in fact we shall need an extra two characters on the right hand side.

Algorithm The algorithm is:

Drawing a border

Check the coordinates
Create a window one character larger on the left and two on the right
Write the top left corner
Write the top line using a loop
Write the top right corner
For each of the lines in between,
        write a bar, go to the right side, write a bar
Write the bottom left corner
Write the bottom line using a for loop
Write the bottom right corner

There is a decision to be made as to whether we should clear the window at the same time as writing the border: sometimes this may be desirable, sometimes not. We could make this option an additional parameter, and treat the centre lines differently depending on which is chosen.

Program

```
PROCEDURE Border (x1, y1, x2, y2 : integer; clear : boolean);
   CONST
      topleft      = 201;
      topright     = 187;
      bottomleft   = 200;
      bottomright  = 188;
      horizontal   = 205;
      vertical     = 186;
      space        = ' ';

   VAR
    x : 1..80;
    y : 1..25;

   BEGIN
    if not ((x1 in [2.. 76]) and (y1 in [2..21])
        and (x2 in [3..78]) and (y2 in [3..23]))
    then begin
      gotoxy (x1, y1);
      writeln('There is no room for the border');
      writeln('with these coordinates:');
      writeln(x1:4, y1:4, x2:4, y2:4);
    end
    else begin
      window(x1–1, y1–1, x2+2, y2+2);
      gotoxy(1,1);
      write(chr(topleft));
      for x := x1 to x2 do write(chr(horizontal));
      writeln(chr(topright));
      for y := y1 to y2 do
```

```
            if clear then
                writeln(chr(vertical), space : x2–x1+1, chr(vertical))
            else begin
                write(chr(vertical));  gotoxy(y2–y1+3);
                writeln(chr(vertical));
            end;
        write(chr(bottomleft));
          for x := x1 to x2 do write(chr(horizontal));
        write(chr(bottomright));
    end;
END; {Border}
```

There are two points to note in this procedure. Firstly, note that the loops for printing the horizontal lines use *x1* and *x2* as their limits. These are values in the original domain – such as 40 and 49 – but are used by the loop simply as counters. They are not used as position markers once the window has been set. Secondly, the writing of:

> space : x2–x1 + 1

means to write a space in a gap of the given size. So if *x1* and *x2* were 40 and 49 respectively, this would write 10 spaces.

| Testing | If we call the procedure with:

> border (15, 5, 65, 10, true);

we should get something like:

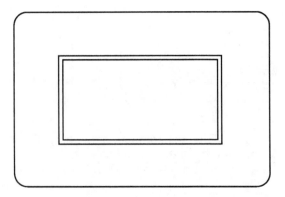

Remember that the grain of the *y*-axis is much coarser than that of the *x*.

The in-operator

Characters form natural subsets. For example, there is the set of digits, the set of capital letters, the set of vowels, and so on. In Pascal, we can construct sets of characters and use the *in* operator to check whether a value is in a given set. *Set membership.*

A set is constructed from a list of items and ranges of items, enclosed in square brackets. The ranges are expressed as starting value and ending value either side of double dots. For example, typical sets are:

```
['A', 'E', 'I', 'O', 'U', 'a', 'e', 'i', 'o', 'u']
['0'..'9']
['+', '–', '0'..'9', '.', 'E']
```

There is more about sets in Chapter 7, but note here that we can also construct sets of integers, and that the elements of a set must all be of the same type. Thus we cannot mix character literals and integer literals in the same set. To use the in-operator for expression *e* and set *s,* we have: *More in Chapter 7.*

```
e in s
```

When checking for something not in a set, we have to use the somewhat clumsy notation:

```
not (e in s)
```

Example 5.2   Validating identifiers

Problem   Suppose we need to be able to check whether words could be valid Turbo Pascal identifiers, that is, that they start with a letter or underscore and contain only letters, digits and underscores.

Solution   Write a program which reads characters and checks that they form a valid sequence, writing out an appropriate message.

Examples   Given the following identifiers, we should reach the results on the right.

limit	true
x5097a	true
5m	false
three_sided	true
_special	true

Algorithm The algorithm can be described as:

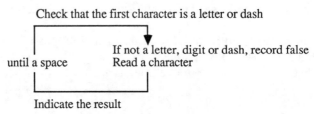

Validate

Check that the first character is a letter or dash

until a space | If not a letter, digit or dash, record false
Read a character

Indicate the result

Program

```
PROGRAM ValidateIdentifiers (input, output);
  CONST
    space = ' ';

  VAR
    correct : boolean;
    ch      : char;

  BEGIN
    writeln('****** Identifier validation ******');   writeln;
    writeln('Type a possible Pascal identifier ',
        'followed by a space');
    correct := true;
    read(ch);
    if not (ch in ['A'..'Z', 'a'..'z','_'])
    then correct := false
    else
      WHILE ch <> space do begin
        if not (ch in ['A'..'Z', 'a'..'z', '0'..'9','_'])
        then correct := false;
        read(ch);
      END;
    if correct then writeln('Correct')
            else writeln('Wrong');
  END.
```

Testing Send a series of different correct and incorrect identifiers to the program in order to check its response.

5.2 Strings

In addition to the type character, Turbo Pascal provides a type called *string*. A string is a sequence of characters with a given maximum length. To declare a string, we specify the length in square brackets.

```
String declaration

string [ maximum length ]
```

For example, we might declare:

```
VAR
    name         : string[20];
    monthname    : string[10];
    line         : string[80];
    filename     : string[12];
    numberplate  : string[7];
```

String values

Strings can be of any length up to 255 characters, and may contain characters from the whole available character set. The maximum length specifies an upper limit on the size of a particular string, but at any one time, it may contain a smaller number of characters, and be recognized as such. For example, we can say:

```
monthname := 'May';
```

in which case, the current length of *monthname* is set to 3, and if we write it out this is taken into account, thus:

```
writeln('I think ', monthname, ' is my favourite month.');
```

yields:

```
I think May is my favourite month.
```

If an attempt is made to assign more characters than the maximum declared, then Turbo Pascal should signal an error.

Reading and writing strings

Strings can be read and written using the usual statements. When reading in a string, it is probable that the number of characters will not always be exactly the maximum allowed. For example, we may say:

>   readln (monthname);

and type in:

>   April

Strings have dynamic lengths.

As long as we type a <return> key at the end of the characters, all is well. Turbo Pascal will store the five characters in *monthname* and set the length of the string to 5. If we then write out the string, only the five characters will be written, not the maximum of 10. Thus we could say:

>   writeln('I think ', monthname, ' is my favourite month.');

and get:

>   I think April is my favourite month.

If the number of characters typed in exceeds the maximum allowed, then the overflow is simply ignored. Thus:

>   readln(name);

with:

>   James Fox-Fox-Robinson

will set *name*, which is only 20 long, to *James Fox-Fox-Robins*.

Writing neat tables of strings.

Often one wishes to tabulate strings, which may, as we have seen, be of different actual lengths. Unfortunately, the effect of a field width is to **right** justify the string, giving a jagged appearance to any table. In order to **left** justify the strings, we have to write them out followed by explicit spaces up to the maximum. The standard formula is:

>   {To write a string left-justified in its maximum length}
>   write(s, space:max−length(s));

So if the maximum length is 20, say, and we write a string 9 long, we get the string followed by a space written in a gap 11 large. The 9 plus the 11 gives 20, which is what we wanted.

<return> is a vital ender for strings.

Turbo Pascal's convenient way of dealing with string input relies on close cooperation between the programmer and the user of the program in the matter of the <return> key. The user will naturally type it at the end of a string, in order to indicate that the string is finished. Turbo Pascal will recognize this, and complete the reading and set the string length accordingly. The <return> character must then be dealt with, which is accomplished by the -ln part of the readln statement. If this is not present, then the <return> character will remain pending and be read in by the next (unsuspecting) statement! Thus we make the golden rule:

> **Golden Rule**
> Always use readln for reading in strings.

String operators and functions

The six relational operators are defined for strings:

$$= \quad <> \quad < \quad > \quad <= \quad >=$$

Comparison is based first on the length and then on the ordering of the individual characters. There is also the additional operator + for joining (or concatenating) two strings together. It is also possible to obtain single characters from a string by indicating their position in square brackets, starting at 1. Thus in the above example, *name*[1] would be *J*, and *name*[2] would be *a* and so on.

+ is the concatenation operator.

There are eight standard procedures and functions defined for strings in Turbo Pascal:

```
FUNCTION Concat (S1, S2, ..., Sn : string) : string
FUNCTION Copy (S : string; Index : Integer; Count : Integer) : string;
FUNCTION Pos (Substr, S : string) : byte;
PROCEDURE Delete (var s : string; index : integer; count : integer);
PROCEDURE Insert (source : string; var s : string; index : integer);

FUNCTION Length (s : string) : integer;

PROECDURE Str (n [: width [: decimals] ]; var s : string);
PROCEDURE Val (S : string; var n; var code : integer);
```

String manipulation procedures.

The purpose of the first five routines is clear from their names. They allow quite complicated string manipulations, and are fully described in the Turbo Pascal Manual.

Str and *Val* allow conversions from numbers to strings and back again, and have the same effect as readln and writeln, except that they use variables instead of files. The *n* parameters in each case are listed without type names: the implication is that any of Turbo's numeric types is acceptable. *Length* gives the current actual length of a string, which will be anything from 0 up to the maximum with which it was declared. The current length of the string is stored in the zeroth position. Thus after *April* had been assigned to *monthname* , *monthname* [0] would have the value 5.

5.3   Text files

Up to now, we have used the terminal for all our communication with our programs. As our programs become more sophisticated and the amount of data they handle and results they produce increases, a single device for all input and output will become inadequate. We need to bring in other devices, such as the printer and disk files. Which device is appropriate at a given time will depend on what the program is doing then, and on the size and meaning of the information.

Input/output streams

A program goes through several **stages** during its running time, and with each we can associate various **input/output streams**, as shown in Figure 5.1. The common stages and streams are:

Input/output streams.

1.   **Initialisation**. During this stage, there is dialogue with the user, consisting of **prompts** and **responses**. These are most typically directed to the screen and accepted from the keyboard of the terminal, respectively.

2.   **Processing**. If there is a large amount of **data** to be processed, or if it consists of permanent information, then the most appropriate place for it is a disk file. Similarly, **results** usually need to be read quietly after a program has run, which means sending them to a printer or to a file again. Also during this phase, errors may occur, or it may be desirable to output comforting status **messages** such as '2000 records processed so far...'. These would go onto the screen, so that the user could be informed immediately, or could go to a printer, to appear intermingled with the results.

3.   **Finalisation**. It is a very good idea to end any program that processes or produces large amounts of information with a simple **message** indicating how much work was done. Once again, this could go to screen or printer.

The two key issues here are how to connect a particular device to the program and, in the case of the streams with the option of various devices, how to leave the decision as late as possible – even to runtime. The ability to

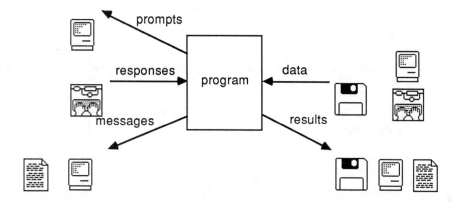

Figure 5.1 Diagram of input/output streams for a typical program

connect and reconnect devices for various streams relies on the Pascal concept of a **file.** In this section we shall consider files of text; Chapter 8 considers files of other types.

Text file statements

In Pascal, all information that is read or written using the standard read and write statements is associated with a **text file.** This fact has been largely hidden from us because we have been using the default files, called *input* and *output.* These files are nearly always connected to the default devices, which are most often the keyboard and screen respectively. In order to use other devices such as the printer or the disk, we must declare other files and indicate in the appropriate read and write statements that we want to use these files, rather than the defaults. There are actually several steps in this process:

1. **Declare** a file in the program.
2. **Assign** a device to the file.
3. **Open** the file for reading or writing.
4. **Refer** to it in all input/output statements.

Steps in accessing a file.

The forms for these operations in Turbo Pascal are:

Declaring a text file
VAR *F* : text;

Assigning a text file

assign (F, *filename*);

Opening a text file

reset (F);   {to open for reading}
rewrite (F);   {to open for writing}

Referring to text files

read (F, ...);
write(F, ...);
readln (F, ...);
writeln(F, ...);
eoln (F)
eof (F)
close (F);

Files and file names

Relationahip
with physical
files.

The file declaration declares *F* as a variable, just like any other variable. The assign procedure then associates it with an actual file on the disk, or with the printer. The filename, in the case of the disk operating under DOS, will be a string 12 characters long. So typical assigns would be:

```
VAR
   markfile, resultsfile : text;

BEGIN
   assign (markfile, 'marks.dat');
   reset (markfile);
   assign (results, 'results.out');
   rewrite(results);
```

It is important always to ensure that the file name has been added to each relevant read and write. Omitting them by mistake is a common source of odd errors in programs. In fact, since the file names may need to be written out many times in a program, it is quite useful to make them short. For example, instead of the above, we could have:

```
VAR
    inp, out : text;

BEGIN
    assign(inp, 'marks.dat');
    reset(inp);
    assign(out, 'results.out');
    rewrite(out);
```

In most programs, the actual name of the file that the program is to use will not be known when the program is written: it will be up to the user to supply it once the program starts running. Thus typically, the assign sequence will usually include a request for a file name, as in:

```
VAR
    inp, out : text;

BEGIN
    write('What file for the marks? ');
    readln(filename);
    assign(inp, filename);
    reset(inp);

    write('What file for the results? ');
    readln(filename);
    assign(out, filename);
    rewrite(out);
```

Linking up to a disk file.

Filename is just a temporary variable, and can be reused, as shown.

It is possible that the file name typed in could be incorrectly spelt, or refer to a file which does not exist, in which case the assign procedure will fail. Ways of recovering from this are discussed when we look at the DOS unit in Chapter 8.

Opening and closing files

Text files can only be accessed in read mode or write mode, not both simultaneously. The difference between setting up a file that is to be used for reading and one that is to be used for writing is in the procedure used to open it: *reset* or *rewrite*. A file can be closed during a program, and reopened again for a different purpose, or it can be associated with a different name.

Other devices

Turbo Pascal allows devices other than disk files to be connected up. Specifically, we can assign text files to *CON* for the terminal and *PRN* for the printer. In addition, we can assign files to the terminal for use by the Crt routines using *AssignCrt* instead of *Assign*. This enables output to be done using *OutText*, which is faster than writeln.

End-of-file

When we discussed loops in earlier chapters, we mentioned four ways of detecting the end of data:

- build in a count;
- preface with a count;
- end with a signal value;
- use a built-in signal value.

The last method has the decided advantage that the data can be of any length and does not need an additional terminating value. It can be achieved in Pascal by using the end-of-file function.

Pascal defines *eof* as a boolean function which returns true or false depending on the value of the end-of-file flag. When we have read the last character in a file, the end-of-file flag is set in the Pascal system, and it can be tested by calling the function *eof*. Pascal defines *eof* as a boolean function which returns true or false depending on the value of the end-of-file flag. Thus a simple loop such as:

```
while not eof (inp) do begin
  read(inp, ch);
  write(out, ch);
end;
```

will copy the contents of one text file to another.

The data that is typed in from a keyboard, and which is shown simultaneously on the screen, also forms a **file**. Its proper name is *input*, but it can be omitted, as we have seen. To indicate the end of this file, we type the special character on the keyboard, CTRL-Z. Thus if we have a simple loop such as:

```
while not eof do
  read(ch);
writeln('All done');
```

data will be accepted from the keyboard, until the end-of-file character is pressed. This will cause the loop to end and the closing message to appear.

The end-of-file character itself is not read because *eof* becomes true when the character is pressed, not when it is read.

One important property of data, when viewed as constituting a file, is that it may not be present at all. In other words, the file may be empty. To guard against this eventuality it is better to use while-loops rather than repeat-loops when processing files, and start off with a check for end-of-file.

End-of-file can also be used with data consisting of numbers, though here we have to be a bit careful. Consider the following list of numbers such as:

```
81  53  12
97
34  2  704
```

The special end-of-file character must be pressed immediately after the 4, without any spaces or returns intervening. If this is not done, then after the 704, end-of-file will not be set, and a program may try to read another number – which isn't there. The special Turbo Pascal function *SeekEof* can be used instead of *eof* to avoid this problem.

SeekEof introduced.

Example 5.3   Document statistics

| Problem | A publisher requires prospective authors to indicate the number of words in a document, as well as the average number of words per sentence.

| Solution | We can write a program which reads the text, character by character, keeping a count of the number of words and the number of sentences. We can define a word as:

Defining the data.

- starting with a letter or an apostrophe,
- containing letters, apostrophes and hyphens,
- ending with anything that isn't one of those.

Similarly, we define a sentence as ending with a punctuation mark such as fullstop, question or exclamation. Examples would be:

It is hot today, isn't it?   words = 6

Good – that's OK.   words = 3

| Algorithm | There are two ways of tackling the algorithm. The first is to regard the sentence as consisting of words and gaps (as it does) and having a loop to process these successively:

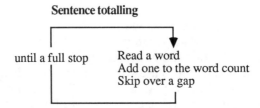

Reading a word and skipping over a gap are actions that would require loops themselves. We can therefore call this the **nested loops** or **structured solution**.

The second approach is to regard the sentence as a single stream of characters, some of which trigger events such as incrementing a count. The structure of this algorithm is quite different:

Two solutions to the same problem.

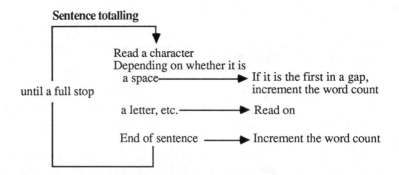

Looking at this algorithm, we can see that it depends on the state of a 'key' – the character just read. This would map into a program based on a case-statement, as described in the next section. This is called the **state solution**.

Both algorithms have their difficult parts. In the nested loops version, the problem is that in order for one of the loops to stop, it will have to have already read the first character of the next item. For example, the end of a gap is determined by the presence of a non-space. If the word-reading loop is phrased as a read-count sequence, then a word with only one letter will be lost from the count. Instead, the loops should follow a read then count-read pattern, so that the read comes at the end of a loop, providing a trigger, but not actually processing the character.

In the state approach, the problem is to distinguish between the first space in a gap (which causes the word count to be incremented) and the other spaces, which must simply be ignored. This is handled by a boolean variable which is set and tested appropriately.

| Program | We shall proceed with the structured solution, using procedures to good effect to emphasise that we are dealing with words and gaps alternately. Notice that we can avoid having to list all possible punctuation marks, by only referring to the ones in words, and using *not* to get the others.

We would like to be free to start the text with a gap, and in fact to have no data at all. This is taken care of by setting *ch* to some gap character such as space, and going straight into the *skipagap* procedure. The while-loop then ensures that nothing happens if in fact no gap or no data exists.

```
PROGRAM DocumentStatistics (input, output);

{Counts the words in the file of text}

VAR
   data        : text;
   ch          : char;
   words,
   sentences   : 0 .. maxint;
   document    : string[12];

PROCEDURE ProcessaWord;
   {called once a letter or apostrophe has been found}
   BEGIN
      WHILE not eof(data) and (ch in  ['A'..'Z', 'a'..'z', '-', ''']) do
            read(data, ch);
   END; {ProcessaWord}

PROCEDURE skipagap;
   {called once a non-word, non-sentence ender has been
      found}
   BEGIN
      while not eof(data) and not (ch in ['A'..'Z', 'a'..'z', ''']) do
         read(data, ch);
   END; {skipagap}

BEGIN
   writeln('****** Document statistics ******');  writeln;
   write('Read from what file? ');
   readln(document);
   assign(data,document);
   reset (data);
   words := 0;
   sentences := 0;
   ch := ' ';

   while not eof (data) do begin
      repeat
         skipagap;
         Processaword;
         words := words + 1;
```

```
                    until eof(data) or (ch in ['.', '!','?']);
                    sentences := sentences + 1;
                  end;

                  writeln('The number of words is ', words:1);
                  writeln('The number of sentences is ', sentences:1);
                  writeln('The average words per sentence is ',
                          round(words / sentences):1);
              END.
```

| Testing | The test data should include all possibilities. Just by looking at the program, consider what would it do if we had text which did not end with a punctuation mark, such as:

> J A Jones

Reasoning about the program's correctness.
When we get into *ProcessaWord* to read Jones, we will read the 's', go round the loop and try to read again. Since this is the end of the file, the loop stops and we exit *ProcessaWord* into the main loop, and hence straight into *skipagap*. Since *eof* is now set, *skipagap* does nothing and we come out of that loop and end gracefully. The ending is not quite so graceful if there are no words at all because then the division at the end will fail. This situation should be checked for.

Lines

Text is composed of characters, as we have seen, but Pascal goes a step further in recognising that characters can also be composed into lines. In text files, the end of each line of data has an additional special **end-of-line** marker. Just before the marker is read an end-of-line flag is set in the system. This flag can be tested using a function called *eoln*. Thus we can find out where lines end in the data, and take appropriate action.

The eoln function.
Pascal defines *eoln* as a boolean function which is true if the character which is just about to be read is the end-of-line marker, and false otherwise. Thus if we wanted to count how many lines there were in a piece of text on a file called *inp*, we would use statements such as:

```
              lines := 0;
              WHILE not eof(inp) do begin
                read(inp, ch);
                if eoln(inp) then lines := lines + 1;
              END;
              writeln('There were ',lines:1, ' lines in that file.');
```

However, Turbo Pascal's string type means that we seldom have to be concerned directly with the end-of-line marker. If we are reading whole lines of characters, then this can be done much more simply and efficiently as follows:

```
lines := 0;
WHILE not eof(inp) do begin
   readln(inp, S);
   lines := lines + 1;
END;
writeln('There were ',lines:1, ' lines in that file.');
```

When reading numbers alone, the fact that data comes on different lines can usually be ignored; this is made possible by the usual interpretation of the end-of-line marker as a space.

Reusing disk files

A disk file can be read to the end, and then read from the beginning again by the same program. All that needs to be done is to call *reset*, which will put the file back at the start. Similarly, a disk file that has been written by a program can be read back by it. What is required here is that the file be closed and then reset, which will open it for reading.

Several devices can be connected to the same file, one after another. For example, suppose the words in several documents have to be counted. An additional loop can be placed around the existing *DocumentStatistics* program and on each iteration a new file can be connected and reset.

Example 5.4   Assessing lecturer performance

Problem   Zanyland University has instituted a lecturer assessment scheme. Lecturers are evaluated on several criteria such as knowledge, manner, rapport with the class, lecturing aids, and so on. Students are asked to mark the lecturers on a scale of five, where each value is given a specific meaning. For example, part of the questionnaire might read:

Voice	Amount of material
Lively and varied	Satisfactory
Fairly lively	Rather too much
Satisfactory	Lacking
Rather dull	Far too much
Monotonous	Insufficient

Five marks are given for the first answer, four for the second, and so on down the scale. We would like to write a program to process lecturer evaluations.

| **Solution** | First of all, we must sort out the input/output streams in the system. We have five: |

1. instructions to the user on the screen;

2. dialogue from the user on the keyboard and screen;

3. the master file of questions to be read in;

4. the lecturer's file of student replies to be read in;

5. the result file of the summary of the answers.

Once we have organised these streams, the processing is fairly simple: we read a question, read the number of replies for it over each choice, output the results in a suitable way, and move on to the next question. Obviously, we would like to maintain a running total of the results so that we can print out an overall score at the end.

| **Example** | The questions file will consist of a list of questions and choices, following one after each other and separated by a blank line, |
for example:

The question file
Voice
Lively and varied
Fairly lively
Satisfactory
Rather dull
Monotonous

Amount of material
Satisfactory
Rather too much
Lacking
Far too much
Insufficient

The answers file has the counts for each option, that is, five numbers per line for each question. In addition, we record at the start of the file:

- the name of the lecturer,

- the date of the assessment,

- the name of the class concerned, and

- the number of students in the class.

These four lines of information are then copied across to the results file, as is, for identification purposes. A sample answers file might start like this:

Sample answers file   Data file 2.
M C Mouse
6 November 1991
CM131 Programming Principles – Pascal section
80 students
16 35 20 9   0
37 20 11 10 2
...

For the output, we would like the question, the sample answers, the percentage who answered each choice, and a little histogram.

| Algorithm | Apart from setting up the files, the program consists of a single loop as follows: |

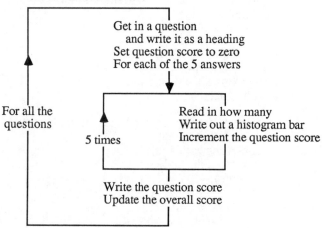

Lecturer assessment
Set overall score to zero

Get in a question
  and write it as a heading
Set question score to zero
For each of the 5 answers

For all the questions

5 times

Read in how many
Write out a histogram bar
Increment the question score

Write the question score
Update the overall score

We go straight to the program, which makes extensive use of files.

| Program |

```
PROGRAM Assessment (input, output);

CONST
   maxquestions = 3;
   maxanswers   = 5;

TYPE
   questions    = 1..maxquestions;
   answers      = 1..maxanswers;
```

Declaring three
files.

```
VAR
  questionfile,
  answerfile,
  resultfile      : text;
  score           : real;
  n               : 0..maxint;

PROCEDURE Initialise;
  VAR
    filename : string[12];
    s : string;
    i : 1..3;
  BEGIN
    writeln ('***** Lecture Assessment Scheme *****');
    write ('What file for the questions? ');
    readln (filename);
    assign (questionfile, filename);
    reset (questionfile);
    write ('What file for the students''s answers? ');
    readln(filename);
    assign (answerfile, filename);
    reset (answerfile);
    write('What file for the results? ');
    readln(filename);
    assign (resultfile, filename);
    rewrite (resultfile);

    writeln('******* Processing students replies for *****');
    for i := 1 to 3 do begin
      readln(answerfile, s);
      writeln(resultfile,s);
      writeln(s);
    end;
    readln(answerfile, n);
    writeln(resultfile, n, ' students');
    writeln(n, ' students');
  END;   {Initialise}

PROCEDURE ProcessandPrint;
  CONST
    space = ' ';
  VAR
    q           : questions;
    i, k, a     : answers;
    question,
    choice      : string[80];
    qscore      : real;
    x           : integer;

  BEGIN
    for q := 1 to maxquestions do begin
      readln(questionfile, question);
      writeln(resultfile, question);
```

```
      qscore := 0;
      for i := 1 to maxanswers do begin
        readln(questionfile, choice);
        read (answerfile, a);
        x := round(a/n*100);
        write(resultfile, chr(i-1+ord('a')), space, choice:28,
             x:3,'%',space);
        for k := 1 to x do write(resultfile, '*');
        writeln(resultfile);
        qscore := qscore + (maxanswers – q + 1)* x;
      end;
      readln(questionfile);
      writeln(resultfile, 'Score ',
                      qscore/(n * maxanswers) * 10:3:1);
      score := score + qscore;
      writeln(resultfile);
    end;
  END; {ProcessandPrint}

BEGIN
  Initialise;
  ProcessandPrint;
  writeln(resultfile);
  writeln(resultfile, 'Total score is : ',
        score/(n*maxanswers*maxquestions)*10:3:1);
  close(resultfile);
END.
```

| Testing |

If we run the program on data such as that described above, then the results file should start off like this:

M C Mouse
6 November 1991
CM131 Programming Principles – Pascal section
80 students

Lecturer
assessment
output.

Voice
a	**Lively and varied**	**20%**	***************
b	**Fairly lively**	**44%**	*********************************
c	**Satisfactory**	**25%**	********************
c	**Rather dull**	**11%**	*********
d	**Monotonous**	**0%**	

Score 7.5

Amount of material
a	**Satisfactory**	**48%**	************************************
b	**Rather too much**	**25%**	********************
c	**Lacking**	**14%**	***********
d	**Far too much**	**13%**	**********
e	**Insufficient**	**2%**	**

Score 8.0

5.4 The case-statement

The if-statement is a two-way selection statement based on conditions. However, if there are several simple tests for given values, successive else-if statements can become unwieldy. Pascal provides for so-called **keyed selection** with the case-statement. The form of the case statement in Turbo Pascal is:

Case-statement

CASE *key-expression* of
  key-values : *statement*,
  key-values : *statement*,

  . . .

  key-values : *statement*,
ELSE *statement;*
END; {CASE}

Rules for the case-statement. The case-statement considers the value of the key-expression and then endeavours to find a match among the lists of key-values. If a match is found, then the corresponding statement is executed, after which control passes to the end of the case-statement. If a match is not found, the statement after the else, if present, is executed. If there is no else part, and no match is found, then control passes to the next statement.

The key-expression must be of type integer, boolean, character or enumerated (as defined in Chapter 7). It may not be real. The key-values are lists of literals or constants of the same type as the key-expression and may also include subranges. The key-values do not have to be in any order, but each may occur only once.

As an example, consider the little jingle which gives the number of days in a month:

Thirty days hath September, April, June and November.
  All the rest have thirty-one, excepting February alone,
  Which has but twenty-eight days clear,
  And twenty-nine in each leap year.

If we assume that the following declarations and read statement have been made:

```
VAR
  month : 1 .. 12;
  days   : 1 .. 31;

BEGIN
  write('What month (1..12)? ');
  readln (month);
```

then a case-statement can be used to look at the month and set *days* to the appropriate value as follows (ignoring leap years):

```
CASE month of
  9, 4, 6, 11            : days := 30;
  1, 3, 5, 7, 8, 10, 12 : days := 31;
  2                      : days := 28;
END; {CASE}
```

As always, the statement mentioned in the form can be a compound statement and include several statements. This is needed to establish the correct day for February, taking account of leap years. To do this, the year has to be known as well and checked for a multiple of four (excluding multiples of 100, 200 and 300). With the extra declaration and read:

```
VAR  year : 0 .. 2500;

write('What year (0 .. 2500)? ');
readln (year);
```

the case-statement now becomes:

```
CASE month of
  9, 4, 6, 11            : days := 30;
  1, 3, 5, 7, 8, 10, 12 : days := 31;
  2 : if (year mod 4 = 0)
         and not ((year mod 100 = 0)
              and not (year mod 400 = 0))
      then days := 29
      else days := 28;
END; {CASE}
```

More complex case actions.

Mapping key values

In the previous example, the key was a single variable, and it mapped directly onto the values. Sometimes there are many values for each statement, and there is a simple way of adjusting them so that there is only one per statement. For example, suppose that given an examination mark, it is required to set a symbol depending on the multiple of ten, with anything over 80 being A, over 70 being B, and so on down to anything under 40 being F. The case-statement to achieve such a mapping is:

```
VAR
    mark    : 0 .. 100;
    symbol  : 'A' .. 'F';

CASE mark div 10 of
    10, 9, 8  : symbol := 'A';
    7         : symbol := 'B';
    6         : symbol := 'C';
    5         : symbol := 'D';
    4         : symbol := 'E';
    3, 2, 1, 0 : symbol := 'F';
END; {CASE}
```

This is the clearest and most efficient way of solving this problem, but it is not the only way. The same effect could be achieved using successive else-ifs and some calculations on characters as follows:

```
if mark >= 80 then  symbol := 'A' else
if mark <   40 then  symbol := 'F' else
                     symbol := chr (ord('B')– mark div 10 + 7);
```

It is certainly easier to see what is going on in a table as opposed to a calculation, so case-statements should be used in preference to if-statements where possible.

Menu handlers

Interactive programs generally have several paths through them, and the user is invited to choose a path from a menu. A common way of expressing a menu is to give each option a letter or number, and invite the user to type in the required choice. This is explored in the next example.

Example 5.5   Menu handler for controlling a database

| **Problem** | A database is being set up with the facilities to:

A standard set of requirements.

- add a new record,

- remove an existing record,

- find a record and display all its details,

- extract records with certain key values,

- sort these, and

- print them.

We have been detailed to write the procedure which interfaces with the user and passes control to a specific procedure which will perform the action required.

Solution   We should start off by doing a screen layout. The following is a fairly good first attempt:

```
    Database Main Menu
    =================

    A   Add
    R   Remove
    F   Find
    E   Extract
    S   Sort
    P   Print
    Q   Quit

        Please type your choice:
```

There are many different styles of menus. Some favour numbers for choices, others letters in sequence. However, an association between the commands and the actions helps the user, and is generally thought to present a good interface. (We were fortunate in this case that the actions all had distinct first letters.)

Options for menu commands.

Algorithm   The natural choice for a control construct is the case-statement. However, we must remember that there could be incorrect commands. In fact, one must program defensively, and **expect** the user to type incorrect commands. A loop around the reading of the command is therefore required. We also allow the user to type in upper- or lower-case letters.

Program defensively!

Program

```
PROCEDURE CommandHandler;
  VAR command : char;
  BEGIN
    REPEAT
      PrintMenu;  {Not shown here}
      repeat
        writeln(chr(bell),'Please type in your choice: ');
        read(command);
        writeln;
```

Alert the user by ringing the bell.

```
        until command in ['A','a','R','r','F','f','E','e','S','s','P','p','Q','q'];
        CASE command OF
          'A','a' : Add;
          'R','r'  : Remove;
          'F','f'  : Find;
          'E','e' : Extract;
          'S','s' : Sort;
          'P','p' : Print;
          'Q','q' :;
        END; {case}
      UNTIL command in ['Q','q'];
    END; {CommandHandler}
```

Once a Q or q is typed, the command module exits, returning control to the program that called it.

5.5 Case study 2: Exam marks

Problem

The Matriculation Board in Zanyland wishes to computerise the calculation of final examination results. Students take six or seven subjects and must pass five subjects with at least 40% in these. The final mark is computed as the average of the best six subject marks, and a symbol is given: A for over 80%, B for 70 – 79%, C for 60 – 69%, D for 50 – 59%, E for 40 – 49% and F for anything under 40%. The exams can be taken at higher or standard grade, and in order to pass overall, there must be at least three passes at higher grade and one of these must be a language or a science.

Solution

The first step is to work out exactly what input is required and what output must be produced, and at the same time, to refine the rules into a more precise form.

For each student there are going to be six or seven subject–mark pairs, as well as a name. There is no indication as to how the subjects are identified, but having acquired a list of subjects offered from the Board, we see that they all start with a different letter. It is therefore a neat idea to use the initial letter of the subject as a code as follows:

Selecting data
codes.

A	Art
B	Biology
C	Chemistry
D	Divinity
E	English
F	French

G   Geography
H   History
L   Latin
M   Mathematics
P   Physics

In this list there are three languages and five sciences. Art, divinity and history do not qualify as either. To distinguish between higher and standard grade we can use capitals and smalls. Thus a typical set of marks would be:

E 67   A 45   f 70   M 80   P 75   C 55   h 60

Adding the name to this list is a bit tricky. If it is added to the start or end, it will be difficult to separate it from the mark list without using special characters. A simpler solution is to have the name on a line by itself, as in:

Jones A D
E 67   A 45   f 70   M 80   P 75   C 55   h 60

Apart from making programming simpler, this scheme has the advantage that other information such as school or age can be added and perhaps processed by some other system, without disturbing the marker program. The marks for one student are therefore assumed to end at the end of a line.

For output, the final result and symbol are required. Since it is likely that the marks will be stored on a disk file somewhere, the name and marks of each student will have to be echoed on the output. It is also useful to have a record of which mark was not used, if seven subjects were taken. Specimen output might be:

Name	Subject marks						Excluded	%	Symbol
Jones A D	E 67	f 70	M 80	P 75	C 55	h 60	A 45	67.83	C

We can see that space is a bit tight, so that it will be necessary to restrict the echoing of the name to, say, 20 characters.

In deciding on the symbol, the specification does not say what is granted if the rules are not met, for example, if there is no higher pass of a language or science. In the absence of any advice from the Board, we decide to add three new symbols as follows:

X – did not pass five
H – did not pass three at higher grade
L – did not pass a language or science at higher grade.

Selecting error codes.

Examples

As with the previous case study, it is going to be important to choose test data carefully to test each of the conditions. One way of doing this is to keep most of the subject marks the same, and vary only one or two so as to produce all the effects required.   A sample set might be:

```
Adams Q T
E 60   a 50   M 65   c 70   h 78   P  55
Bright A B
E 60   a 50   M 65   c 70   h 78   P  35
Cairns J K
E 37   a 50   M 65   c 70   h 78   P  35
Dobson B N
E 37   A 50   m 65   c 70   H 78   D  70
```

with the corresponding results:

Name	Subject marks						Excluded	%	Symbol
Adams Q T	E 60	a 50	M 65	c 70	h 78	P 55	–	63.00	C
Bright A B	E 60	a 50	M 65	c 70	h 78	P 35	–	59.67	H
Cairns J K	E 37	a 50	M 65	c 70	h 78	P 35	–	55.83	X
Dobson B N	E 37	A 50	m 65	c 70	H 78	D 70	–	61.67	L

The 'Excluded' column was not needed as all the candidates took six subjects in these examples.

Algorithm

This problem is best tackled from the top level downwards. We start by identifying the main sections and loops of the solution as follows:

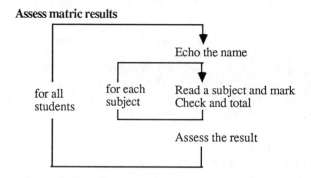

Echoing the name can be done by reading and writing a string. By setting the string maximum to 20, we can arrange to truncate any longer names, as they would not fit in the table. Moving on to reading the individual subjects and marks we realise that a simple:

read (subject, mark);

will only work once: the next time the read-statement will assign to the subject the space after the number, not the letter which is further on. Therefore, the spaces in between each pair have to be skipped. The skipping process will end when the next subject code is encountered, or in the last case, at the end of a line. Taking these possibilities into account, the following algorithm emerges.

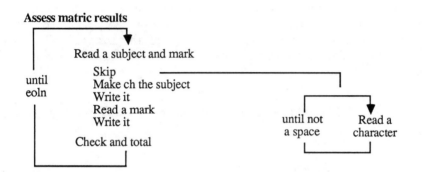

Assess matric results

Read a subject and mark

Skip
Make ch the subject
Write it
Read a mark
Write it

Check and total

until
eoln

until not
a space

Read a
character

Refining the top
level.

An important point is that the skipping loop is only meant to be used if a symbol is imminent, since it does not look for the end of the line. The reading will therefore only end correctly if the last mark is right at the end of the line. This assumption must be made clear to the person putting in the data. (How would the algorithm have to be changed to take account of random spaces at the end of the line?)

The checking and totalling procedure has several operations to perform. One of these is to find the lowest mark as the pairs are read in. This process was covered in Chapter 2 for finding the *highest* number, and can be reused with the obvious change of < for >. The top level of this section is:

Check and total

Add to total
Reset lowest if necessary
Increment subjects taken
Consider as a pass
Consider as a higher pass
Consider as a language or science

More
refinement.

The three checks follow one after each other, with the conditions in increasing order. That is, we first check for a pass, then a higher pass, then a language or science higher pass. The appropriate construct is therefore successive else-ifs.

Finally, assessing the result involves removing the lowest mark (if applicable), dividing by 6 and then calculating the symbol. Mapping a mark to a symbol was developed in the previous section, and the case-statement from that section can be brought straight across, with the special symbols for breaking the rules being handled first.

Program

Each of the four sections is programmed as a separate procedure. Even though they are each only called once, having the procedures enables the calls at the outer level to reflect the structure of the program. Two extra procedures are added to clear all totals, and to print the instructions for the data.

```
PROGRAM MatricResults (input, output, data, list);

  CONST
    space       = ' ';
    passmark    = 40;
    studentmax  = 4000;
    NeedToTake  = 6;
    namemax     = 20;

  VAR
    {Input values}
      subject   : char;  {letters}
      mark      : 0 .. 100;

    {Checks and totals}
      total     : 0 .. 700;
      lowest    : 0 .. 100;
      taken,
      passes,
      highers   : 0 .. 7;
      language,
      science   : boolean;

    {results}
      symbol    : 'A' .. 'X';
      result    : real; {0.00 .. 100.00}

    {files and counts}
      data,
      list      : text;
      n         : 0 .. studentmax;

  PROCEDURE EchoName;
    VAR  name : string[namemax];
    BEGIN
```

```
          readln (data, name);
          write(list, name, space:namemax - length(name));
       END; {EchoName}

   PROCEDURE Clear;
     BEGIN
       total := 0;
       lowest := 100;
       taken := 0;  passes := 0;  highers := 0;
       language := false;
       science := false;
     END; {Clear}

   PROCEDURE ReadSubjectandMark;
     VAR ch : char;
     BEGIN
       repeat
         read (data, ch);
       until ch <> space;
       subject := ch;
       write (list, subject);
       read (data, mark);
       write (list, mark:3, space:2);
     END;  {ReadSubjectandMark}

   PROCEDURE CheckandTotal;
     BEGIN
       total := total + mark;
       if mark < lowest then lowest := mark;
       taken := taken + 1;
       if mark >= passmark then begin
         passes := passes + 1;
         if subject in ['A'..'P'] then begin
           highers := highers + 1;
           case subject of
             'E', 'F', 'L'          : language := true;
             'B', 'C', 'G', 'M', 'P'  : science := true;
             'A', 'D', 'H'          : {Don't count}
           end; {case}
         end;
       end;
     END; {CheckandTotal}

   PROCEDURE AssessResult;

     PROCEDURE CalculateSymbol;
       BEGIN
         if passes < 5 then symbol := 'X' else
         if highers < 3 then symbol := 'H' else
         if not (language or science)  then symbol := 'L' else
         case round(result) div 10 of
           10, 9, 8  : symbol := 'A';
           7          : symbol := 'B';
```

```
6          : symbol := 'C';
5          : symbol := 'D';
4          : symbol := 'E';
3, 2, 1, 0  : symbol := 'F';
end; {case}
END; {CalculateSymbol}

BEGIN
if taken > NeedToTake
then begin
  total := total − lowest;
  write (list, lowest:5);
end else write (space:5);
result := total / 6;
write(list, result:9:2);
CalculateSymbol;
writeln (list, symbol:3);
END; {AssessResult}
```

End of the nested procedure.

```
PROCEDURE Instructions;
BEGIN
  writeln('The file of data must have each student''s ');
  writeln('information on two lines as follows:');
  writeln;
  writeln('    Jones A D');
  writeln('    E 67   A 45   f 70   M 80   ',
          '  P 75   C 55   h 60');
  writeln;
END; {Instructions}

PROCEDURE ConnectFiles;
VAR filename : string[12];
BEGIN
  write('What data file?');
  readln(filename);
  assign(data, filename);
  reset (data);
  write('What results file?');
  readln(filename);
  assign(list, filename);
  rewrite(list);
  writeln(list, '   Name      Subject marks      ',
          '  Excluded   %   Symbol');
END; {ConnectFiles}

BEGIN
  writeln('****** Exam results ******');
  Instructions;
  ConnectFiles;
  n := 0;

  WHILE not eof(data) do begin
    EchoName;
```

```
         Clear;
         while not eoln (data) do begin
            ReadSubjectandMark;
            CheckandTotal;
         end;
         readln(data);
         AssessResult;
         n := n + 1;
      END;
      close(list);
      writeln (n:1, ' students processed');
   END.
```

Testing

Some test data was given above in the examples. Much more is needed, but
remember to keep it as simple as possible so that it is relatively easy to check
the results that the computer produces. For the record, this is what might
appear on the screen when this program is run:

****** Exam results ******
The file of data must have each student's
information on two lines as follows:

Jones A D
E 67   A 45   f 70   M 80   P 75   C 55   h 60

What data file? Green School
What results file? PRN
86 students processed

The results themselves would appear on the printer, as requested.

5.6   Turbo Pascal's graphic input/output

Interactive programs have a freedom not accorded their linear counterparts,
and can display and request information making use of position as well as
text. We shall consider here how to use the screen with both the Crt unit and
the Graphics unit.

Crt input and output

Input and output when the Crt unit is in operation can be done in the normal
manner with reads and writes. However, the Crt provides additional routines

to assist with positioning questions and answers. These were discussed in Section 3.3, and are further illustrated in the next example.

Example 5.6   Using windows for menus

In a program that is going to run for some time, offering choices to the user, a menu will be an important anchor point. As such, it should remain on the screen, and not be scrolled off or overwritten while other activities take place.

A popular choice for the menu is a **menu bar** at the top or bottom of the screen. Provided the available options can fit on one line, this is an attractive choice, since it makes minimal impact on the space available for the actual processing of the program.

Setting up a menu bar, say, at the top of the screen is easy. We can write one out such as:

A menu bar.   **Menu: Add Remove Find Extract Print Quit**

where the implication is that the first character of each option is the command character. We then define the rest of the screen as a window, and let the program run.

The problem is how to enable the selection of options, and where this should take place. There are two approaches:

- return to the top line after each action and wait for a command; or
- designate some character such as <escape> as a means of getting out of any operation and into the menu.

The second is more difficult to implement, as it requires inspection of every character that comes in. The first is relatively straightforward. We change the menu bar to:

Menu: Add Remove Find Extract Print Quit | Command?

and wait after the question mark for a command to be selected.

An alternative approach to menu bars is to have a proper menu window, and use a procedure similar to command handler in Example 5.6. We may wish to keep the menu in the top left corner of the screen, and handle commands there. The following shows an extract from a simple database program which adopts this approach. Notice the use of constants for the coordinates, not only of the menu window, but also of the message and

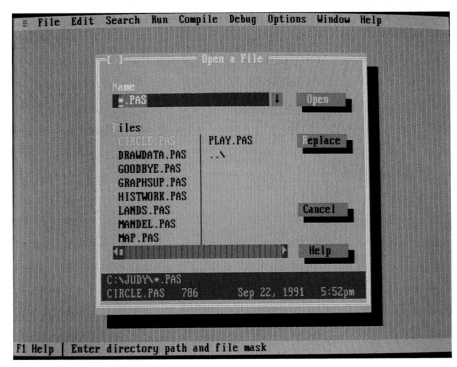

The Turbo Pascal environment, showing a dialogue box.

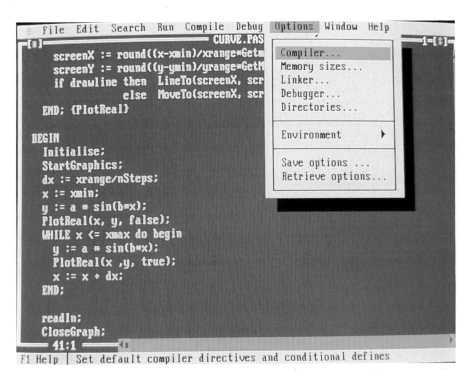

The Turbo Pascal environment, showing a pull-down menu.

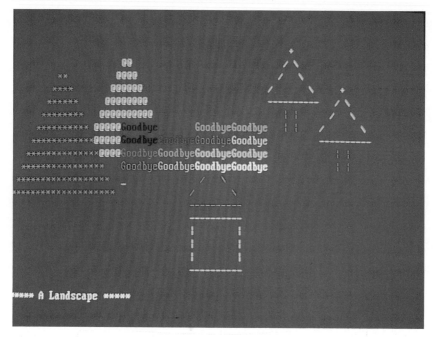

The Landscape program and Goodbye procedure.

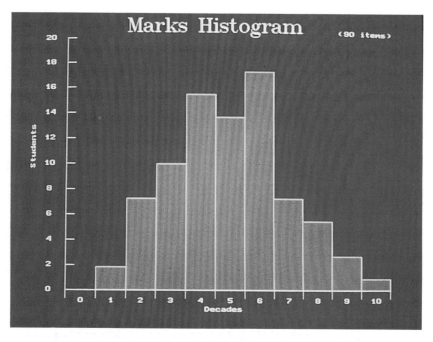

The Histogram procedure, using the Graph unit.

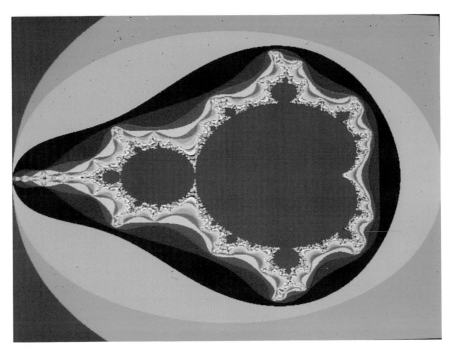

The Mandelbrot program, illustrating pixel graphics.

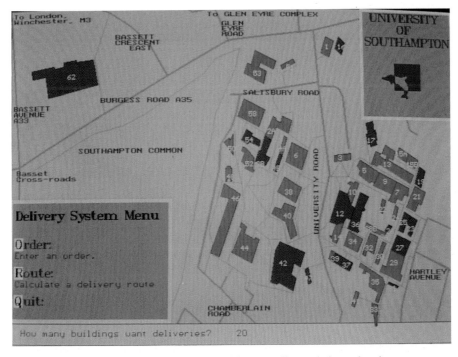

The Campus program, showing text features, line and shape drawings.
(Map © Crown copyright.)

The Circles procedure, illustrating flood filling.

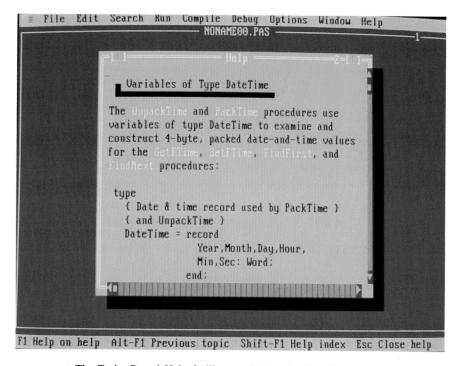

The Turbo Pascal Help facility, explaining the DateTime record.

command lines. Endeavour to work out on paper what the screen will look like, and how the commands are handled. Notice the use of *ClrEol* to erase a previous answer.

A useful pair of procedures.

```
CONST
  {Window coords}
    {Command window}
      cx1 = 1;   cx2 = 39;   cy1 = 3;   cy2 = 12;
      mx = 1;    my = 8;     {for messages}
      rx = 22;   ry = 7;     {for commands}

PROCEDURE DisplayMenu;
  BEGIN
    window(cx1, cy1, cx2, cy2);
    writeln('1  Read in');
    writeln('2  Display');
    writeln('3  Sort );
    writeln('Q  Quit');
    gotoxy(1,ry);
    write('Type in your choice ');
  END; {DisplayMenu}

PROCEDURE GetRequest;
  BEGIN
    window (cx1, cy1, cx2, cy2);
    repeat
      gotoxy(rx,ry); clreol;
      readln(command);
      gotoxy(mx, my);  clreol;
      if not (command in  ['1', '2', '3', 'Q', 'q']) then
        writeln('Not a valid command');
    until command in ['1', '2', '3', 'Q', 'q'];
    gotoxy(mx, my);  clreol;
  END; {GetRequest}
```

Integrating such routines into a program should be straightforward.

Graphic text input

The ReadKey function.

Reading values via the graphic unit is not as simple. Readln cannot be used, and each character has to be brought in via the Crt's *ReadKey* function and processed as part of a string or number, as required. *ReadKey* returns the next character typed on the keyboard, whatever it is, whereas read looks for a specific item of the required type (numeric or character). The character read is not echoed to the screen. If *KeyPressed* was true before the call to *ReadKey* , the character is returned immediately. Otherwise *ReadKey* waits for a key to be typed. The use of *ReadKey* with extended character codes is discussed in Example 8.6.

Example 5.7 A general graphic input routine

The ReadKey
function.

| Problem | Develop a general procedure for reading in replies to questions when the Graphics unit is operating.

| Solution | We can use the *ReadKey* procedure to pick off characters one by one and construct a string, until the return key is pressed. Thereafter, the calling routine can decide whether to convert the string to a number, using the *Val* function.

| Algorithm | The algorithm consists of a simple repeat loop, passing each character through a case-statement and appending it to the reply string. If a number is expected, then the procedure can ignore non-numeric characters. By detecting a backspace character (ACSII value 8), the routine can also respond to user's mistakes. The parameters it will need are:

```
VAR
  Reply    :string;
  Prompt   :string;
  x, y     :word;
  Letters  :boolean;
```

where *x* and *y* are the screen positions at which the question must be posed.

ReadKey
needs
OutTextxy.

Unlike read, *ReadKey* does not echo the character on the screen, so each time round the loop, the current value of the reply is actively displayed using *OutTextxy*.

| Procedure |

```
PROCEDURE GetInput (VAR Reply:string;
                    Prompt:string;
                    x, y:word;
                    Letters:boolean);
  CONST
    backspace = 8;
    return    = 13;
  VAR ch :char;

  BEGIN
    OutTextXY(x,y,prompt);
    Reply:='';

    repeat
      ch:=readkey;
      CASE ch of
        'A'..'Z',
        '(',')',' ',','  : if letters then reply:=order+ch;
        'a'..'z'         : if letters then
                              reply:=reply+chr(ord(ch)-ord('a')+ord('A'));
```

```
        '0'..'9'     : reply:=reply+ch;
        chr(backspace)   :delete(reply,length(reply),1);
        chr(return) : {do nothing};
      end;{case}
      OutTextXY(x,y,reply);
    until ch=chr(return);
  END;{GetInput}
```

| Testing |

This routine is used in the map drawing program of Case Study 3 in Chapter 7.

Graphic text output

Turbo Pascal provides a variety of text fonts and styles for output. These are controlled by the procedures:

```
PROCEDURE SetTextStyle
            (Font : word; Direction : Word; CharSize : word);
PROCEDURE SetTextJustify(Horiz, Vert : word);
```

where the following constants apply:

```
CONST
{Fonts}
  DefaultFont    = 0;
  TriplexFont    = 1;
  SmallFont      = 2;
  SansSerifFont = 3;
  GothicFont     = 4;

{Directions}
  HorizDir   = 0;
  VertDir    = 1;

{Horizontal justifying}
  Lefttext      = 0;
  CenterText = 0;
  RightText   = 2;

{Vertical justifying}
  BottomText = 0;
  CenterText = 1;
  TopText     = 2;
```

A serif is a line on a letter: our text is seriffed, the program font is not.

Not a redefinition.

Character sizes are expressed as multiplications of the basic size, from one up to 10. A *charsize* of one will use an 8x8 pixel rectangle, and so on. Normally one is used for the default font, and four for the others.

Example 5.8 Investigating fonts

| Problem |

What do the fonts look like, and how big are they? How will they fit into a proposed screen design?

| Solution |

To answer these questions, we should set up a text program to look at the effects of the different font styles and sizes. In addition, we note that there are two useful functions:

```
FUNCTION TextHeight (S : String);
FUNCTION TextWidth (S : String);
```

which will return the height and width of a given string or character in pixels.

| Algorithm |

To illustrate the variety offered, we choose various styles and sizes, displaying the parameters in their own font.

| Program |

```
PROGRAM FontTester (input, output);
 USES graph;
VAR
  driver, mode    : integer;
  y, font,
  hori, verti, size  : word;
  s               : string;

PROCEDURE ShowFont(font,size,hori,verti, x : word;
                            var Y : word);
  VAR
    hs, ws : string[2];
    fs      : string[16];

  BEGIN
    SetTextStyle (font, horizdir, size);
    SetTextJustify (hori, verti);
    y := y + 40;
    Str(TextHeight('M'),hs);
    Str(TextWidth('M'),ws);
    case font of
      0 : fs := 'DefaultFont';
      1 : fs := 'TriplexFont';
      2 : fs := 'SmallFont';
      3 : fs := 'SanSerifFont';
      4 : fs := 'GothicFont';
    end;
    s := fs +' size '+chr(size+ord('0'));
    OutTextxy(x, y, s);
    s := 'Height ' + hs + ' Width ' + ws;
```

```
      y := y + 40;
      OutTextxy(x, y, s);
    END;

  BEGIN
    driver := detect;
    InitGraph(driver, mode, '');
    Y := 0;
    ShowFont(DefaultFont,0,CenterText,BottomText,GetMaxX div 2,Y);
    ShowFont(TriplexFont,0,LeftText,BottomText,0,Y);
    ShowFont(TriplexFont,2,LeftText,BottomText,0,Y);
    ShowFont(SmallFont,0,RightText,BottomText,GetMaxX,Y);
    ShowFont(SmallFont,8,RightText,BottomText,GetMaxX,Y);
    ShowFont(SansSerifFont,0,LeftText,BottomText,0,Y);
    ShowFont(GothicFont,0,RightText,BottomText,0,Y);
    readln;
    CloseGraph;
  END.
```

| Testing |

This program will run on any screen with a graphics adapter. However, to print out the results, we need a high quality printer, and sometimes even special software. The following is an example of output that could be thus obtained.

`DefaultFont size 0`

`Height 8 Width 8`

TriplexFont size 0
Height 31 Width 24

TriplexFont size 2

Height 20 Width 16

`SmallFont size 0`

`Height 9 Width 6`

Height 22 Width 15

SmallFont size 8

SanSerifFont size 0
Height 32 Width 21

Summary 5

1. The type *char* includes the 256 ASCII characters. Some **characters** are printable, some have control functions such as ringing the bell. Those not on the keyboard can be accessed via their codes.

2. **Operations** on characters include the six relations and the in-operator for testing for set membership. There are four **functions** applicable to characters namely, *succ, pred, ord* and *chr.*

3. The **end of a file** (*eof*) is set when a control character is typed on the keyboard (CTRL-Z) or when the end of a disk file is reached.

4. **End of line** (*eoln*) is set when RETURN is pressed on the keyboard, or when the last character in a line on a file is read.

5. Interactive programs usually have several input/output **streams** for prompts, responses, messages, data and results. Most of these benefit from being handled by redirectable text files.

6. Turbo Pascal provides facilities for declaring, assigning, opening and referring to **text files**.

7. The **case-statement** provides for selecting from a group of statements based on a key value.

8. Case statements can only be used with integer, char, boolean or enumerated **keys**, not with real or string keys.

9. Input in **graphics mode** must be handled at the character level.

10. Turbo Pascal provides special procedures for reading and writing in a variety of **font** styles, when in graphics mode.

Self-check quiz 5

1. How does one get the computer to ring its bell?

2. Would it be correct to say: for s := 'AAA' to 'ZZZ' do write(s); Why?

3. What is the expression for obtaining the numerical value of a character that you suspect is a digit?

4. Write a while loop that reads and writes characters while they are not digits. Use the in-operator in the condition.

5. How is end-of-file signalled when typing from the keyboard on your computer?

6. How are files assigned to devices in Turbo Pascal?

7. If a file has been assigned to a disk, can it later be assigned to the printer without restarting the program?

8. Identify all the mistakes in the following case statement.

```
case letter of
  'b' : write('banana');
  'a' : write('apricot');
  'g', 'gr' : write('grapes');
  'a' : write('apple');
end case;
```

9.   In Turbo Pascal, what happens if the value of the key is not one of those listed in the case-statement?

10.   Write calls to Graphics unit routines to print your name in the centre of the screen in a seriffed font, about 2 cms high.

Problems 5

Answers are provided for problems marked with a §

5.1§   **Converting names** A very old file of people's names was created using all capital letters. Convert it to the usual capital and lower-case letters. Take account of initials, but do not go as far as handling surname prefixes properly, for example:

R A JONES	R A Jones
J. FOX-ROBINSON	J. Fox-Robinson
P DU PLESSIS	P Du Plessis

5.2§   **Word length profile** We already have a program to calculate the average length of words in a piece of text. Following on from this, reprocess the same file, counting how many words are above the average length.

5.3§   **Splitting a file** Suppose we have a file of numerical readings, some of which are negative and some of which are positive. We wish to create two new files, one with all the positive numbers, and one with the negative numbers, and then go back and print both out from the program, with the positive numbers file first.

5.4§   **Comments** A piece of text is stored on a file. It is divided into paragraphs separated by blank lines. Write a program which reads in the text and prints it out again, ignoring all text between Pascal comment brackets { }. Print suitable warning messages if:

  • a { is found inside a comment;

  • a } is found without a matching { ;

  • a paragraph ends without a matching }.

At the end of each paragraph print the percentage of text (excluding spaces) that occurred in comments.

Sample input	Sample output
This is the same length	This is the same length
as the comment {This	as the comment rest assured.
assured comment is the	*** No ending bracket
same length as the rest}	
rest assured. {And so	Comment is 50% of the text

5.5   **Standards** A piece of text is stored on a file. It is divided into paragraphs separated by blank lines. Write a program which reads in the text and prints it out again, having made any changes necessary to have the text conform to the following standards:

  •   three spaces at the start of a paragraph;

  •   capital letter at the start of each sentence;

  •   two spaces between sentences or main clauses, that is, after a fullstop, question mark, exclamation mark, semicolon or colon;

  •   only one space between words otherwise.

Sample input	Sample output
It is always hard to type	It is always hard to type
to a standard.Some people	to a standard. Some people
use different ones: single	use different ones: single
or double or no	or double or no spaces
spaces before a sentence.	before a sentence. I think
i think double looks best.	double looks best.

5.6 **Contents page** Write a program to produce a contents page for a book using data supplied in a fixed format. The data should be read off a file and the output sent to a printer. Consider the following input:

(First steps (The Computer, 5) (Problem Solving (Definition, 10) (Outline, 15) (Algorithms, 20)) (Programs and Procedures, 25)) (Types and Looping (Types (Integer, 30) (Character, 36) (Boolean, 43)) (Looping (Counting Loops, 49) (Conditional Loops, 52)))

The parentheses indicate the chapters, sections and subsections and the numbers following them are the page numbers. Page numbers are only given when there is no further subdivision. The output for the data above would be:

CONTENTS

1. First Steps
    1.1   The Computer 5
    1.2   Problem Solving
      1.2.1 Definition   10
      1.2.2 Outline   15
      1.2.3 Algorithms   20
    1.3   Programs and Procedures   25
2. Types and Looping
    2.1   Types
      2.2.1 Integer   30
      2.2.2 Character   36
      2.2.3 Boolean   43
    2.2   Looping
      2.2.1 Counting Loops   49
      2.2.2 Conditional Loops   52

5.7 **Lecturer assessment extended** The lecturer assessment program of Example 5.4 handles one lecturer very well. However, most lecturers would like to know how they are doing in comparison to other lecturers. Thus we keep a further file which contains the current average score for each of the questions. As we process a new questionnaire, we read the current average, merge it with the new score and write out the new current average to a new file. Implement this extension to the program. You will need to make some decision about the names of the old and new average files.

5.8 **Rectangles and squares** Positions on a computer screen are measured in pixels. These are not normally the same size in the horizontal (X) and vertical (Y) directions. The ratio of these sizes is called the **aspect ratio**, and can be obtained from the Graph unit through the procedure:

PROCEDURE GetAspectRatio (var xaspect, yaspect : word);

Write a procedure which has the same action as procedure *Rectangle*, but which works out if your computer screen has an aspect ratio of 1.0 (the same size in the X and Y directions), and adapts if it does not. Use your program to plot rectangles and squares of various sizes and positions on the screen.

6

Functions and arrays

To complete the development of procedures, we take another look at parameters and introduce functions. The chapter then concentrates on arrays, together with the subrange types they need, and ends with a look at Turbo Pascal's facilities for picture graphics.

6.1 Parameters again

Why do we use procedures? Our experience to date would probably suggest:

- to avoid duplication;
- as a conceptual tool for breaking up a problem into subproblems;
- as a documentation aid.

We have also seen that procedures can be made more powerful by allowing the effect to differ slightly each time the procedure is called, using the parameter mechanism. We can now consider parameters in a more formal way.

The parts of the procedure that are to be generalised are listed in the declaration, straight after the procedure name. These are the **formal parameters**. Correspondingly, when we call the procedure we list the specific instances for those parts and these are known as **actual parameters**.

Formal and actual parameters.

Procedure declaration

PROCEDURE name *(formal parameters)*;
   declarations
   BEGIN
      statements
   END; {name}

Procedure call

name *(actual parameters)*;

The list of formal value parameters acts as a declaration of variables that are to be used in the procedure. As for any other variables, therefore, the appropriate types must be specified. Actual parameters can be variables, expressions, procedures or functions. Parameters fall into two categories, depending on the way in which the correspondence between the formals and actuals is set up, that is:

Value and VAR
parameters.

- **value parameters** for passing values in only, and

- **VAR parameters** for passing access to variables.

With value parameters, the value of the actual parameter is passed into the procedure, and may be changed under its formal name there, but any changes do not affect the actual parameter, even if it is a variable rather than an expression. For example, the following program:

```
PROGRAM Passing (input, output);
VAR
  a : integer;
  b : char;

PROCEDURE swallow (head : integer; tail : char);
  BEGIN
    writeln ('Swallow 1: ',head:4, tail:4);
    head := head*2;
    tail := succ(tail);
    writeln ('Swallow 2: ', head:4, tail:4);
  END; {swallow}

BEGIN
  a := 25;
  b := 'X';
  writeln ('Main 1: ', a:4, b:4);
  swallow(a, b);
```

```
        writeln ('Main 2: ', a:4, b:4);
    END.
```

would produce the following output:

Main 1:	**25**	**X**
Swallow 1:	**25**	**X**
Swallow 2:	**50**	**Y**
Main 2:	**25**	**X**

The situation is different with VAR parameters. A procedure may have the task of calculating a result which needs to be passed back to the calling program. Pascal provides for this by means of parameters which are specially designated in the list of formals as VAR. These formal parameters act as channels to the actual parameters and any changes made to a formal parameter affect the actual parameter.

The form of a VAR parameter declaration is simply:

VAR parameter declaration

VAR formal parameter identifiers : type identifier;

Example 6.1   A swapping procedure

Suppose we have a number of occasions when we need to place two values in order. We could write a procedure that has two parameters, and alters them so that their values are in numeric order. The parameters would have to be declared as VAR.

```
        PROCEDURE order (VAR n, m : integer);
          VAR temp : integer;
          BEGIN
          if n > m then begin
            temp := n;  n := m;  m := temp;
          end;
          END; {order}
```

If we have x as 9 and y as 5, then the call:

```
        order (x, y);
```

will result in x becoming 5 and y becoming 9. If the parameters had been declared as value then although the values of n and m would have been interchanged, this effect would not have been transmitted back to x and y.

Example 6.2 Special integer read

Another useful procedure is one that can read in an integer followed by any character, not necessarily a space. In Turbo Pascal, integers must be followed by a space, tab or end-of-line. So to read in an integer such as a measurement, for example, 6m or 5s, we shall need to decode the characters ourselves. The procedure follows the description of integers in Section 4.2.

A useful
procedure.

```
PROCEDURE readinteger (VAR n : integer);
    {Assumes at least one digit after a sign,
    but the sign is not compulsory}
VAR
    negative  : boolean;
    ch        : char;
BEGIN
    n := 0;
    read(ch);
    if ch in ['+','−'] then begin
        negative := ch = '−';
        read(ch);
    end else negative := false;
    while ch in ['0'..'9'] do begin
        n := n * 10 + ord(ch) − ord('0');
        read(ch);
    end;
    if negative then n := −n;
END; {readinteger}
```

There will be an example of how this could be used in the next section.

Behind the scenes

In order to reinforce the notion of VAR parameters being channels to their actual counterparts, let us look at how they operate inside the computer. In essence, the formal VAR parameter is a variable which is supplied with the **reference** of the actual parameter at the time of the call. The effect of the actual parameters being changed by any changes to the formal parameters is a facility that should not be used lightly. It is also possible that it may not be exactly what is intended in a particular situation, as illustrated in the following example.

Suppose we wish to use the *order* procedure in another context, that is, we have my age and your age in two variables and we wish to put them in numerical order. If we call:

order (myage, yourage);

then the following pictures apply to the variables concerned.

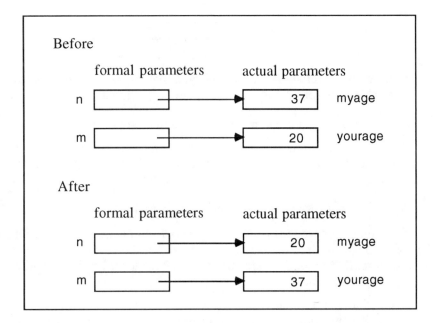

What has happened here? The actual parameters have been altered, which is not what we wanted in this case. We probably only wanted to *know* who was younger. What we need is a procedure with these two parameters as value parameters and another, VAR, parameter for the result. This gives:

```
PROCEDURE firstisyounger (n, m : integer; VAR b : boolean);
BEGIN
  b := n > m;
END; {firstisyounger}
```

and we could call this with:

```
firstisyounger (myage, yourage, me);
if me then writeln('I am younger);
```

Parameter passing rules

There are certain rules that apply to the correspondence of formal and actual parameters, known as parameter passing. When talking about value parameters, we refer to **pass-by-value** and when referring to VAR parameters, the term is **pass-by-reference**. The rules are:

1.   The actual parameters supplied must agree with the formal parameters in number, order and type. Thus the following are all incorrect calls.

order (p);   needs two parameters
swallow ('+', 7);   wrong order
swallow (4, 8);   *tail* must be a *char*

2.   For value parameters, the actual parameters can be any constants, variables or expressions. For example, we could have:

swallow (sqr(trunc(pi)) + 1, chr(ord(b) − ord('A')));

For var parameters, the actual parameters must be variables. They may not be constants, because values of the actual parameters may be changed. It would therefore be incorrect to say:

order (x, 8);   8 is not a variable

3.   The names chosen for actual parameters are quite independent of those for the formals. However, one need not make them deliberately different. Comments are often useful to describe the meaning of formal parameters.

4.   A variable should only be used once as a VAR parameter in any one call. The reason for this is that a variable used, say twice, as an actual parameter would end up having two formal names, with confusing results. For example, we should not write *order (a,a);*

Example 6.3   Counterfeit cheques with parameters

Parameters reduce global usage and repetition.

| Problem | We would like to consider whether the *Checkacheque* program in Example 4.3 cannot be better written using parameters.

| Solution | First look for global variable usage. Both the procedures make use of globals, so we should declare them with parameters instead. Next we should look for repetition. In fact, the two procedures *RecordZero* and *RecordNonzero* are nearly identical, and we can rationalise by making them into one, with parameters.

| Program | Consider the two procedures:

```
PROCEDURE RecordZero;
    {Uses and updates globals        : CountofZeros,
                                       CountofNonzeros
                                       Counterfeit}
    BEGIN
      CountofZeros := CountofZeros + 1;
      CountofNonzeros := 0;
      if CountofZeros = 3 then counterfeit := true;
    END; {RecordZero}
```

```
PROCEDURE RecordNonzero;
  {Uses and updates globals       : CountofZeros,
                                    CountofNonzeros
                                    Counterfeit}
  BEGIN
    CountofNonzeros := CountofNonzeros + 1;
    CountofZeros := 0;
    if CountofNonzeros = 4 then counterfeit := true;
  END; {RecordNonzero}
```

We can write a single procedure which does the same operation as either, and would be called by one of:

```
if digit = 0
then Register (CountofZeros, CountofNonzeros, 3, counterfeit);
else Register (CountofNonzeros, Countofzeros, 4, counterfeit);
```

The procedure can be written generally in terms of runs as follows:

```
PROCEDURE Register (VAR CurrentRun, OtherRun : integer;
                    max : integer;
                    VAR counterfeit : boolean);
  BEGIN
    CurrentRun := CurrentRun + 1;
    OtherRun := 0;
    if CurrentRun = max then counterfeit := true;
  END; {Register}
```

Inserting this in the program and rerunning it is left as an exercise.

This example emphasises that the choice of formal parameter names is important, but that one should not feel obliged to think of new names for the sake of it: *counterfeit* is a perfectly adequate name as a formal and an actual.

6.2 Functions

We have already seen the use of built-in functions such as *sin, sqrt, abs* and *eof.* In Pascal, we can also define our own functions, with the properties that they:

- return a single value as the function value, and
- are called as part of an expression.

Functions can have parameters, along the same lines as procedures. However, it is considered bad practice to have functions that alter their environment, and so generally, by convention we restrict parameters to passing by value.

Form of a function

A function is declared in much the same way as a procedure, with the added bit of information being its type which may be integer, real, boolean or character. (Subranges of these and enumerated types are also permitted, as described in Chapter 7.) The form below shows how a function is declared. There is no form for a call: calls have to be part of an expression, appearing in another statement such as an assignment or writeln.

Function calls are part of expressions.

Function declaration

FUNCTION name *(formal parameter declarations)* : type;
   declarations
   BEGIN
     statements
   END; {name}

The function must be assigned a value at least once somewhere inside its body before it terminates, and that value must be of the correct type. Although a function is called as part of an expression or assignment statement, the function name may not be used as if it were a variable inside its own body.

For example, suppose we wish to calculate the sum of all the numbers up to *n*. The temporary variable used to keep the running total is essential, and its value is assigned to the function name at the end.

```
FUNCTION Sigma (n : integer) : integer;
   VAR i, total : integer;
   BEGIN
     total := 0;
     for i := 1 to n do
       total := total + i;
     Sigma := total;
   END; {Sigma}
```

Example 6.4   Ticking clock

| Problem | We wish to provide a digital clock which ticks over at the right speed. |

| Solution | Looking at a clock, the counters for the minutes and seconds go from 0 to 59 and round again, while the hour counter goes |

from 1 to 12. So we shall provide a function called *next* which has three parameters – the counter and its upper and lower bounds. The function will check the counter against the upper bound and reset it if necessary.

Function

```
FUNCTION next (c, lower, upper : integer) : integer;
  BEGIN
    if c = upper then next := lower else next := succ(c);
  END; {next}
```

Extension We also need to consider the positioning of the clock, and *Introducing the* calibrating it to make it tick at the right speed. The Crt unit *delay* will help with both issues. *Gotoxy* can be used to have the values written on *procedure.* the same place each time, and the *delay* procedure can endeavour to simulate real seconds. *Delay* takes a single parameter in milliseconds. We can ask the user to type in a delay value, so as make the clock as realistic as possible.

Testing A suitable test would be to print out the time until a key is pressed.

```
PROGRAM TestTicker (input, output);
  {Testing the next function using a clock}

  USES Crt;

  VAR
    H        : 1..12;
    M,
    S        : 0..59;
    interval : 0..1000;

  FUNCTION next (c, lower, upper : integer) : integer;
    BEGIN
      if c = upper then next := lower else next := succ(c);
    END; {next}

  BEGIN
    ClrScr;
    writeln('***** Testing the next function *****');
    write('Starting hours, minutes and seconds : ');
    readln (H, M, S);
    write('Give a delay for the ticking (around 800) : ');
    readln(interval);

    WHILE not keypressed do begin
      gotoxy (35, 10);
      write(H:2,':',M:2,':',S:2);
      if S = 59 then begin
        if M = 59 then H := next (H,1,12);
        M := next (M, 0, 59);
      end;
      S := next (S, 0, 59);
      delay(interval);
    end;
  END.
```

A common data
checking
tecnique.

Testing   The program will print the time in the centre of the screen, and carry on doing so until told to stop. This could be a useful 'screen filler' program that could be left running when nothing else is happening.

Exercise   Adapt the program to run on a 24 hour clock.

Example 6.5   Checksums

Problem   Zanyland University gives each student a student number which consists of four digits and ends with a checksum character which is computed by taking the sum of the preceding digits modulo 4. These checksums need to be verified.

Solution   Define a function which will take a number, analyse it, and return true or false, depending on whether the checksum digit is correct or not.

Examples   Some sample numbers might be:

1234 2	$1+2+3+4 = 10;$	$10 \bmod 4 = 2;$	correct
5682 1	$5+6+8+2 = 21;$	$21 \bmod 4 = 1;$	correct
7007 1	$7+0+0+7 = 14;$	$14 \bmod 4 = 2;$	incorrect

Algorithm   The number will have to be decomposed, digit by digit. This can be done simply by repeatedly taking modulo 10. At the same time, the digits can be added and then the sum checked against the check digit.

Program

```
FUNCTION checksum (number, digit: integer; ) : boolean;
  VAR
    i    : 1 ..4;
    sum  : 0 .. 9999;

  BEGIN
    sum := 0;
    for i := 1 to 4 do begin
      sum := sum + number mod 10;
      number := number div 10;
    end;
    checksum := (sum mod 4) = digit;
  END; {checksum}
```

Notice that in this function, one of the value parameters, *number*, is used as if it were a variable. This is quite permissible, and any changes made to *number* will not be reflected back in the calling program.

Example 6.6 Length of a number

| Problem | We would like to know how much space a number will occupy if printed. |

| Solution | Two solutions spring to mind. Working from first principles, we can deduce how many digits an integer needs by looking at the characteristic of its logarithm. Alternatively, we can use the Turbo Pascal routine *str* to first transform the number into a string and then work out how much of the string is occupied. This method has the advantage that it would work for both integers and reals. |

Alternative methods.

| Function 1 |

```
FUNCTION digits (n : integer) : integer;
  VAR d : integer;
  BEGIN
    if n < 0 then begin
      d :=1; n := abs(n);
    end else
    d := 0;  {plus sign not printed}
    d := d + trunc (ln(n) / ln(10) + 1);
    digits := d;
  END; {digits}
```

This will work for integers only.

The function could be used in cases where formatting is required. For example, to find out if a number will fit on a line 60 characters wide on which *count* characters have already been written, we could use:

```
if  count + digits(number) > 60  ...
```

Notice that the function name cannot be used as a variable and therefore the local variable *d* had to be defined for the summing, and assigned to *digits* at the end.

| Function 2 | This time we must define what we mean by counting the digits. In the case of real numbers, we assume that we want to know the whole number of digits occupied when the number is written, including one for the decimal point. |

This will work for reals as well.

```
FUNCTION digits (n : real) : integer;
  CONST
    max = 30;
  VAR
    s : string[max];
```

```
           i : 0 ..max;
        BEGIN
          str(n,s);
          i := 0;
          repeat i := i + 1 until s[i] <> ' ';
          digits := max − i + 1;
        END; {digits}
```

This version illustrates well the power of combining existing functions to make new ones.

Designing procedures and functions

In designing a Pascal program with procedures and functions, the easy part is breaking the work up into logical components. It is more difficult to do this well. Doing it well means creating components which are as self-contained as possible, and have a safe interface with the rest of the program.

It is generally held that parameters provide the best interface, because the names of the formals are defined by the procedure, and therefore do not depend on or conflict with anything that may be declared elsewhere. Thus we should strive to have procedures that only communicate via parameters, and do not make use of global variables.

Maximising self-containedness. This rule applies to constants as well. A procedure can rely on implicit constants, but this weakens its usefulness as a building block in other programs. Take for example the *checksum* function in Example 6.5. It mentions three constants: 1, 4 and 10. One may argue that 10 is genuinely intrinsic to the computation, since numbers are written in base 10, and that 1 is the start of a counting range. But the presence of 4 ties us to the specific case of a four digit number. It would be more general to have this as a parameter, giving:

A better version of checksum.

```
FUNCTION checksum (number, digit, size: integer) : boolean;
   VAR
      i    : 1..maxint;
      sum : 0..9999;

   BEGIN
      sum := 0;
      for i := 1 to size do begin
         sum := sum + number mod 10;
         number := number div 10;
      end;
      checksum := (sum mod size) = digit;
   END; {checksum}
```

Not all procedures, of course, are intended to be reused in other programs. Some, particularly those that are declared nested inside another, serve a very specific purpose, and it is sometimes convenient for them to make use of nonlocal variables. These choices are illustrated in Example 6.7.

Choosing a procedure or a function

The choice of whether to use a function or procedure, when both are possible, can be made according to:

- how many values need to be returned, and
- how the routine is to be called.

If more than one value is to be returned, then necessity dictates that we use a procedure with VAR parameters. If we are only talking about a single value result, then a function is a nicer way of expressing things. However, if we need to know the result of the computation again later in the program, then we won't want to call the function again, and so would like to have the result stored somewhere. A procedure with the VAR parameter serves this purpose, but there is another way of doing it. The essential point is to record the result of the routine, and this can be done with the function.

Recall the procedure:

```
PROCEDURE firstisyounger (n,m : integer;  VAR b : boolean);
  BEGIN
    b := n > m;
  END {firstisyounger }
```

We could replace this with a function:

```
FUNCTION isyounger (n, m : integer) : boolean;
  BEGIN
    isyounger := n > m;
  END; {isyounger }
```

and call it with:

```
answer := isyounger (myage, yourage);
```

Both are correct, and the choice will depend largely on circumstances.

Example 6.7   Calculating floor areas

Problem   Estate agents frequently provide information about houses that includes the dimensions of each room. It is very useful when comparing houses to be able to have a figure for the total floor area, based on these.

Solution   Enter the room dimensions into a data file, and have a program which reads them and calculates the area. We shall assume that the dimensions are given initially in feet and inches but that we wish to have them in metric as well.

| Example | Assume we are dealing with input and output such as this:

```
14 Highfield Lane
------------------------
Lounge  23'8"x11'2"   264.28sq ft   7.21m x 3.40m   24.55sq m
Bedroom1  12'3"x11'3"   137.81sq ft   3.73m x 3.43m   12.80sq m
```

| Algorithm | We use stepwise refinement and start at the outer level, itemising the tasks that need to be done, in the correct order, and making assumptions about procedures and parameters as seems fitting.

Stepwise
refinement.

```
BEGIN
  Setupfiles;
  Copyheadings;
  CalculateRoomsandTotal;
END.
```

The idea is that there are no global variables at all (except the files), and that all the work is done inside the procedure *CalculateRoomsandTotal*. At the next level down, a likely sequence of events is given by this portion of the procedure:

```
BEGIN
  aBlankLine := false;
  WHILE not aBlankLine do begin

    Echoto(' ');
    readftins (ft1, ins1);
    Echoto('x');
    readftins(ft2, ins2);
    multiply (ft1, ins1, ft2, ins2, area);

    convert(ft1, ins1, m1);
    convert(ft2, ins2, m2);
    writeln(area, m1, m2, m1*m2);  {with units, of course}

    Addtototals;
    Checkforablankline;
  END;
END;
```

Each procedure can then be elaborated in turn, using as much old material as we can. For example, *Readftins* can make use of a version of the previously developed procedure, *readinteger* from Example 6.2.

```
PROCEDURE readftins (VAR ft, ins : integer);
  VAR a : integer;
```

```
next : char;

PROCEDURE readinteger(var n : integer; var follow : char);
    {Reads an integer and returns the following character}
VAR ch : char;
BEGIN
  n := 0;
  while ch in ['0'..'9'] do begin
      n := n * 10 + ord(ch) - ord('0');
    read(f, ch);
  end;
  follow := ch;
END; {readinteger}

BEGIN
  readinteger(a, next);
  if next = "" then begin {feet}
    ft := a;
    readinteger (ins, next);
  end;
  ins := a;
END; {readftins}
```

This procedure illustrates nicely the use of a nested procedure called with different parameters. In fact, we could not have done without the parameters here.

Finally, consider the case of checking for a blank line being the end of the data. (We do not wish to use end-of-file because we are anticipating several sets of data coming in.) The results of the check will be stored in a boolean variable, which is defined outside the procedure, giving:

```
PROCEDURE Checkforablankline;
    BEGIN
    readln(data);  writeln(results);
    if eoln(data) then begin
      aBlankline := true;
      readln(data);  writeln(results);
    end;
    END; {Checkforablankline}
```

Alternative
versions.

Alternatively, the outer procedure could send its boolean variable as a parameter which *Checkforablankline* could call the same name, and do exactly the same with it, that is:

```
PROCEDURE Checkforablankline (VAR aBlankline : boolean);
    BEGIN
    readln(data);  writeln(results);
    if eoln(data) then begin
      aBlankline := true;
      readln(data);  writeln(results);
    end;
    END; {Checkforablankline}
```

Which is better, is a moot point. *Checkforablankline* is a one-off procedure, defined entirely for ease of reading and it does not actually need a parameter. *Addtototals* is in a similar position. However, if the procedure were either at the outer level, or could conceivably be called more than once, then a parameter should be used. The full text for this program is given later, as it will benefit from features yet to be introduced.

6.3 The type statement

There are six main predefined types in Turbo Pascal – integer, real, char, boolean, string and text. The first four are known as **scalar** types. The last two are **structured** types in that they form collections of characters in a certain structure. In the next few chapters we shall be looking at the seven ways Pascal provides for creating new types from existing values and types. The table gives the full list of standard Pascal's predefined types and existing type mechanisms. Turbo Pascal has extra predefined types which are mentioned when their 'parent' types are discussed.

	Predefined types	**Mechanisms for user-defined types**
Scalar	integer real char boolean	subrange enumerated
Structured	string text	record set array file pointer

The user-defined types are created by means of a type statement, which gives a name to a chosen new structure. Each of the type mechanisms has its own form, as we shall see in the next few chapters. In any one declaration section, the keyword TYPE may appear more than once, and several types may be listed under it each time. Normally, though, we tend to group type declarations in one place, and follow the standard Pascal order of the three sections as : CONST, TYPE, VAR.

Form of the type statement

A type statement associates a name with a type formation as follows:

Type declaration
TYPE
identifier = *type*;
identifier = *type*;
. . .
identifier = *type*;

Form of subrange types revisited

The first type enables constraints to be placed on the range of values available in three of the other scalar types – integer, char and enumerated. This is done by specifying precise lower and upper bound values. In earlier chapters, bounds were given for individual variables; now they will have official status and can be used over and over again by name. As before, any such bounds will used by the Pascal system to check that the use of variables conforms with their declaration. The form for defining a subrange type is:

Subrange type
identifier = *lower bound* .. *upper bound*;

where the bounds must both be of the same type, known as the **base type**. Permissible base types are integer, char or enumerated. The bounds must be constant values or named constants: they may not be expressions. Note that the symbol .. must not have a space between the dots. Examples of subrange types are:

```
TYPE
    weights       = 0..200;      {kgs}
    temperatures  = -50..60;     {degrees Celsius}
    money         = 0..maxint;
    initials      = 'A'..'Z';
    digits        = '0'..'9';
    counters      = 1..10;
    marks         = 0..100;
```

Variables of these types can then be declared, as in:

```
VAR
    myweight,
    yourweight      : weights;
    income, tax     : money;
    initial         : initials;
    i, j, counter   : counters;
```

The importance of subrange types

Variables of subrange types can only take values in the specified range. If assignment of a value outside this range is attempted, the program should stop with a 'value out of range' error. For example:

initial := 'p';   and   counter := 0;

are erroneous. In Turbo Pascal, this checking has to be explicitly turned on, whether through the environment menu, or by including {$R+} at the start of a program.

It is possible to assign an expression of the base type to a subrange variable, and the Pascal system will then check at runtime that the values are compatible. For example, in:

counter := counter + 1;

the Pascal system should always check that the range of *counter* is not exceeded.

'Value out of range' is better than nothing.

'Value out of range' errors often indicate that the original algorithm is defective in some way. In other words, the declarations stated that the variables have certain properties, but the statements were not keeping the values within these. Without the proper use of subranges, many of these errors go undetected or are very hard to find.

A subrange type inherits the operators and functions from its base type. However, care must be taken with the functions *succ* and *pred* so that the range is not exceeded.

Example 6.8   Expiry dates

Problem   A library lends books for ten days at a time. Given a date of issue, calculate the return date.

Solution   The basic calculation is to add the 10 days to the day of issue, and to check whether this takes us into the next month. By making various simplifying assumptions, the solution breaks up into several parts. In the first place, we assume that all months have the same number of days, say 31, and we set this up as a named constant in the CONST section. Then we assume that the months will be known by number, not by name, as we intend doing simple arithmetic on the months. Given these assumptions, the calculation becomes:

> Add 10 to the issue day, taking modulo days in the month
> If the issue day plus 10 is more than the days in the month
> add 1 to the issue month

| Program | Because this seems such a simple solution, we go straight into the program, using suitable subranges for the day and month types, and a named constant for the borrowing period.

```
PROGRAM LibraryReturns1 (input, output); {$R+}
CONST
  daysinmonth   = 31;  {for now}
  period        = 10;  {days}

TYPE
  days          = 1..daysinmonth;
   months       = 1..12;

VAR
   issueday,
   returnday    : days;
   issuemonth,
   returnmonth  : months;

BEGIN
  writeln('****** Book dates ******');
  write('Type in the day and month: ');
  readln(issueday, issuemonth);
  returnday := (issueday + period) mod  daysinmonth;
   if issueday + period > daysinmonth then
     returnmonth := issuemonth + 1
   else
     returnmonth := issuemonth;
   writeln('Due back on ', returnday:1, '/', returnmonth:1);
END.
```

| Testing | Running the program with a selection of values seems to work, until we try to take out a book on the 21st. The Pascal system stops the program and complains that a value is out of range on the line:

```
returnday := (issueday + period) mod daysinmonth;
```

The program
does not work.

Studying this, we see that the computer *has* detected a mistake: (21 + 10) mod 31 is 0, which is not a valid day. The correct answer is 31. Suppose we quickly change the statement to:

```
returnday := (issueday + period) mod daysinmonth − 1;
```

and rerun the program. The 21st is still incorrect and now the 22nd gives the wrong answer as well: 0 instead of 1.

From all this, we realise that this statement is really not correct, and that using *mod* is not going to work because it will sometimes return a zero, which we don't want. The answer is to treat the two cases of being within a month and going over a month boundary separately. The revised program becomes:

| Program 2 |

Fix No. 1.

```
PROGRAM LibraryReturns2 (input, output);
  CONST
    daysinmonth = 31; {for now}
    period      = 10;  {days}
  TYPE
    days        = 1..daysinmonth;
    months      = 1..12;
  VAR
    issueday,
    returnday   : days;
    issuemonth,
    returnmonth : months;

BEGIN
  writeln ('****** Book dates ******');
  write ('Type in the day and month: ');
  readln (issueday, issuemonth);
  if issueday + period > daysinmonth then begin
      returnday := issueday + period – daysinmonth;
      returnmonth := issuemonth + 1;
    end else begin
      returnday := issueday + period;
      returnmonth := issuemonth;
    end;
  writeln('Due back on ', returnday:1, '/', returnmonth:1);
END.
```

| Testing 2 | Testing proceeds as before, and all seems well until we try Christmas Day – 25 and 12. The system stops again and says a value is out of range on the line:

Caught again!

```
returnmonth := issuemonth + 1;
```

This makes sense, because there is no such month as 13! The use of a subrange has caused another silly error to be detected. To fix this one, another circular addition is needed, as in:

```
if issuemonth = 12
  then returnmonth := 1
  else returnmonth := issuemonth + 1;
```

| **Solution 2** | Turning now to the days in the month, we recall that a case statement was used in Chapter 5 to set this up. This can be |

incorporated in the beginning of the program.

| **Program 3** |

```
PROGRAM LibraryReturns3 (input, output);                    Right at last.
  {Calculates the date 10 days hence}

  CONST
    period   = 10;  {days}

  TYPE
    days     = 1..31;
    months   = 1..12;
    years    = 1900 .. 2500;

  VAR
      issueday,
      returnday     : days;
      issuemonth,
      returnmonth   : months;
      daysinmonth   : days;
      year          : years;

  FUNCTION daysof(month : months): days;
  BEGIN
    CASE month of
      9, 4, 6, 11          : daysof := 30;
      1, 3, 5, 7, 8, 10, 12 : daysof := 31;
      2  : begin
            write('In what year? ');
            readln(year);
            if (year mod 4 = 0)
                          and not ((year mod 100 = 0)
                          and not (year mod 400 = 0))
            then daysof := 29
            else daysof := 28;
          end;
    END; {CASE}
  END; {daysof}

  BEGIN
    writeln ('****** Book dates ******');
    write ('Type in the day and month: ');
    readln (issueday, issuemonth);
    if issueday + period > daysof(issuemonth) then begin
      returnday := issueday + period − daysof(issuemonth);
      if issuemonth = 12
        then returnmonth := 1
        else returnmonth := issuemonth + 1
    end else begin
```

```
        returnday := issueday + period;
        returnmonth := issuemonth;
      end;
    writeln('Due back on ', returnday:1, '/', returnmonth:1);
  END.
```

| Testing |

For the record, a sample run would produce:

****** Book dates ******
Type in the day and month: 22 2
In what year? 1986
Due back on 4/3

Reading into a subrange

There is a general method for reading integer subranges which makes use of the following procedure:

```
PROCEDURE readrange (VAR x : integer;  min, max : integer);
BEGIN
  REPEAT
    read(x);
    if (x < min) or (x > max)
    then writeln('NO!  Range is ',min:1,'..',max:1,' : ');
  UNTIL (x >= min) and (x <= max);
END; {readrange}
```

The caller supplies an integer variable with the two relevant ranges and *readrange* will repeatedly read numbers until it receives one within the given range. The caller follows this up with an assignment into the actual variable that is to be read. So, for example, with the declarations:

```
TYPE
  weights      = 0..200;
  temperatures = -50..60; {degrees Celsius}
VAR
  myweight     : weights;
  temperature  : temperatures;
  num          : integer;

readrange (num, 0, 200);    myweight := num;
readrange (num, -50, 60);  temperature := num;
```

Similar procedures could be written for the other base types.

Hints on using subranges

1. The **bounds** required for a subrange are not always as clear cut as the above examples for days or months might suggest. Numbers of children, amount of tax, even the year should have upper limits, but these have to be decided on the basis of what is sensible. A comment to the effect that the bounds are 'for now' or 'approximately' will be useful as documentation.

2. Notice that subranges cannot apply to **real numbers**. Instead, we continue to use comments to define the range of reals to be used for each variable.

3. Subranges are always checked when a variable is **assigned to** or when an expression is passed as a **value parameter** to a procedure or function. Turbo Pascal does not check the value when a subrange variable is read into.

4. The **shorthand** for subrange types with the range specified directly on a variable declaration as in:

    VAR age : 0..140;   Avoid this from
                                                now on.
    is not good practice. Often the same range is needed again, for example as a parameter type, and without a type name to unify the properties, mismatches can occur.

5. To distinguish between **type names** and variable names, a nice convention (used in this book and elsewhere) is to make types plural. Thus we have the variable *day* of type *days*, and so on.

6. Making use of **named constants** as subrange bounds is very helpful if the ranges have to be changed.

6.4 Arrays

We are beginning to realise that there is a need to be able to store and manipulate multiple values in a program. If there are relatively few values, simple variables can possibly be used, but consider the following example.

Suppose we have several hundred scores between 0 and 20 which have to   The need for
be analysed for frequency of occurrence of each score. We could set up 21   arrays.
counters, one for each score. As the scores are read in, the counter corresponding to the score could be incremented. It would be very unwieldy if we had to invent 21 different names for the counters, and then use a big case-statement every time one of them needed updating. What we need is the concept of the ***i*th variable** so that we can read a value, say i, and then update *counter*$_i$. Pascal provides for this facility with the **array**.

Form of an array type

An array is a bounded collection of elements of the same type, each of which can be selected by indexing. The relevant form is:

Array type
TYPE *identifier* = ARRAY [*bound type*] OF *element type*;

where the bound type is a subrange of integer, char, boolean or enumerated type and the element type is any type not containing a file type. Examples of declarations are:

```
TYPE
    scores      = 0..20;
    classrange  = 0..100;
    frequencies = ARRAY [scores] of classrange;
    capitals    = 'A'..'Z';
    occurrences = ARRAY [capitals] of boolean;
    daysofweek  = 1..7;
    daycounts   = ARRAY [daysofweek] of integer;
```

To use an array, we must first declare a variable of that type, then each element can be accessed by mentioning the name of the array variable and an index expression enclosed in square brackets. The index is sometimes known as the **subscript**. For example, we have:

```
VAR
    counter    : frequencies;
    occurred   : occurrences;
    daycount   : daycounts;

FOR score := 0 to 20 do counter[score] := 0;
occurred['Z'] := false;
daycount[5] := daycount [5] + 1;
```

Example 6.9   Counting frequencies

Problem   The frequencies of several hundred scores between 0 and 20 have to be calculated as well as the frequency of occurrence of the code for the club they belong to, which is a character.

Example   Suppose we have a file with the data:

```
19 J    Smith A
10 B    Jones P G
19 A    Brown T
```

then the result required would be that all the score frequencies would be zero, except:

$$scorecount_{19} = 2 \qquad scorecount_{10} = 1$$

and all the club frequencies would be zero except those for J, B and A which would be one.

| Solution |

The solution has already been outlined in the previous example. We set up two arrays and as each score is read, the appropriate element of the array is incremented. Similarly for the clubs. The algorithm is so simple that we go straight on to the program.

| Program |

```
PROGRAM CountingFrequencies (input, output, inp);
  CONST
    maxscore   = 20;
    playerlimit  = 250;

  TYPE
    scores      = 0..maxscore;
    players     = 0..playerlimit;
    clubs       = 'A'..'Z';
    scorearrays = ARRAY [scores] of players;
    clubarrays  = ARRAY [clubs] of players;

  VAR
    scorecount  : scorearrays;
    clubcount   : clubarrays;
    score       : scores;
    club        : char;
    filename    : string[12];
    inp         : text;

  BEGIN
    writeln('****** Frequency counting ******');
    write('What file for tor the data? ');
    readln(filename);
    assign(inp, filename);
    reset (inp);

    {Initialise the arrays}
    FOR score := 0 to maxscore do
      scorecount[score] := 0;
    FOR club := 'A' to 'Z' do
```

Initialising is important.

```
                    clubcount[club] := 0;

                    {Count the scores and clubs}
                    WHILE not eof(inp) do begin
                      read(inp, score);
                      scorecount [score] := scorecount [score] + 1;
                      repeat read(inp, club) until club <> ' ';
                      clubcount[club] := clubcount[club]+ 1;
                    END;

                    {Print the frequencies}
                    writeln('Table of Score Frequencies');
                    for score := 0 to maxscore do
                      writeln(score, scorecount[score]:6);
                    writeln;
                    writeln('Table of Club Frequencies');
                    for club := 'A' to 'Z' do
                      writeln(club, clubcount[club]:6);
                  END.
```

Try this.
This program has been written without procedures or functions. Clearly, it could have been formally broken up and parameter interfaces created. However, in this case, we deemed it simpler to present the program as one unit, so that the idea of arrays can be understood on its own. In later examples, we shall see how arrays can be passed as parameters and procedures written which operate on arrays.

Properties of array types

Arrays can be formed of any type. This includes arrays themselves, leading to multi-dimensional arrays, discussed in detail later. The size of an array is limited only by the computer's memory, which is usually adequate for most applications. Most computers, though, will probably baulk at an array with subscripts given as [integer].

As with records, there are no operators that apply to whole arrays. However, assignment is possible. For example, given:

```
              TYPE
                range   = 1..100;
                vectors = array[range] of real;

              VAR a, b    : vectors;
```

we can say:

```
              b := a;
```

Operations on the elements of an array depend on their type. Additional operators apply to strings, as described previously in Section 5.2.

Unlike strings, whole arrays cannot be read or written from text files; they must be treated element by element.

Array constants

In Turbo Pascal, we can write out values for an array, enclosed in parentheses. The form for an array constant is:

Array constant
(*constant*$_1$, *constant*$_2$, ... *constant*$_n$)

where the constants apply to each element of an array of length n. Enough   For short arrays. constants must be supplied for every value, so that one would only use this facility for short arrays. For example, useful constants in an assignment statement would be:

```
daycount := (31,28,31,30,31,30,31,31,30,31,30,31);
```

The type of *daycount* is known to be *daycounts*, defined previously as:

```
TYPE
   daycounts = ARRAY [daysofweek] of integer;
```

More often, we shall use array constants in the constant section, and in this case the type name must be specified first, as in:

```
CONST
   daycount : daycounts = (31,28,31,30,31,30,31,31,30,31,30,31);
```

A note on security

Pascal is quite firm about only allowing access to array elements that actually exist. Every time an array is accessed, the index supplied is checked against the bounds given in the type definition. If the index is out of bounds, an error message such as 'Invalid subscript' is given and the program halts.

These checks are done at compile time whenever possible. Thus the following may all result in compilation errors:

```
scorecount[25]
initialcount['a']
```

initialcount['*']

Always wear
your 'seat belt'. However, Turbo Pascal allows this checking to be switched off, and may even have it switched off by default. The idea is to make the program run faster by omitting checks. This is false economy: during development, most programs contain errors, and any checks the system can make to enable those errors to be detected as soon as possible will probably reduce the number of times the program needs to be compiled and tested. Thus it is worthwhile turning the checks on for every program. To do this, put the compiler directive {$R+} at the start of the program, or turn on subrange checks through the environment menu.

Example 6.10   Scalar product of two vectors

Problem   One of the more common operations on vectors is finding the scalar product. We would like to develop a self-contained function to do this for vectors of various lengths.

Handling arrays
of different
lengths. **Solution**   The scalar product is defined as the sum of the product of each of the elements of the two vectors, that is:

$$\sum_{i=1}^{n} a_i b_i$$

The calculation involves a straightforward looping algorithm. However, let's consider how to accommodate vectors of different lengths in different runs of the program. That is, in run 1 we may want to find:

$$(1, 2) . (0, 3)$$

and in run 2:

$$(1, 2, 2, 3, 4, 5) . (7.5, 2, 3.1, 4, 5, 5).$$

The problem is that an array must be defined with a fixed number of components, so that the compiler may allocate a definite region of storage for the array. However, although the number of components is fixed, we do not have to use them all. We decide on some maximum and then specify the precise size within that maximum. This size is passed to the procedure and used by it as its upper bound.

Algorithm   The declarations related to defining an array with the flexibility required are:

```
CONST
  nmax = 100;
TYPE
  range  = 1 .. nmax
  vector = array [range] of real;
VAR
  a, b : vector;
  n    : range;
```

So the arrays *a* and *b* will run from 1 to *n*, where $n \leq nmax$. The data will consist of *n*, an integer of type *range*; then *n* real numbers for a_i, then another *n* real numbers for b_i, ($i = 1$ to *n*). Many array programs involve large amounts of data, which are usually read from a file, and the procedure *Getdata* reads the data from a file 'scalar.dat'.

Simulating variable length arrays.

Program

```
PROGRAM ScalarProduct (input, output); {$R+}

CONST
  nmax = 100; {Maximum vector size handled}

TYPE
  range = 1..nmax;
  vector = ARRAY[range] of real;

VAR
  a,b : vector;
  n   : range;

FUNCTION product (n: range; a, b : vector) : real;
  VAR
    i     : range;
    sum  : real;
  BEGIN
    sum := 0.0;
    FOR i := 1 to n do
      sum := sum + a[i] * b[i];
    product := sum;
  END; {product}

PROCEDURE initialise;
  BEGIN
    writeln('********Vector Scalar Product********');
    writeln;
    writeln('Scalar product of 2 vectors  a, b  of dimension n');
    writeln('with n <= 100 at present; the data n, a, b ');
    writeln('are read from a file: scalar.dat');
    writeln;
  END; {initialise}
```

```
PROCEDURE getdata(VAR a,b : vector; VAR n: range);
VAR
  f   : text;
  i,j : range;
BEGIN
  assign(f,'scalar.dat');
  reset(f);
  read(f,n);
  FOR i := 1 to n do
    read(f, a[i]);
  FOR i := 1 to n do
    read(f, b[i]);
END; {getdata}

BEGIN
  initialise;
  getdata(a,b,n);
  writeln('The scalar product is: ',product(n,a,b):10:6);
END.
```

Testing	Given the data in the file:

```
5
3.0 4.5 6.0 7.5 9.0
2.0 2.0 2.0 2.0 10.0
```

Then the program will produce

********Vector Scalar Product*********

**Scalar product of 2 vectors a, b of dimension n
with n <= 20 at present; the data n, a, b
are read from a file: scalar.data
The scalar product is 132.000000**

If the file declares more than the maximum values, say 150, then the *read(n)* will still succeed, but the first loop will eventually crash, since we had put the range checking option on.

Multi-dimensional arrays

Arrays are very useful for storing tables of information, such as data in rows and columns, or matrices. Since Pascal permits array elements to be of any type, including arrays themselves, arrays of multiple dimensions can be built up. For a typical matrix such as:

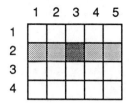

the declarations might be:

```
CONST
    rowmax     = 4;
    columnmax  = 5;

TYPE
    rowrange    = 1..rowmax;
    columnrange = 1..columnmax;
    rows        = array [columnrange] of real;
    matrices    = array [rowrange] of rows;

VAR
    matrix : matrices;
    r,i,j  : rowrange;
    c      : columnrange;
```

Then a single row of the matrix is represented by:

```
matrix[r]
```

Each element of the row can also be selected, as in:

```
matrix [r] [c]
```

or:

```
matrix [r, c]
```

The two forms are equivalent, although the second one is more natural when a matrix is defined as a single type, without defining the row type first. This can be achieved by declarations such as:

A row of a matrix is a vector.

```
TYPE
    rectangles  = array [rowrange, columnrange] of real;
```

The difference between the two forms is that an array declared with subscripts listed in one declaration, like *rectangles*, cannot then be broken up into rows that can be manipulated independently. With the two-stage declaration, as for *matrices*, a row variable could be defined such as:

```
VAR
    row : rows;
```

and rows from the matrix assigned directly to it. Thus to swap two rows of the matrix, we could say:

```
row := matrix[i];
matrix[i] := matrix[j];
matrix[j] := row;
```

Example 6.11 Rainfall statistics

| Problem | The Zanyland Weather Department has kept statistics on monthly rainfall figures for the past 20 years. Now they would like to calculate:

- the average rainfall for each month, and

- the standard deviation for each month.

| Solution | The table of rainfall figures that is provided by a clerk will look something like this:

	Jan	Feb	Mar	Apr	May	Jun	Jul	Aug	Sep	Oct	Nov	Dec
1971												
1972												
...												
1988												
1989												
1990												

Each entry is a real number for the rainfall

The data can be read in nicely by drawing such a table on the screen and letting the user type in each value in turn, or by reading the values off a file. As the values are read in, they are stored in a matrix which is indexed by both the months and the years. Since the rainfall for a month seems to be the crucial figure, the matrix should be structured so that a whole column can be moved around at once. To do this, we make months the first subscript, and the range of years the second, that is:

```
CONST
  maxyear = 30;

TYPE
  months       = 1..12;
  yearrange    = 1..maxyear;
  rainfalls    = real;
  monthlyrains = array[yearrange] of rainfalls;
  raintables   = array[months] of monthlyrains;
```

```
VAR
   raintable : raintables;
```

Once the figures are safely in the matrix, procedures can be designed to perform the required calculations. Each will make use of the matrix and be passed either a column of one month's rainfall figures or an index to such a column.

Algorithm The function to calculate the monthly average would be:

```
FUNCTION monthlyaverage
            (rain:monthlyrains; n : yearrange) : rainfalls;
```

Alternatively, the declaration could be:

```
FUNCTION monthlyaverage (m : months; n : years) : rainfalls;
```

where the parameter indicates an index into the rain table. If the index alone is sent as a parameter, then the function has to access the rainfall table as a global variable, which affects its self-containedness, and it has to perform double indexing to get to each element. If the whole column is sent, there is an initial overhead in copying the values into the function, but accessing the elements is by single indexing, and the self-containedness of the function is preserved. On balance, the first is a better choice.

If the value calculated by *monthlyaverage* is assigned to a variable *a* it can be passed to the next function which uses it to calculate the standard deviation. The declaration for this function is therefore:

```
FUNCTION monthlystddev (rain : monthlyrains;  n : years;
                        mean : rainfalls) : rainfalls;
```

Program This version of the program assumes input from a file, though by replying CON to the request for a filename, the screen can be used.

```
PROGRAM Weather (input, output, data);
  CONST
    maxyear = 30;
  TYPE
    months       = 1..12;
    years        = 1950..2100;
    yearrange    = 1..maxyear;
    rainfalls    = real;
    monthlyrains = array[yearrange] of rainfalls;
    raintables   = array[months] of monthlyrains;

  VAR
    raintable          : raintables;
    m                  : months;
```

```
                        startyear, endyear  : years;
                        nyears              : yearrange;
                        data, results       : text;
                        a                   : rainfalls;
```

Calculating the
mean.

```
FUNCTION monthlyaverage
                (rain:monthlyrains; n : yearrange) : rainfalls;
    VAR
      total : rainfalls;
      y : yearrange;
    BEGIN
      total := 0.0;
      for y := 1 to n do total := total + rain[y];
      monthlyaverage := total / n;
    END; {monthlyaverage}
```

Calculating the
standard
deviation.

```
FUNCTION monthlystddev
        (rain:monthlyrains; mean : rainfalls; n : yearrange) : rainfalls;
    VAR
      total : rainfalls;
      y : yearrange;
    BEGIN
      total := 0.0;
      for y := 1 to n do total := total + sqr(mean-rain[y]);
      monthlystddev := sqrt(total / (n-1));
    END; {monthlystddev}
```

```
PROCEDURE Openfiles;
  VAR filename : string[20];
  BEGIN
    write('What file for the data? '); readln(filename);
    assign (data, filename);
    reset(data);
    write('What file for the results (CON for the screen)?');
    readln(filename);
    assign(results, filename);
    rewrite(results);
  END; {Openfiles}
```

```
PROCEDURE ReadinData(var startyear, endyear : years);
  VAR
    year : 0..maxyear;
    y    : years;
  BEGIN
    year := 0;
    while not eof(data) do begin
      read(data,y);
      if year = 0 then startyear := y;
      year := year + 1;
      for m := 1 to 12 do
      read(data,raintable[m][year]);
    end;
```

```
        endyear := y;
        writeln('Data read for years ',startyear, ' to ', endyear);
      END; {ReadinData}

    BEGIN
      writeln('******* Rainfall statistics ******');
      Openfiles;
      ReadinData(startyear, endyear);
      nyears := endyear-startyear+1;
      writeln('Month Average      Std Deviation');
      for m := 1 to 12 do begin
        a := monthlyaverage(raintable[m],nyears);
        writeln(results,
            m:4, a:12:2,
            monthlystddev(raintable[m],a,nyears):12:2);
      end;
      close(results);
      readln;
    END.
```

6.5 Turbo Pascal and picture graphics

We saw in Chapter 2 how simple line drawings can be constructed using writeln statements, and by using windows, can be placed at will on the screen. We can do the same with the Turbo Pascal's Graph unit, but this time we can actually draw shapes in graphics, rather than using characters.

Drawing shapes

We can draw the following shapes with the Graph unit:

```
PROCEDURE Arc (x, y : integer;  Startangle, Endangle, Radius : word);
PROCEDURE Bar (X1, Y1, X2, Y2 : integer);
PROCEDURE Bar3D (X1, Y1, X2, Y2 : integer;
                    depth : word, Top : boolean);
PROCEDURE Drawpoly (Numpoints : word; var Polypoints);
PROCEDURE Circle (X, Y : integer;  radius : word);
PROCEDURE Ellipse (X,Y : integer;
                    StAngle, EndAngle, XRadius, YRadius : word);
PROCEDURE Line (X1, Y1, X2, Y2 : integer);
PROCEDURE Pieslice (x, y : integer;  Startangle,
                    Endangle, Radius : word);
```

Routines for shapes.

```
PROCEDURE Rectangle (X1, Y1, X2, Y2 : integer);
PROCEDURE Sector (X, Y : integer;
                        StAngle, EndAgle, XRadius, YRadius : word);
```

All of these except *bar* and *Bar3D* produce outlines; the bar procedures draw solid coloured rectangles, one in two dimensions, the other representing three dimensions. The colour used for drawing the outlines is defined by:

Routine for outline colour.

```
PROCEDURE SetColor (Colour : word);
```

The colour used for filling in the bars is defined by the current **fill style**, which can be set with:

Routine for filling patterns.

```
PROCEDURE SetFillStyle (Pattern : word;  Colour : word);
```

There are many options for the pattern, but the most useful is *SolidFill*. Thus to draw a red bar we would call:

```
SetFillStyle (SolidFill, Red);
Bar (0,0, 50, 50);
```

Shapes drawn in outline by the other procedures can also be filled with colour using:

Routines for filling colour.

```
PROCEDURE FloodFill (X, Y : integer;  Border : word);
```

This will fill the area bounded by the border colour with the current fill colour. If the point (x,y) is in the border, then the interior is filled, otherwise the exterior is filled. So to draw a circle with a green outline, filled in yellow, we could call:

```
SetColor(Green);
Circle (200, 200, 100);
SetFillStyle (SolidFill, Yellow);
FloodFill (200, 200, Green);
```

Remember that the colour mentioned in *FloodFill* is the colour of the boundary it must look for, not the colour it will use to do the filling.

Drawpoly is a special procedure in that it accepts an **untyped** array provided the array contains the x,y coordinates of the polygon to be drawn. The use of *Drawpoly* is illustrated in Example 6.14.

Example 6.12 Graphics screen filler

| Problem | We would like to convert the screen filler program of Example 3.7 to draw graphics shapes until told to stop.

| Solution | Choose an appropriate shape drawing routine and randomly generate the vertices of the shape until a key is pressed.

| Algorithm | Suppose we choose a circle shape. We can randomly generate the line and fill colour, the centre and radius in a repeat loop. We shall set maximum size of a circle as one tenth of the screen depth, given by *GetMaxY*.

The algorithm can operate in two nested loops. The inner loops reacts to any key press, and allows the screen to 'freeze' at a particular state. If a space–return sequence is pressed, then the program will actually stop. Clearly, the user should be advised of this before the program begins: such an enhancement is left up to the reader.

A user-friendly procedure.

| Program |

```
PROGRAM GraphicsScreenFiller;

USES
  Crt, Graph;

PROCEDURE Initialise;
  VAR driver, mode : integer;
  BEGIN
    driver := detect;
    InitGraph(driver, mode, ' ';
    ClearDevice;
  END; {Initialise}

PROCEDURE Circles;
{ Draws random circles on the screen }
  VAR
    MaxRadius  : word;
    X, Y, C    : word;
    ch         : char;
  BEGIN
    MaxRadius := MaxY div 8;
    SetLineStyle(SolidLn, 0, NormWidth);
    C := 1;
    repeat
      repeat
        SetColor(C);
        SetFillStyle(1,C);
        X := Random(MaxX);
        Y := Random(MaxY);
```

```
            Circle(X, Y, Random(MaxRadius));
            FloodFill(X,Y,C);
            C := C+1;
            if C = 15 then C := 1;
          until KeyPressed;
          readln(ch);
        until ch=' ';
      END; { Circles }

      BEGIN { program body }
        Initialise;
        Circles;
        CloseGraph;
      END.
```

Testing   Output from the program can be seen in the colour plate section.

Now let us consider using shape drawing in a meaningful way with arrays. We shall look at two examples. The first builds on the frequency counting examples of Section 6.4. Here we look at how to draw a histogram of the frequencies represented in a wide range of array types. The second example looks at a data-driven way of drawing shapes, and leads into the case study at the end of the next chapter.

Example 6.13 Histogram drawing

Problem   We would like to be able to draw a histogram of a given set of frequencies, computed from a wide variety of input data.

Solution   There are two concerns here: to draw the histogram, and to allow for a range of input data. Essentially, we are looking at producing something like this:

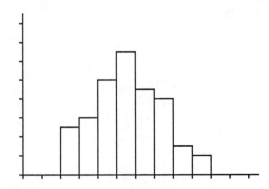

together with annotations along the x and y-axes. These will depend on the range of the index and item types for any particular frequencies.

Thus we need to consider the following parameters:

Parameters for a histogram.

- the range of the index (for the x-axis annotations);

- the range of the frequencies (for the y-axis annotations);

- the titles of the histogram and its axes;

- the frequency values in an array.

The number of bars can be deduced from the range of the index, and should be restricted to a maximum of 26. This will allow for a range of letters, but any more would become crowded on the screen.

In order to have a uniform notation on the y-axis, we will fix the number of intervals at 10, and annotate them accordingly.

| Algorithm | As with the graph printing procedure in Chapter 4, a major consideration is how to scale the values onto the physical screen. The important equations are:

Scaling for a histogram.

Physical step sizes on the axes:

$$xstep = xaxis \ / \ xrange$$
$$ystep = yaxis \ / \ 10$$

Logical step sizes on the axes:

$$xtick = 1$$
$$ytick = \ yrange \ / \ 10$$

Relation between physical and logical axes:

$$xscale = xaxis$$
$$yscale \ = yaxis \ / \ yrange$$

In drawing the histogram, we must consider colours. Blue makes an excellent background, and yellow and light red (orange) contrast well. We use the default font for most of the lettering, and the larger triplex font for the heading.

| Procedure |

```
TYPE
    range   = min ... max;
    vectors = array[range] of integer;

PROCEDURE Histogram (
              xmin, xmax : range;
```

```
                                   ymin, ymax : integer;
                                   n : integer;
                                   title, xtitle, ytitle : string;
                                   F : vectors);

{Assumes that graphics has been initiated}
CONST
  H = 25; {The space allowed for ticks and titles}

VAR
  MaxX, MaxY          : integer;
  xstep, ystep, yscale : real;
  H, J, ytick,
  x1, x2, y1, y2      : word;
  num                 : string[3];
  bignum              : string[6];

BEGIN
  GraphDefaults;
  ClearDevice;
  SetBkColor(blue);
  SetColor(yellow);
  SetFillStyle(SolidFill, LightRed);
  SetTextJustify (CenterText, CenterText);

  {Calculate limits and scaling factors}
  MaxX := GetMaxX;
  MaxY := GetMaxY;
  x1 := 50 + 2*H;
  y1 := 50;
  x2 := MaxX - 100;
  y2 := MaxY - 10 - 2*H;
  xstep := (x2-x1) / (xmax-xmin);
  ystep := (y2-y1) / 10;
  yscale := (y2-y1) / (ymax-ymin);
  ytick := round((ymax-ymin+1)/10);

  {Display the title}
  SetTextStyle (TriplexFont, HorizDir, 4);
  OutTextxy(MaxX div 2, y1 div 2, title);
  SetTextStyle(DefaultFont,HorizDir,1);
  Str(n,bignum);
  OutTextxy(MaxX-100,y1-10,' ('+bignum+' items)');

  {Draw y axis, title, annotation and ticks}
  Line (x1, y1, x1, y2);
  SetTextStyle (DefaultFont, VertDir, 1);
  OutTextxy(x1 -2*H, y2 div 2, ytitle);
  SetTextStyle (DefaultFont, HorizDir, 1);
  J := y2;
  for i := 0 to 10 do begin
    Line (x1+H div 2, J, x1, J);
```

```
            Str(round(i*ytick),num);
            OutTextXY(x1-H, J, Num);
            J := round(J - ystep);
        end;

        {Draw x axis, title, annotation, ticks and bars}
        Line (x1, y2, x2, y2);
        SetTextJustify(CenterText,TopText);
        SetTextStyle(DefaultFont, HorizDir, 1);
        OutTextxy((x2+x1+H) div 2, y2+H, xtitle);

        J := x1;
        for i := xmin to xmax   do begin
            Str(i, num);
            Line(J, y2, J, y2 + H div 2);
            OutTextxy(J+round(Xstep/2), y2 + H div 2, num);
            Bar(J, round(y2-F[i] * yscale), round(J + xstep), y2);
            Rectangle(J, round(y2-F[i] * yscale), round(J + xstep), y2);
            J := round(J + Xstep);
        end;
        Line(J,y2,J,y2 + H div 2);

    END; {Histogram}
```

| Testing |

To test the procedure, we could put it in the *Counting Frequencies* program of Example 6.9 and call it for both the score and club data. Unfortunately, Pascal's strict type checking will first require the values in the *scorecount* and *clubcount* arrays to be copied into an array of type *vectors*, before *Histogram* can be called. This is the price we pay for generality.

The program below is an adaptation of the *CountingFrequencies* program to print three histograms. The first grades the bars from nothing to a maximum, showing the full *y* range of a histogram. The second has random values for all of 26 bars. The last one reads in data from a file, and displays a histogram which approximates to a normal curve. Two of these are shown in the colour plates.

```
        PROGRAM HistogramTester (input, output, inp);
        USES graph;

        CONST
            maxscore      = 20;
            playerlimit   = 250;

        TYPE
            scores        = 0..maxscore;
            players       = 0..playerlimit;
            clubs         = 'A'..'Z';
            scorearrays   = ARRAY [scores] of players;
            clubarrays    = ARRAY [clubs] of players;
```

```
range       = 0..30;
vectors     = ARRAY[range] of integer;

VAR
  scorecount  : scorearrays;
  clubcount   : clubarrays;
  score       : scores;
  club        : char;
  inp         : text;
  filename    : string[12];
  i           : players;
  n           : integer;
  vector      : vectors;
  driver, mode : integer;

PROCEDURE Histogram ...
  ... as before
END; {Histogram}

BEGIN
  driver := detect;
  InitGraph(driver, mode, 'd:\lang\turbo6\bgi');

  {Create scores for testing purposes}
  n := 0;
  FOR score := 0 to maxscore do begin
    scorecount[score] :=score*5;
    n := n + score*5;
  end;
  {Copy the score data to a vector and draw the histogram}
  for score := 0 to maxscore do
    vector[score] := scorecount[score];
  Histogram (0, maxscore, 0, 100,n, 'Scores Histogram',
      'Scores', 'Number of players', vector);
  readln;

  {Generate clubs randomly for testing purposes}
  FOR club := 'A' to 'Z' do
    clubcount[club] := random(playerlimit);

  {Copy the club data to a vector and draw the histogram}
  for club := 'A' to 'Z' do
    vector[ord(club)-ord('A')+1] := clubcount[club];
  Histogram (1, 26, 0, playerlimit, playerlimit, 'Club Histogram',
      'Clubs (1 is A etc)', 'Number of players', vector);
  readln;

  {Read in marks data and draw the histogram}
  assign(inp,'marks.dat');
  reset(inp);
  for i := 0 to 10 do vector[i] := 0;
  n := 0;
```

A possible home for the graphics drivers.

```
while not eof(inp) do begin
  read (inp,i);
  vector[i] := vector[i]+1;
  n := n+1;
end;
Histogram(0,10,0,n div 4, n,'Marks Histogram',
              'Decades','Students',vector);
readln;
Closegraph;
END.
```

| Testing | The output from a typical use of *Histogram* is shown in the colour plates. |

The *Histogram* procedure has a fair number of calls to the Graphics unit, and these generally have explanatory parameters. However, when we come down to drawing freehand shapes, we are faced with the prospect of having actual pixel positions mentioned in the calls to procedures such as *LineTo*, *MoveTo*, *LineRel*, and so on. These can rapidly become unintelligible, and moreover, any change to the lines, however small, will require changing and recompiling the program. It would seem that the function of activating the graph routines could be separated from the data required to drive them. This suggestion is investigated in the next example, and incorporated in the case study at the end of Chapter 7.

Taking it further.

Example 6.14 Data-driven drawing

| Problem | We would like to be able to drive the graphics routines from a data file. |

| Solution | Set up a single character command for each of the routines normally used. Create the data with the command followed by the values for the parameters. |

| Procedure | The procedure is really very simple. The character commands have been chosen as closely as possible to the initial letter of the routine's name, but as there are conflicts, compromises had to be made. All the user must provide is the name of the file containing the data, and *DrawData* does the rest. |

```
PROCEDURE DrawData(filename:string);
  {Assumes that Graphics has been initialised}
  VAR
    f            : text;
  command,ch  : char;
```

```
                          a,b,c,d          : integer;
                          s                : string;
                       BEGIN
                          assign(f,filename);
                          reset(f);
                          while not eof(f) do begin
                            read(f, command);
                            case command of
                              'C' : begin readln(f,c);        SetColor(c); end;
                              'S' : begin readln(f,d,c);      SetFillStyle(d,c); end;
                              'V' : begin readln(f,a,b,c,d);  SetViewPort(a,b,c,d,true); end;
                              'R' : begin readln(f,a,b,c,d);  Rectangle(a,b,c,d); end;
                              'M' : begin readln(f,a,b);      MoveTo(a,b); end;
                              'E' : begin readln(f,a,b);      LineRel(a,b); end;
                              'F' : begin readln(f,a,b,c);    FloodFill(a,b,c); end;
                              'T' : begin readln(f,a,b,c);    SetTextStyle(a,b,c); end;
                              'O' : begin readln(f,a,b,ch,s); OutTextXY(a,b,s); end;
                              'B' : begin readln(f,a,b,c,d);  Bar(a,b,c,d); end;
                              'I' : begin readln(f,a,b,c);    SetLineStyle(a,b,c); end;
                              'L' : begin readln(f,a,b);      LineTo(a,b); end;
                              'K' : begin readln(f,a);        SetBkColor(a); end;
                            end;
                          end;
                          close(f);
                       END;{DrawData}
```

The choice of command characters is arbitary.

Testing To test the procedure, we need a data file and a small program. The following data file is used to produce the menu in the campus map shown in the colour plates.

```
S 1 15
B 5 475 635 445
R 5 475 635 445
S 1 15
B 0 443 228 270
S 1 7
B 5 438 223 275
T 1 0 1
C 4
O 10 280 Delivery System Menu
S 1 15
B 8 324 21 341
B 8 364 21 381
B 8 404 21 421
C 4
O 10 320 O
O 10 360 R
O 10 400 Q
C 8
O 23 320 rder:
O 23 360 oute:
O 23 400 uit:
T 2 0 5
O 10 340 Enter an order.
O 10 380 Calculate a delivery route
```

While one can, at a push, follow what is going on here, it is clearly a good idea to keep such data to one side, and not to embed it in procedure calls in a program.

Summary 6

1. Values can be sent into a procedure or function by means of **parameters** using either value parameters or VAR parameters.

2. Values can be **returned** from a procedure by means of a function value (only one) or VAR parameters (many).

3. Parameters listed in the procedure are termed **formal parameters**, while those listed in a call are termed actual parameters. **Actual parameters** may be any expression or variable for value parameters, but only variables for VAR parameters.

4. **Value parameters** are used for passing values into a procedure and provide security against accidental changes. They are the default and should be used unless the particular facilities of call-by-reference are needed.

5. **VAR parameters** are used for passing values into and out of a procedure. They should only be used in preference to value parameters when passing values out is necessary.

6. **Functions** must execute an assignment to the function name before returning. A function name may not be used as a variable within the function.

7. The **type statement** associates a name with a user-defined scalar or structured type.

8. **Subranges** can be based on any scalar type but real, and enable a restriction to be placed on the values permitted from the base type.

9. **Array subscripts** should be declared as subrange types. Subscripts can be subranges of integer, boolean, char or enumerated types. The elements of an array can be another array, creating a multi-dimensional structure.

10. An array can be assigned to another of the same type, or passed as a parameter. These are the only **operations** available on whole arrays.

11. To ensure that the Pascal system checks that subscripts are **valid** at runtime, it may be necessary to turn on the compiler option {$R+}.

12. Turbo Pascal provides routines for **drawing shapes** and colouring them in.

13. Drawing can best be done via a **data-driven procedure**, rather than through fixed calls in a program.

Self-check quiz 6

1. Write the declaration for a procedure *P* which needs two integer value parameters, a real VAR parameter and real value parameter.

2. Is it permissible for an actual parameter and a formal parameter to have the same name?

3. Is it permissible for a formal parameter to have the same name as a local variable in its procedure?

4.   Is the following a valid subrange? kilograms = 0.4 .. 20.0;

5.   Can subscripts be negative integers?

6.   What happens if a value outside a given subrange is assigned?

7.   What happens if an array is accessed with a subscript of the wrong type, such as character instead of integer?

8.   What happens if an array is accessed with a variable which has the right type but has a value outside those specified?

9.   Can part of a matrix be passed as a parameter? If so, what part?

10.   Can a function return a vector as a result?

Problems 6

Answers are provided for problems marked with a §.

6.1§   **Sum of squares**   Write a function which is given two integers as parameters, and returns as its value the sum of the squares of the numbers between and inclusive of the two parameters. Show how to call the function to print the value of $\sum i^2$ where i runs from 1 to 10.

6.2§   **Parameter passing**   Study the following program.

```
PROGRAM Picture (output);
  VAR row, length : integer;
  PROCEDURE modify (v : integer; VAR x : integer);
    BEGIN
      x := v * v - v;
    END; {modify}

  PROCEDURE line (long : integer);
    VAR index : integer;
    BEGIN
      for index := 1 to long do write(row:2);
      writeln;
    END; {line}

BEGIN
  FOR row := 1 to 4 do begin
    modify (row, length);
    write (row:2, length:4);
    line (length);
  END;
END.
```

What will *Picture* print out when it is run? Explain why *v* and *x* are listed separately in the formal parameter list for *modify*.

6.3   **Highest and lowest**   Write a procedure to read in a given number of real numbers and return the maximum and minimum values found. Test the procedure with a small program.

6.4   **Validating identifiers**   In Section 5.2, there is an example program which checks whether a word is a valid Pascal identifier. Convert the checking part into a boolean function and verify that the program still works correctly.

6.5§ **Exam marks revisited** Consider the program in the case study in Section 5.5. Decide whether the program could have been better designed from the point of view of procedures, and whether parameters should be used. Give good reasons for any changes that you suggest.

6.6   **Mains voltage** The mains voltage supplied by a substation is measured at hourly intervals over a 72 hour period, and a report made. Write a program to read in the 72 readings and determine:

- the mean voltage measured;
- the hours at which the recorded voltage varies from the mean by more than 10%;
- any adjacent hours when the change from one reading to the next was greater than 15% of the mean value.

Include in your program an option to display a histogram of the voltage over the 72 hours, using the procedure developed in Example 6.14.

6.7   **Useful procedures** Write and test procedures which take an array of integers as one of their parameters and do the following:

- find the maximum of all the elements;
- find the maximum of all the elements, plus all the positions where it occurs;
- determine the range of values spanned by the array;
- determine whether all the quantities in the array are equal;
- determine the number of times a value greater than a given level occurs.

7

User-defined types

We look at three data types – enumerated, records and sets, and then see how Turbo Pascal units can be built around them. The chapter concludes with a case study of drawing a map using data stored on a file.

7.1 Enumerated types

The objects that programs have to deal with go beyond the predefined types, which provide only for numbers, characters and boolean values. Good examples come from the data in a passport, with the following three items not falling into any predefined category:

sex   – male or female
marital status – single, married, widowed, divorced, separated
colour of eyes – blue, grey, brown, hazel, green

In older languages, such values had to be forced into one of the predefined types, leading to **codes**, which were usually numeric. For example, male would be 1 and female 2. The disadvantage of this scheme is that it can easily lead to errors by using the wrong code, and there is no obvious check that a code is valid at all.

Pascal recognises that its predefined types do not cover everything and provides for new types to be constructed with the individual values listed as identifiers. This is known as **enumerating** the values, and hence these types are called **enumerated types**.

Form of an enumerated type

An enumerated type is declared in a type statement, with the type formation being a list of identifiers. Formally, this gives:

Enumerated type

identifier = (*list of identifiers*);

Examples are:

```
TYPE
    sex         = (male, female);
    status      = (single, married, widowed, divorced, separated);
    eyecolours  = (blue, grey, brown, hazel, green);
    machines    = (micro, mini, mainframe);
    states      = (found, notthere, looking);
    suits       = (clubs, diamonds, hearts, spades);
```

Enumerated values

All enumerated values in a program must be different.

Each enumerated type can have as many values as one likes, but each must be a distinct identifier, and the identifiers must not clash with other identifiers within the same scope. Specifically, a given identifier cannot be a value in two different types, as in:

```
TYPE
    lights      = (red, amber, green);
    eyecolours  = (blue, grey, brown, hazel, green);
```

However, subranges of newly-declared enumerated types are possible, and can often be used to good effect, as in:

Subranges are allowed.

```
TYPE
    daysoftheweek = (Monday, Tuesday, Wednesday, Thursday,
                     Friday, Saturday, Sunday);
    weekdays      = Monday..Friday;
    weekend       = Saturday..Sunday;
    midweekbreak  = Tuesday..Saturday;
```

Unfortunately, these types are linear, and do not 'wrap around'. Subranges therefore must refer to values in order. For example, we cannot follow the above declarations with:

> longweekend = Friday..Monday;

The notation for an enumerated value is simply an identifier like *boolean*. As for any other identifier, the case of letter is unimportant. Thus the following all refer to the same value:

> Monday
> monday
> MONDAY

Enumerated functions and operators

There are three functions that apply to all enumerated types:

ord (id)	gives the ordinal value of *id* in the list of the type
succ(id)	gives the next value in the list, if it exists
pred(id)	gives the previous value in the list, if it exists

The values in an enumerated type are said to be ordered, and there exist equivalent ordinal values starting from 0. Thus in the *eyecolours* type, *ord(blue)* is 0 and *ord(brown)* is 2. The ordering can be used to loop through the values, either using a for-statement, as in:

> VAR day : daysoftheweek;
>
> for day := Tuesday to Saturday do

or with *succ* or *pred*, as in:

> day := Tuesday;
> while day <= Saturday do begin
>   {whatever}
>   day := succ(day);
> end;

Moving through enumerated values.

One problem with using *succ* and *pred* is that they are not defined for the last and first values in a list respectively. Thus *succ(Saturday)* is alright, but *succ(Sunday)* should cause a value out of range error.

The operators that are available for enumerated types are the same as those for characters, namely, the conditional operators = <> <= >= < and >. The interpretation of the inequalities is once again based on the order of the values as specified in the declaration of the type.

Example 7.1 Calculating bills

The Relaxeeze Holiday Camp in Zanyland has a basic charge of D120 per person per week, but has three billing strategies, depending on the season and the day on which the guests arrive:

> Arrive on Saturday, Sunday or Monday : standard charge
> Arrive after Monday : half price
> In summer : add 50%

Given the day of arrival, the season and the number of people, we can write a function which will use these to work out the cost of the holiday.

```
TYPE
    daysofweek  = (Saturday, Sunday, Monday,Tuesday,
                     Wednesday, Thursday, Friday);
    seasons     = (spring, summer, autumn, winter);
    peoplerange = 0..100;  {can't take more}
    dollies     = 0..maxint;  {sky's the limit}

FUNCTION holidaycost (
              arrival    : daysofweek;
              season     : seasons;
              people     : peoplerange) : dollies;

CONST
  basicrate = 120;  {dollies}
VAR
  sofar : dollies;
BEGIN
  sofar := basicrate;
  if arrival > Monday then sofar := sofar div 2;
  if season = summer then sofar := round(sofar * 1.5);
  holidaycost := sofar * people;
END;  {holidaycost}
```

The order is defined in the type declaration.

Notice that the declaration for the days of the week was altered to start on Saturday so that the > could be used to good effect with the arrival day.

Input and output of enumerated types

Input and output is not available for enumerated types in Pascal. Thus the use of enumerated types is often confined to manipulations inside a program. However, it is sometimes essential to get values from the outside world into a program and to store them in an enumerated type. In order to do this, the ordinal values referred to above might have to be employed. Alternatively, the words used as the values can be read in and decoded.

In the same way, outputing an enumerated value involves a translation from the identifier values to items that can be printed, that is, numbers or strings or characters. Both of these processes can be neatly packaged in procedures, so that for any given new enumerated type, *x*, *readx* and *writex* routines can be written. For debugging purposes, the *ord* of a value can be printed.

A quick way to print an enumerated value.

Example 7.2   Decoding days

| Problem | The days of the week form a very useful type in many applications. Inevitably, it will be necessary to read in a day, store it as an enumerated type, and print it out. We wish to write two procedures to do this.

| Solution | Printing is easy, as it simply employs a case statement to map the non-printable enumerated values onto printable strings.

```
PROCEDURE writeday (d : daysofweek);
  BEGIN
    case d of
      Monday    : write ('Monday');
      Tuesday   : write ('Tuesday');
      Wednesday : write ('Wednesday');
      Thursday  : write ('Thursday');
      Friday    : write ('Friday');
      Saturday  : write ('Saturday');
      Sunday    : write ('Sunday');
    end;
  END; {writeday}
```

Writing days.

Reading is more difficult. We have to take an unknown quantity in the input – suspected of being a day name – and check it against one of the seven possibilities. There are two ways of tackling this:

1. Check each letter as it comes in, and make a decision based on the first few letters.

2. Read in the whole word and check it against a table of possibilities.

| Algorithm | The procedure must read characters until it can be sure as to what day is intended, then it can skip characters until a space. Monday, Wednesday and Friday can be established on the first letter, but the others need two letters. The procedure is:

Reading days.

```
PROCEDURE readday (var d : daysofweek);
VAR
  ch    : char;
  valid : boolean;
BEGIN
  REPEAT
    valid := true;
    read(ch);
    if ch in ['M','T','W','F','S'] then
    case ch of
      'M'  : d := Monday;
      'W'  : d := Wednesday;
      'F'  : d := Friday;
      'T'  : begin
             read(ch);
             if ch = 'h' then d := Thursday else
             if ch = 'u' then d := Tuesday else
             valid := false;
             end;
      'S'  : begin
             read(ch);
             if ch = 'a' then d := Saturday else
             if ch = 'u' then d := Sunday else
             valid := false;
             end;
    end
    else valid := false;
    if not valid
    then writeln('*** Wrong spelling.  Try again');
  UNTIL valid;
  repeat read(ch) until ch = space;
END; {readday}
```

Problems with readday.

One feels slightly uneasy about this procedure because it is only checking one or sometimes two letters, and making an assumption that these are the beginnings of words for days. Thus, given any of the following:

> Saturn
> Saturday
> Sat.
> Satsuma

readday would decide that the word was Saturday.

Discussion   Within the confines of reading a date, the dangers of the procedure being given something quite silly are minimal. However, the next example explores the second option, and shows how enumerated types can be used to make programs more general.

Example 7.3 Multilingual interfaces

Problem A program is being written for general use within several countries, and it is a requirement that the output should be in whatever language is spoken in that country. However, we do not want to change the program every time. How can the words printed out be made independent of the Pascal code?

Solution The solution is to make the words data and store them in files, *Abstract away* one for each language. At the start of the program, the *from the data.* language required is set, and the words from that file are read into one or more arrays. Instead of writing out actual strings, the program is altered to write out the contents of the array instead.

Algorithm As an example, take the days of the week. Within the program, we can refer to these by means of an enumerated scalar, in English.

```
TYPE
    daysofweek    = (Monday, Tuesday, Wednesday, Thursday,
                     Friday, Saturday, Sunday);
```

However, the actual words to be printed will come from a file. For example, the French versions are:

lundi
mardi
mercredi
jeudi
vendredi
samedi
dimanche

and could be stored in a file called *French.days*.

Day names in most languages will not exceed 10 in length, so we can declare *names* as a string 10 long. The array of day names is then simply an array of this type.

Algorithm The declarations required are:

```
TYPE
    namerange     = 1.. daynamemax;
    names         = string[10];
    daysofweek    = (Monday, Tuesday, Wednesday, Thursday,
                     Friday, Saturday, Sunday);
    daynames      = array [daysofweek] of names;
```

```
VAR
    dayfile        : text;
    filename       : names;
    dayname        : daynames;
```

Then the reading in of the French names and writing them can be done by first reading in the filename, and then the strings, as in:

```
write('Which file for the day names? ');
readln(filename);
assign(dayfile, filename);
reset(dayfile);

for day := Monday to Sunday do
    readln(dayfile,dayname[day]);
```

Testing   Supposing *French.days* was the file used, then:

```
write(dayname[Friday]);
```

would produce:

vendredi

Switching to another language would be done by changing the file name, and reading in the new words.

Discussion   So far we have not shown how we would take in a word and translate it to a day. In essence, we have to read in the whole word, and search through the *dayname* array for a match. This warrants another example!

Example 7.4   Searching string tables

Problem   In the program that wrote out foreign spellings for days of the week (Example 7.3), there is also a requirement that it read them. Moreover, it is desirable that the program should work for any set of foreign names specified as data.

Solution   The words for days are stored in a file, and read into an array of strings. A potential day can then be read and passed to a **search** procedure, which will return the index to the array for that string, or some error code if the string is not a valid name.

If we reflect on this, we realise that searching is an operation that could be applicable in many circumstances. Reading a month name, or a department name, or even a person's name, and checking that it appears on a list could be done in the same way. The only difficulty is that different enumerated types could not be used for the subscripts. If we sacrifice the use of enumerated types at this level, and use integer subranges instead, we can come up with a very nice generalised procedure for reading and identifying strings.

Searching is a standard technique.

| Examples | Given a table containing days of the week in French:

Generalised tables.

lundi	vendredi
mardi	samedi
mercredi	dimanche
jeudi	

then passing the word:

> vendredi

as a parameter to the proposed search procedure should return a 5. With the data:

> spring
> summer
> autumn
> winter

a call to the same search procedure with a parameter:

> summer

will return a 2. The only difference is the number of valid words in the table: seven in the first case, and four in the second. We can declare a general table of a reasonable size, and pass the actual length of it to the search procedure.

| Algorithm | The searching algorithm is an example of a double-exit loop: either the word is found in the table, or the end of the table is reached before the word is found. We use a technique known as **state indicators** to keep track of the state of the search while it is progressing. This state starts out as searching, then can change to either found or not found, depending on the outcome. We are therefore looking towards an enumerated type defined as:

```
TYPE
  state = (searching, found, notthere);
```

Table Search

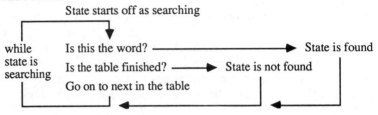

State starts off as searching

while
state is
searching

Is this the word? ───────────────────────▶ State is found

Is the table finished? ──────▶ State is not found

Go on to next in the table

The one issue to settle, then, is how the procedure should report that a word did not match any in the table. The best way is to have a boolean as a parameter, and to rely on the caller checking it before assuming that the index returned is meaningful.

| Program | In the program that follows, three string tables are set up and searched. Moreover, reading in a table is also an operation that can be generalised, and this is done as well in *ReadStringTable*.

```
PROGRAM Searchingtables (input, output);

   CONST
      tablemax = 30;
      wordmax = 20;

   TYPE
      words        = string[wordmax];
      tablerange   = 1..tablemax;
      tableindex   = 0..tablemax;
      stringtables = array[tablerange] of names;
      dayrange     = 1..7;
      seasonrange  = 1..4;
      deptrange    = 1.. 20;

   VAR
      daytable,
      seasontable,
      depttable    : stringtables;
      word         : words;
      there, stop  : boolean;
      ndays,
      nseasons,
      ndepts
      n            : tableindex;

   PROCEDURE ReadStringTable (
                     VAR n : stringindex;
                     VAR T : stringtables;
                     s : string);
      VAR f : text;
```

*A generalised
procedure.*

```
BEGIN
  write('What file for the ', s);
  readln(filename);
  assign(f, filename);
  reset (f);
  n := 0;
  while not eof(f) do begin
    n := n + 1;
    readln(f,T[n]);
  end;
  writeln('Table with ', n, ' elements read.');
END; {getintable}

PROCEDURE Search (
    T : stringtables;
    n : stringindex;
    x : words;
    VAR index : stringrange;
    VAR result : boolean);
TYPE
  states = (searching, found, notthere);
VAR
  i      : stringrange;
  state : states;
BEGIN
  if i = 0 then state := notthere else begin
  state := searching;
  i := 1;
  REPEAT
    if x = T[i] then state := found else
    if i = n then state := notthere else
    i := succ(i);
  UNTIL state <> searching;
  end;
  CASE state of
    found :   begin
                      index := i;
                      result := true;
                  end;
    notthere :  result := false;
  END;
END; {search}

BEGIN
  writeln('****** Searching string arrays ******');
  ReadStringTable(daytable, ndays, 'day names');
  ReadStringTable(seasontable, nseasons, 'season names');
  ReadStringTable(f, depttable, ndepts,'department names');

  stop := false;
  repeat
```

Another
generalised
procedure.

```
                    writeln('Type in a day, a season, a department or QUIT');
                    readln(word);
                    if word = 'QUIT'
                    then stop := true
                    else begin
                       Search (daytable, ndays, word, n, there);
                       if there
                       then writeln('This is day No. ', n)
                       else begin
                          Search (seasontable, nseasons, word, n, there);
                          if there
                          then writeln('This is season No. ', n:1)
                          else begin
                             search (depttable, ndepts, word, n , there);
                             if there
                             then writeln ('This is department No. ', n:1)
                             else writeln ('This word is not in any of the tables.');
                          end;
                       end;
                    end;
                 until stop;
         END.
```

| Discussion | The *Search* procedure implements a **linear search**. If the data to be searched is ordered, then there are far more efficient searching methods, but these are beyond the scope of this book.

Another point to note is that in standard Pascal (but not in Turbo), there is a facility to pass arrays that are actually of different lengths to a procedure. These are called **conformant array parameters**. Details of these can be found in the other *Pascal Precisely* texts.

7.2 Records

Many programming applications are centred around the processing of data, which may assume a fairly complicated form. An example would be the full information required for a passport, which would include names, date of birth, sex, marital status, various facial characteristics and so on. All these items combine to form a single unit and there will be times when they need to be treated as such. Pascal provides for such a grouping mechanism in its record construct.

Form of a record type

A record type is declared as a list of fields of other types, enclosed in keywords. The types of the fields can be anything, either all different or all the same or a mixture.

```
Record type

   identifier  =  RECORD
                     field : type;
                     field : type;
                        . . .
                     field : type;
                  END;
```

An example of a natural application of a record type would be a date: this comprises three fields, but may well be treated as a unit by itself on occasion. Such a definition, with its subsidiary definitions, would be:

```
CONST
     past      = 1750;
     future    = 2500;

TYPE
     days      = 1..31;
     months    = 1..12;
     years     = past..future; {The limit of the program's lifetime!}

     dates     = RECORD
                     day    : days;
                     month  : months;
                     year   : years;
                  END;
```

Since a field can be of any type, it could be a record itself. For example:

```
TYPE
     sexes      = (male, female);
     newborns = RECORD
                     sex    : sexes;
                     birth  : dates;
                  END;
```

Records within records.

And finally, a useful record definition is:

```
TYPE
     point = RECORD
                 x, y : real;
              END;
```

Record values

The range of values for any one record is the product of every value of every field. In other words, any kind of composite value can be accommodated in a record type.

In Turbo Pascal, we can write down literal values for records by listing each field and then giving its value. For example, we could establish constants for the above records as follows:

Record
constants.

```
CONST
    StartDate : date      = (day: 1;  month : 1;  year : startyear);
    origin     : point     = (x: 0; y: 0);
    king       : newborns  = (sex: male;
                              birth: (day: 12; month: 4; year: 1984);
```

Record operators and functions

It went without saying for the scalar types that assignment was defined, but it is worth emphasising that this is also true for records. If we declare:

```
VAR mybirthday, today, happyday : dates;
```

and define appropriate values for the first two, then we can say:

```
if mybirthday = today then writeln('Happy Birthday to me!');
happyday := mybirthday;
```

The dot
operator.

The important operator as far as records are concerned is that for **field selection**, which is indicated by a dot. Any field of a record can be selected by giving the record variable name (not the type name) followed by a dot and the field name. If there are records within records, then several dots can be used to access the lower fields as in:

```
VAR baby : newborns;

baby.sex := female;
baby.birth.day := 21;
baby.birth.month := 3;
baby.birth.year := 1986;
```

Record values cannot be read or written in their entirety by the predefined read and write statements. It is necessary to treat each scalar field separately. As for enumerated types, it is a good idea to construct procedures for each of these operations. So, for example, one would define *readdate* and *writedate* procedures to handle variables of the type *dates*. However, entire records can be input from and output to files as discussed in Section 8.5.

The with-statement

Writing out long selected field names can be tedious. Pascal provides a shorthand which factorises out the common parts of a field name – the with-statement. The usual form of the with-statement is:

With statement
WITH *record variable name* DO BEGIN   *statements;* END; {with}

The scope of the with-statement extends from the BEGIN to the END and within this scope any reference to the fields of the record mentioned can be given without their prefix. For example, the group of statements above could be rewritten as:

```
baby.sex := female;
WITH baby.birth DO BEGIN
    day := 21;
    month := 3;
    year := 1986;
END; {WITH}
```

A useful
shorthand.

This version is not any shorter, but it is perhaps easier to read and to write, because there is less repetition.

The syntax of the with-statement includes a version for having a list of record names, an example of which would be:

```
WITH baby, baby.birth DO BEGIN
    sex := female;
    day := 21;
    month := 3;
    year := 1986;
END; {WITH}
```

It is permissible to mention a record more than once, as was done here, but it is not correct to mention two records of the same type. In this case, the Pascal system would not know to which record each field belonged.

It is also possible to have a with-statement applying to only one statement, in which case the begin-end is omitted. The good use of this option is with read and write statements, as in:

```
with baby.birth do write(day, month, year);
```

An example program using records is given in the next section, when we extend the idea to encompass abstract data types.

Variant records

The information that is gathered together to form a record type could have inherent variations. For example, in a record that has a field for marital status, there may be additional fields for the name and occupation of the spouse. However, if a particular record of this type had the marital status listed as single, then these latter fields would not apply. In fact, it may well be erroneous to store or access them. Pascal provides for this eventuality in a limited way with the concept of records with variants.

Form of a variant record type

For more complex data.

A record type may specify one field as a **tag field.** Thereafter, for each value of the tag field, a different group of fields may be specified. Each of these groups is known as a **variant**. The form of a record with variants is:

```
Variant record type

identifier = RECORD
   fixed fields
   CASE tag-field : tag-type OF
      tag-values : (variant fields);
      tag-values : (variant fields);
      . . .
      tag-values : (variant fields);
   END; {RECORD}
```

The tag-field may be of any of the discrete types, that is, integer, character, boolean, enumerated, or subranges of these. Each value of this type must be listed with a corresponding list of fields. There may be none, one or more fields for each tag-value. The fixed fields are always listed first in the record, and are optional. Examples of variant record declarations are:

```
TYPE
   status = (married, divorced, single, widowed);
   kinds  = (cartesian, polar);
```

```
person = RECORD
    name  : names;
    birth  : dates;
    CASE MaritalStatus : status of
        married  : (spouse : names;
                          occupation : occupations);
        divorced  : (since : dates);
        single  : ( );
        widowed  : (dependents : integer);
    END;

coordinates = RECORD
    CASE kind : kinds of
        cartesian : (x,y : real);
        polar      : (theta : angles;
                          radius : real);
    END;
```

When a variable is declared of one of these types, initialising the tag field becomes important. For example, if we declare:

```
VAR
    P, Q : person;
    C, D : coordinates;
```

then valid assignments of values would be:

```
readname(P.name);                              Tags provide
P.MaritalStatus := single;                      essential control
readdate(Q.birth);                              over variants.
Q.maritalStatus := widowed;
read(Q.dependents);

C.kind := cartesian;
read(C.x, C.y);
D.kind := polar;
read(D.theta, D.radius);
```

Once the tag field has been given a value, only those fields of the corresponding variant are defined. Thus a variant record provides a secure way of hiding unwanted information. It would not be valid to refer now to *P.dependents* or *C.radius*, since these fields are incompatible with their respective records' tag-fields.

Example 7.5 Roots of a quadratic

| Problem | We would like to solve the quadratic equation $ax^2 + bx + c = 0$ for given values of $a,\ b$ and c. The first thing to remember is |

the formula for the roots of the equation. It is:

$$x = \frac{-b \pm \sqrt{b^2 - 4ac}}{2a}$$

| **Solution** | We would like to construct a procedure that can be reused. In order to do so, it must be made self-contained and |

communicate through parameters only. The input parameters will be the coefficients, a, b and c. The output parameters will be the roots. But how are these to be expressed? The number of roots and their meaning will differ according to the discriminant calculated on the basis of the coefficients. We have the following possibilities:

Catering for all possible cases.

- no roots,

- one root,

- two real roots (possibly equal),

- two imaginary roots, each with two components.

We therefore employ a variant record to express all these variations in a single type.

| **Algorithm** | The definition of the fields for the record follows the list above. Before defining the record, though, we should consider |

how to represent the imaginary roots. These are given by:

(realpart, impart) and (realpart, –impart)

so that we could just include the two values *realpart* and *impart* in the record, and have the caller work out what to do with them. A much better method would be define a separate record for the imaginary type, and use that in the root record. This is done in the full program that follows.

| **Program** |

```
PROGRAM TestQuadratics (input, output);
  TYPE
    rootsorts  = (none, onereal, tworeal, twoimaginary);
    imaginary  = record
                     realpart,
                     impart        : real;
                 end;
    rootrec    = record
                     case sort : rootsorts of
                        none           : ( );
                        onereal        : (R : real);
                        tworeal        : (R1, R2 : real);
                        twoimaginary   : (i1, i2 : imaginary);
                 end;
  VAR
```

```
    a,b,c : real;
    roots : rootrec;

PROCEDURE quadratic (a,b,c : real;  var roots: rootrec);
   VAR D : real; {discriminant}
   BEGIN
     with roots do begin
       if (a=0) and (b=0) then
         sort := none
       else
       if a = 0 then begin
         sort := onereal;
         R := -c/b;
       end else begin
         D := b*b - 4*a*c;
         if D = 0 then begin
           sort := tworeal;
           R1 := -b /(2*a);
           R2 := R2;
         end else
         if D > 0 then begin
           sort := tworeal;
           R1 := (-b + sqrt(D))/(2*a);
           R2 := (-b - sqrt(D))/(2*a);
         end else begin
           sort := imaginary;
           i1.realpart := -b/(2*a);
           i2.realpart := i1.realpart;
           i1.impart := sqrt(-D)/(2*a);
           i2.impart := - i1.impart;
         end;
       end;
     end;
END; {quadratic}


BEGIN
writeln('***** Solving quadratics ******');
write('Type the coefficients ');
readln(a,b,c);
quadratic(a,b,c,roots);
with roots do
case sort of
  none           : writeln('Not a quadratic');
  onereal        : writeln('One real root ', R:6:2);
  tworeal        : writeln('Two real roots ', R1:6:2, '  ', R2:6:2);
  twoimaginary   : writeln('Two imaginary roots (',
                        i1.realpart:6:2,',',i1.impart:6:2,')  ',
                        '(',i2.realpart:6:2,',',i2.impart:6:2,')');
end;
END.
```

A clean, self-contained interface.

| Testing | The program should be tested with quadratics for which the answers are known, for example, cooefficients 1 –2 1 should |

The program should be tested with quadratics for which the answers are known, for example, cooefficients 1 –2 1 should give two real roots equal to 1. A useful extension to the program would be to put the main program in a loop so that several equations can be factorised in one run.

Abstract data types

Records provide a very powerful means of grouping data together, as we have seen from the many examples in the previous section. Several of these examples involved modelling familiar concepts that have well-accepted formats, such as dates, polar coordinates or imaginary numbers. Using records allows us to extend the repertoire of predefined Pascal types to make a richer language for our particular needs.

Consider, however, that the predefined types have, in addition to their specified range of values, sets of properties, operations, functions and input/output facilities. The record structuring facility does not automatically provide these for user-defined types However, it would be desirable if we could create them, so that we could, for example, read a date or add two imaginary numbers.

Such extensions are known as **abstract data types** (adts). The theory is that a data type consists not only of a set of values, but also of the operations that are applicable to it. Then any variables defined of that type can **only** use the operations provided. In other words, one would provide operations to subtract and compare days, but certainly not to multiply or divide them!

Example 7.6   Floor dimensions revisited

Continuing with the program to calculate the area of a house given the dimensions of its rooms (discussed in Example 6.7), we can now pay attention to the data structuring. Feet and inches together form a linear imperial measurement, and should go in a record, and be treated as an adt. The operations that we could define would be:

- read a linear length,
- write out a linear length,
- compare two lengths for equality and inequality.

Not all of these are needed in our program. Furthermore, once it comes to comparing, it may be easier just to deal with the metric measurements. For this reason, we shall store both sets in a composite record for the room. The data types are:

```
TYPE
{Abstract data type for Imperial Length and area}
    feet         = 0..feetmax; {something reasonable}
    inches       = 0..11;
    ImperialLinear= record
                        ft   : feet;
                        ins : inches;
                      end;
    ImperialArea  = real; { sq ft}
{End of adt declarations}

    MetricLength  = real;  {metres}
    MetricArea    = real;  {sq metres}

    RoomDimensions = record
       length, breadth      : ImperialLinear;
       area                 : ImperialArea;
       mlength, mbreadth    : MetricLength;
       marea                : MetricArea;
      end;

VAR
    room : RoomDimensions;
```

We shall assume that the metric measurements are recalculated as needed. The program can now be far more readable, with the *length* and *breadth* field names being used for the dimensions, rather than *ft1* and *ins1*, and so on. For example, the multiply procedure can be called by:

```
WITH room do
    multiply (length, breadth, area);
```

compared to:

```
multiply (ft1, ins1, ft2, ins2, area);
```

as previously. Within the procedure itself, we still need to refer to the first and second dimensions in turn.

```
PROCEDURE multiply (dim1, dim2 : ImperialLinear;
                    VAR a : ImperialArea);
BEGIN
  a := (dim1.ft + dim1.ins/12) * (dim2.ft + dim2.ins/12);
END;
```

Discussion The abstract data type and its operations form a unit, and in Turbo Pascal, there is a facility for actually creating such units and using them from many programs. This is discussed in Section 7.4, when this example is concluded.

7.3   Sets

Pascal is one of a few languages that provides for grouping and manipulating items without respect to order. The type mechanism is the **set**, which has most of the properties and operations of the mathematical concept of a set.

By far and away the most common use of sets is the test for set membership. This has already been introduced in Chapter 5, along with the *in* operator. To recap, examples of such uses of **set literals** are:

Familiar uses of set membership.

```
if month in [sep, apr, jun, nov] then days := 30;
borderlines := mark in [49, 59, 69, 74];
isadigit := ch in ['0'..'9'];
```

If the sets are to be used more often, or manipulated in any way, then a **set type** should be defined, along with **set variables** of that type. The declaration can be split into four stages.

Form of a set type

Four steps in defining a set.

1.   **Define the base type.** A set has to be defined on a base type, which may be a small subrange of integer, char, boolean or enumerated or any subrange of these. Examples of base types are:

```
TYPE
  months       = (jan, feb, mar, apr, may, jun, jul, aug, sep, oct,
                   nov, dec);
  markrange    = 0..100;
  smallrange   = 'a'..'z';
  capitalrange = 'A'..'Z';
```

2.   **Define the set type.** The form of a set type definition is:

Set type
identifier = SET OF *base type*;

Examples of set types are:

```
TYPE
    monthsets    = set of months;
    marksets     = set of markrange;
    smallsets    = set of smallrange;
    capsets      = set of capitalrange;
    charsets     = set of char;
```

Notice the use of the suffixes '-range' and '-set' to distinguish between bases and the sets themselves.

3. **Declare the set variables.** Set types, like any other types, do not exist as items that can be manipulated. We first have to declare variables of that type. Examples are:

```
VAR
    allmonths, months30  : monthsets;
    class, border        : marksets;
    smalls               : smallsets;
    letters, digits      : charsets;
```

4. **Initialise the sets.** Like any other variable, a set variable does not have an initial value. That is, it does not start off as the empty set, any more than an integer variable starts off as zero. It is necessary, therefore, to initialise the set to some value, by listing the elements, or ranges of them, in square brackets, for example:

It is easy to forget this part!

```
allmonths  := [jan..dec];
months30   := [sep, apr, jun, nov];
class      := [50, 60, 70, 75];
digits     := ['0'..'9'];
letters    := [ ]; {to start with}
smalls     := ['a' ..'z'];
```

Note the special case of [ ] which denotes the empty set, and is a set literal compatible with any set type.

Set values and operators

Theoretically, the range of a set is restricted only by the range of its base type. However, because of the way sets are implemented, there is usually a limit placed on the maximum ordinal value in a base type. Turbo Pascal's limit is 256, so that the following would be valid base types:

```
TYPE
    secondcentury = 100..199;
    charsets      = set of char;
```

but the following would not be valid:

```
TYPE
   numbers      = integer;
   fifthcentury = 400..499;
```

Even though *fifthcentury* has only 100 possible values, it exceeds the limit on the maximum ordinal value.

As we have already noted, literal sets are enclosed in square brackets, and may contain individual elements and ranges of elements, where the elements can be constants or expressions of the base type. As described earlier, literal sets cannot be given names under the CONST section, for example:

```
CONST
   class : marksets := [50, 60, 70, 75];
```

There are several operators applicable to sets. The relational ones are:

in	set membership
= <>	set equality and inequality
<= >=	set inclusion

For manipulation of sets, the three operators are:

+	set union
*	set intersection
–	set difference

We shall now see how these are used in typical cases.

There are no predefined functions defined for whole sets. Sets can be passed as parameters to user-defined functions.

Neither input nor output to text files is possible for whole sets – a restriction that we have already seen for whole records and whole arrays. Procedures for accomplishing this are described below.

Manipulating sets

Four common uses of sets.

1. **Creating sets from sets.** A large set may have disjoint subsets, which can be formed by set difference, rather than by listing the elements in each case. For example, we can declare and initialise:

    ```
    VAR months31 : monthsets;

    months31 := allmonths – months30 – [feb];
    ```

(This is exactly what the old rhyme says: '... all the rest have thirty-one, excepting February alone ...'.) Notice that the set operations work on sets, not elements, and it would have been incorrect to say − *feb* instead of − [*feb*].

2. **Creating sets from data.** The elements of a set cannot always be fixed as constants in a program. For example, not all schools and universities have the same class borders for marks as given earlier. To create a set dynamically, we initialise it to the empty set and use set union:

    ```
    class := [ ];   border := [ ];
    for i := 1 to 4 do begin
      read (mark);
      class := class + [mark];
      border := border + [mark − 1];
    end;
    ```

3. **Printing a set.** A set is not a simple type, and it cannot be printed in its entirety using a simple Pascal write statement. To print all the elements present in a set, we have to loop over the whole base type and use tests on set membership. For example:

    ```
    for mark := 0 to 100 do if mark in classes then
      write (mark);
    ```

    There is no simpler way. In fact, to perform any operation on all elements of a set, we need such a combination of a for-statement and an if-statement.

4. **Cardinality of a set.** Sometimes it is necessary to know how many elements there are in a set (its cardinality). To count the elements, once again we have to loop through all possibilities and use tests on set membership. In general, such a function could be defined as:

    ```
    FUNCTION cardinality (s : someset) : integer;
      VAR
        i       : somebase;
        count : integer;  {0..maxsetsize}
      BEGIN
        count := 0;
        for i := lower to upper do if i in s then
          count := count + 1;
        cardinality := count;
      END; {cardinality}
    ```

    The parts in italics will need to be specified for the particular set type and different versions of the function will have to be included for each set type for which it is required.

Example 7.7 Generalised menus

Problem After Example 5.5, we investigated ways of making good menus for controlling programs that will run for some time. We would like to create a menu system where the options and the commands can vary as data, rather than be built into the program.

Solution There are actually two problems here:

- varying the messages associated with each choice, and

- varying and checking the commands.

To solve the first, we can declare an array of messages and read the appropriate strings off a file. For the second, we can declare a set of commands – assuming they are single characters. We then read them off the file as well, put them in the set, and use this to check the user's responses. The file may look something like this:

Alternative
menu layouts.

```
R   Read in data
D   Display
S   Sort
Q   Quit
```

or a different file for the same menu system might be:

```
1.   Read
2.   Extract
3.   Sort
4.   Save
5.   Restore
Q.   Quit
```

Algorithm The routines discussed after Example 5.5 will need to be primed, but otherwise remain much the same.

Program Extracts from the program that would use such a system are given. Note that the constants for controlling the menu window have been made to depend on the maximum size of the menu, which is set at 10. Also note that we read the whole string from the file into the options array, and then extract off the first character to add to the command set.

```
CONST
  maxmenu = 10;

TYPE
  command      = char;
  commandsets  = set of command;
```

```
  options       = string[50];
  optionrange   = 1..maxmenu;
  optionarrays  = array [optionrange] of options;

VAR
  commands  : commandset;
  optionslist  : optionarrays;
  noptions   : optionrange;

PROCEDURE SetUpMenu;
  VAR
    menu     : text;
    filename : string[12];

  BEGIN
    write('What menu file? ');
    readln(filename);
    assign(menu, filename);
    reset (menu);
    noptions := 0;
    commands := [ ];

    while not eof(menu) do begin
      noptions := noptions + 1;
      readln(optionslist[noptions]);
      commands := commands + optionslist[noptions][1]);
    end;
    close(menu);
  END; {SetUpMenu}

CONST
  {Window coords}
    {Command window}
      cx1  = 1;   cx2 = 39;          {for the command window}
      cy1  = 3;   cy2 = 12;
      mx   = 1;   my = maxmenu+2;    {for messages}
      rx   = 22;  ry = maxmenu+1;    {for commands}

PROCEDURE DisplayMenu;                       Taken from an
  BEGIN                                       earlier example.
    window(cx1, cy1, cx2, cy2);
    for i := 1 to noptions do
      writeln (optionslist[i]);
    gotoxy(1, ry);
    write('Type in your choice ');
  END; {DisplayMenu}

PROCEDURE GetRequest (var c : commands);
  BEGIN
    window (cx1, cy1, cx2, cy2);
    repeat
      gotoxy(rx,ry); clreol;
```

```
                            readln(c);
                            UpCase(c); {will make a q a Q}
                            gotoxy(mx, my);  clreol;
                            if not (c in  commands) then
                                writeln('Not a valid command');
                        until c in commands;
                        gotoxy(mx, my);  clreol;
                    END; {GetRequest}
```

Example 7.8   Training schedules

Problem   Employees at Zanyland Inc. attend training courses and a record of each course attended is kept on a file. We wish to discover which employees have attended which course, and which courses overall have been used.

Solution   One could construct arrays with the names of each employee who has done a course. Alternatively, if the employees are identified by number, and the courses by letters, then sets can be used.

Algorithm   Assume that the data has employee numbers followed by a list of course letters. A typical file would look like this:

```
        100 AHF
        123 JHU
        99 U
        77 JHAF
        213 BAF
        190 AB
        180 AJHUF
        170 JHUF
        110 BHAF
        115 AHF
```

We need to keep a set of employee numbers for each course, and a set of all courses taken. This is done with the data structures:

```
        CONST
          numbermax  = 250;

        TYPE
          courses     = 'A'..'Z';
          coursesets  = set of courses;
          numbers     = 000..numbermax;
          numbersets  = set of numbers;
```

```
VAR
   classlist      : array[courses] of numbersets;        An array of sets.
   taken          : coursesets;
```

The algorithm then consists of reading in a number followed by courses until an end of line, and for each course, we add the number to the set in the array indexed by its character. The important statement is:

```
classlist[c] := classlist[c] + [number];
```

To get the full set of courses taken, we construct the union of all courses read in, as in:

```
taken := taken + [c];
```

The rest of the program is concerned with printing out the sets neatly, four numbers to a line.

Program   The program is suprisingly simple. A striking feature of it is that the procedures do not use parameters. This is because there are only two main data structures, they are used from all parts of the program, and it would be superfluous to keep passing them in and out of the procedures. We do, of course, declare all other variables locally where they are needed.

Procedures without paramteres can be justified.

```
PROGRAM Trainingschedule (input, output);
  CONST
    numbermax      = 250;
    space          = ' ';
  TYPE
    courses        = 'A'..'Z';
    coursesets     = set of courses;
    numbers        = 000..numbermax;
    numbersets     = set of numbers;

  VAR
    data       : text;
    classlist  : array[courses] of numbersets;
    taken      : coursesets;

  PROCEDURE InitialiseSets;
  VAR c : courses;
  BEGIN
    for c := 'A' to 'Z' do
      classlist[c] := [ ];
    taken := [ ];
  END; {InitialiseSets}
```

```
PROCEDURE ReadEmployee;
 VAR c : courses;
   number : numbers;
 BEGIN
  read(data,number);
  write(number);
  read(data,c); write(c:5); {the space}
  while not eoln(data) do begin
    read (data,c); write(c);
    classlist[c] := classlist[c] + [number];
    taken := taken + [c];
  end;
  readln(data); writeln;
 END; {ReadEmployee}

PROCEDURE PrintClassLists;
 var c : courses;

 PROCEDURE PrintSet(class : numbersets);
  CONST numbersperline = 4;
  VAR
   n   : numbers;
   i   : 1..numbersperline;
  BEGIN
   i := 1;
   for n := 0 to numbermax do
     if n in class then begin
       write(n:8);
       if i = numbersperline
       then begin
         writeln;
         i := 1;
       end else i := i + 1;
     end;
 END; {PrintSet}

BEGIN
  writeln;
  writeln('Class Lists');
  for c := 'A' to 'Z' do
    if classlist[c] <> [ ] then begin
      writeln('Course ',c);
      PrintSet(classlist[c]);
      writeln;
    end;
  writeln;
  write('Courses used were :');
  for c := 'A' to 'Z' do
    if c in taken then write(c,space);
  writeln;
 END; {PrintClassLists}
```

```
BEGIN
  writeln('**** Employee Training Statistics ****');
  assign (data, 'train.dat');
  reset(data);
  InitialiseSets;
  writeln('Number  Courses');
  WHILE not eof(data) do
    ReadEmployee;
  PrintClassLists;
END.
```

Testing   A sample run would give:

**** Employee Training Statistics ****
```
Number   Courses
100      AHF
123      JHU
99       U
77       JHAF
213      BAF
190      AB
180      AJHUF
170      JHUF
110      BHAF
115      AHF
```

Class Lists
Course A
```
   77   100   110   115
  180   190   213
```
Course B
```
  110   190   213
```
Course F
```
   77   100   110   115
  170   180   213
```
Course H
```
   77   100   110   115
  123   170   180
```
Course J
```
   77   123   170   180
```

Course U
```
   99   123   170   180
```

Courses taken were : A B F H J U

7.4 Turbo Pascal units

In chapter one, we talked about modular decomposition and how parts of a solution can be 'hived off' into a separately compiled and maintainable module. Turbo Pascal is one of the few Pascals that provides a means of doing this, with its unit facility.

We have already encountered some predefined units – Crt and Graph – and have seen that these provide both operations and data for our use. For example, the Crt unit provides procedures such as *gotoxy* but also provides constants for the colours, such as *red*. We shall now look at how to define our own units.

The interface and the implementation

Public and private information.

Each unit consists of two parts – the interface and the implementation. In the interface, we list all the parts that we wish to make available to the user of the unit. In the implementation, we include everything that we do not wish to 'export' in this way, as well as the actual bodies of any routines we mention. Those declarations made in the interface are therefore public, and the rest are private.

Form of the unit

Unit

UNIT *unitname*;
  INTERFACE
    public declarations
  IMPLEMENTATION
    private declarations
    bodies
  END
  or
Initialisation .

The unit concludes with a third and optional part, which is a statement that can be used to initialise the unit before it is used. Thus the unit ends with either a simple END followed by a full stop, or a compound statement (BEGIN–END) containing initialising instructions.

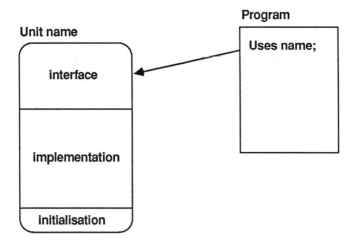

Figure 7.1 Diagram of the use of a unit

The unit is typed into a separate file, stored away and compiled through Turbo Pascal as if it were a program. When the unit is error-free, it will be stored in a file with the suffix .TPU (Turbo Pascal Unit).

The relationship between a unit and the program calling it is depicted in Figure 7.1.

Using units

To incorporate a newly declared unit in a program we give the USES command at the start of the program, as we have already seen. The effect of USES is to include in the program everything from the interface. This means that if the unit has an identifier which is the same as one in the program, then there will be a 'redefined identifier' error. For this reason, the names in units are often coupled with the unit name, especially if there is a likelihood of them being reused elsewhere. This is illustrated in the example that follows.

The best way to understand the use of units is by example. We have been following an example for some time now which is an excellent candidate for a new unit.

Example 7.9   Measurement units

Problem   We would like to have the work put into the metres and feet and inches operations of Example 7.6 packaged up nicely for use, and then to try it out with the floor dimensions problem (Examples 6.7 and 7.6).

| Example | Remember that the input and output is intended to look like this:

```
14 Highfield Lane
------------------------
Lounge     23'8"x11'2"  264.28sq ft  7.21m x 3.40m   24.55sq m
Bedroom1  12'3"x11'3"  137.81sq ft  3.73m x 3.43m   12.80sq m
```

where the plain type could be typed on the screen or read from a file, and the bold type represents the output. The input must be echoed to the output as well. We should set up *x*-coordinates for the various columns. These could be: 1, 15, 30, 45, 65.

| Solution 1 | Example 7.6 explored abstract data types and concluded that the operations on feet and inches were complicated and should be grouped as an adt. We can now formalise this as a unit. To do so, we must select the declarations that we want to be public, and those that can be considered private. In this example, there are no private operations as such, although *readinteger* is declared 'privately' inside *Readftins*. Let us consider the resulting unit before proceeding with the rest of the solution.

| Unit | One decision that has to be made is whether the conversion from feet and inches to metric should be provided by the *Imperial* unit. It would certainly be a useful feature, but would require the metric types to be known. It would not be correct to define a second type in the unit, so instead we define a second unit, in which metric is defined, and use this in *Imperial*. The first unit is:

A small data
type unit.

```
UNIT Metric;
INTERFACE
  MetricLength = real;
  MetricArea   = real;
IMPLEMENTATION
END.
```

This is a fairly rudimentary unit! It has no implementation at all, just the definition of two types. But it serves the purpose of being able to use these definitions in the next unit, without defining them there. The procedures and types developed in Examples 6.7 and 7.6 are now renamed to reflect the unit name.

A typical type
conversion unit.

```
UNIT Imperial;
  USES Metric;
  INTERFACE
```

```
CONST
  feet              = 0..maxint;
  inches            = 0..11;
  ImperialLinear    = record
                        ft   : feet;
                        ins  : inches;
                      end;
  ImperialArea      = real;  { sq ft}

  PROCEDURE ReadImperial ( var f : text;
                                var L : ImperialLinear);
  PROCEDURE WriteImperial (var f : text;
                                L : ImperialLinear);
  PROCEDURE MultiplyImperial (dim1, dim2 : ImperialLinear;
                                var a : ImperialArea);
  PROCEDURE ConverttoMetric (L : ImperialLinear;
                                var M : MetricLinear);
IMPLEMENTATION

  PROCEDURE ReadImperial (var f : text;
                          VAR L : ImperialLinear);
  VAR
    a    : integer;
    next : char;

  PROCEDURE readinteger(var n : integer; var follow : char);
  VAR ch : char;
  BEGIN
    n := 0;
    while not ch in  ['0'..'9'] do read(f,ch);
    while ch in ['0'..'9'] do begin
     n := n * 10 + ord(ch) − ord('0');
     read(f, ch);
    end;
    follow := ch;
  END; {readinteger}

BEGIN
  L.ft := 0;
  readinteger(a,next);
  if next = '''' then begin
    L.ft := a;
    readinteger(a,next);
  end;
  L.ins := a;
END; {ReadImperial}

  PROCEDURE WriteImperial (var F : text; L : ImperialLinear);
  BEGIN
    write(f, L.ft, '''', L.ins, '''');
  END; {WriteImperial}
```

```
        PROCEDURE MultiplyImperial (dim1, dim2 : ImperialLinear;
                        VAR a : ImperialArea);
        BEGIN
          a := (dim1.ft + dim1.ins/12) * (dim2.ft + dim2.ins/12);
        END;

        PROCEDURE ConvertToMetric (L : ImperialLinear;
                    var m : MetricLinear);
        BEGIN
          m := (L.ft + L.ins/12) * 0.3048;
        END;

    END.
```

Obviously, we can add further operations to this unit, such as adding, subtracting and comparing imperial measurements.

Solution 2   Now that the unit has been settled, we can consider other types in the program. The major ones are the metric units and the floor dimensions themselves. The metric units are based on the predefined type real, and can use its operations as-is. There is therefore no call to create a unit for them.

Program   The complete program is given here. A striking feature of the program is that only the text files are global: all other type and variable declarations are in units or in procedures themselves.

```
        PROGRAM Floorspace (input, output);

        USES Metric, Imperial, Crt;

        {Reads dimensions of rooms in feet and prints the area
         in sq ft and sq metres, together with total area}

        VAR data, results : text;

        PROCEDURE CopyHeadings;
          var s : string;
          BEGIN
            readln(data,S);
            writeln(results, s);
            readln(data,S);
            writeln(results,S);
          END; {CopyHeadings}

        PROCEDURE CalculateRoomsandTotal;

        TYPE
          RoomDimensions = record
            itslength, itsbreadth  : ImperialLinear;
```

```
      area               : ImperialArea;
      mlength, mbreadth  : MetricLinear;
      marea              : MetricArea;
   end;

VAR
   room        : RoomDimensions;
   totalsqft   : ImperialArea;
   totalsqm    : MetricArea;
   aBlankLine  : boolean;

PROCEDURE Checkforblankline;
 BEGIN
   readln(data);
   if eoln(data) then begin
    aBlankLine := true;
    readln(data); writeln(results);
   end;
 END;  {Checkforblankline}

PROCEDURE echoto(target : char);
 VAR ch : char;
 BEGIN
   repeat
    read(data,ch);  write(results,ch);
   until ch = target;
 END; {echoto}

BEGIN
  aBlankLine := false;
 totalsqft := 0;
 totalsqm := 0;
 WHILE not aBlankLine do begin
 with room do begin
   Echoto(' ');
   gotoxy(15,wherey);
   ReadImperial (data, itslength);
   WriteImperial (results, itslength);
   EchoTo ('x');
   ReadImperial (data, itsbreadth);
   WriteImperial (results, itsbreadth);
   MultiplyImperial (itslength, itsbreadth, area);
   write (results, ' ':8,area:6:2, 'sq ft');
   ConverttoMetric (itslength, mlength);
   ConverttoMetric (itsbreadth, mbreadth);
   marea := mlength*mbreadth;
   writeln (results, ' ':8,mlength:5:2, 'm x',
             mbreadth:5:2, 'm ', marea:6:2,'sq m');
   totalsqft := totalsqft + area;
   totalsqm := totalsqm + marea;
   Checkforblankline;
 end;
```

```
          END;
          writeln(results, 'Total area :', totalsqft:6:2,'sq ft',
                  totalsqm:6:2,'sq m');
       END; {CalculateRoomsandTotal}

       PROCEDURE OpenFiles;
         VAR filename : string[12];
         BEGIN
           write('For the data file ');
           readln(filename);
           assign(data, filename);
           reset (data);
           write('For the results ');
           readln(filename);
           assign(results, filename);
           rewrite(results);
           writeln;
         END; {openfiles}

     BEGIN
       ClrScr;
       writeln('***** Calculating floor areas *****');
       OpenFiles;
       Copyheadings;
       CalculateRoomsandTotal;
     END.
```

| Testing | The program should produce a run such as this:

***** Calculating floor areas *****
For the data file High14.dat
For the results CON

14 Highfield Lane

Lounge   23'8"x11'2" 264.28sq ft 7.21m x 3.40m   24.55sq m
Bedroom1 12'3"x11'3" 137.81sq ft 3.73m x 3.43m   12.80sq m

7.5   Case study 3: Drawing a map

Problem

The Central Delivery Service of a certain university undertakes to handle deliveries of larger items between buildings on the campus. As the university is very computer orientated, it has been decided to use a computer to show the buildings involved in a delivery session, and to plan the routes. Route planning is an area of computer science that relies on the efficiency of algorithms, and is beyond the scope of this book. Our task is to provide that part of the system that draws the map and highlights the routes, as shown in the colour plates.

Solution

In order to obtain a computerised version of any line drawing, such as a map, it is necessary to **digitise** it. This involves putting a grid of suitable fineness over the original drawing, and picking off the coordinates of the lines that go through it. Over a weekend, a student at the university did this, and we can assume that we have, as data: Getting the data in.

- coordinates for the university's logo, within its own frame of reference;

- coordinates for each of the buildings, on a scale of about 30x16;

- coordinates for the roads and road names on the full screen scale of 640x480 (VGA).

We have to write a program to process these, draw them on the screen, and add in the following:

- choice of background colours, and colours for the roads and buildings;

- a menu box and status line;

- a system for selecting buildings for deliveries.

As we are only writing part of the complete system, we can assume that the selection can be done randomly, for our testing purposes.

Clearly, most of the drawing should be done by adding to the coordinates commands for the *DrawData* procedure defined in Example 6.14. So, for example, to set the background colour to light green and draw a dark gray line around it, we would have the following data:

```
K 10        The background for the map
S 0 0
B 0 0 639 479
C 8
I 0 0 1
R 0 0 639 479
```
Sample data.

The K command sets the background colour to 10 (light green). S sets the fill style to SolidFill. Then we draw a bar over the whole screen. After this, the line colour is set to dark gray, the line style to Solid with a thickness of 1, and a rectangle is drawn at the edge of the screen.

A building, however, has information associated with it in addition to its shape and position, namely, its name and number. Thus we shall treat buildings slightly differently, and use records to hold the information.

For the orders, sets spring to mind, as we can start off with an empty set, and then add to it as the orders come in.

Algorithm

The basic strategy is to draw the map, and to have a small menu with the few options needed for this part of the system. Drawing the map consists of setting up command files for each of the groups of data mentioned above, and calling *DrawData* several times. Then special arrangements are made for the buildings. The overall picture is this:

The overall
algorithm.

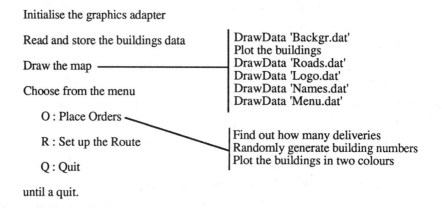

```
Initialise the graphics adapter

Read and store the buildings data        DrawData 'Backgr.dat'
                                          Plot the buildings
Draw the map ───────────────────────     DrawData 'Roads.dat'
                                          DrawData 'Logo.dat'
Choose from the menu                      DrawData 'Names.dat'
                                          DrawData 'Menu.dat'

   O : Place Orders
                                          Find out how many deliveries
   R : Set up the Route                   Randomly generate building numbers
                                          Plot the buildings in two colours
   Q : Quit

until a quit.
```

From the point of view of data types, the buildings are the most interesting. We start by defining a record for *x-y* coordinates, as follows:

```
coordinates = RECORD
                 xc : word;
                 yc : word;
              END;
```

Then we note that to draw a building, we need a number of such coordinates, call them *vertices*. So we declare:

An array of
records.

```
vertexrange = 1.. maxvertices;
vertices    = array[vertexrange] of coordinates;
```

and the building record itself becomes:

```
Buildings  = RECORD
                   outcode  :string[3];          {e.g. 4a, 15b}
                   building :string[64];         {building name}
                   n        :integer;            {number of vertices}
                   xy       :vertices;           {vertices}
                   centre   :coordinates;        {for the number}
            END;
```

A record with arrays.

The data about the buildings is read into an array declared as follows:

```
buildingrange = 1.. maxbuildings;

VAR
  map : array[buildingrange] of Buildings;
```

To actually draw a building, say *b*, we can use the *FillPoly* procedure as follows:

```
with map[b] do FillPoly (n, xy);
```

Use of FillPoly.

assuming that all the appropriate colours and fill styles have been set. To handle the orders, we declare:

```
VAR
  Orders   : set of buildingrange;
```

and proceed in the usual way to add elements in, and check the set through when redrawing the map. This would be done as follows:

```
for i := 1 to numbuildings do
  if i in Orders
  then PlotBuilding (i, LightRed) else PlotBuilding (i, LightBlue);
```

Program

The program given below is relatively short for the impressive picture it draws, as shown in the colour plates. It relies on the data, of course, and this is given in full in the disk which is available for this book. Notice that the program uses the Graph and Crt units: the latter is for reading the key values off in the *GetInput* routine, which was developed earlier in Chapter 5.

```
PROGRAM Campus (Input,Output);

USES Graph, Crt;

CONST
  maxBuildings   = 75;
```

```
                    maxvertices    = 20;

            TYPE
                buildingrange   = 1..maxbuildings;
                buildingindex   = 0..maxbuildings;
                coordinates     = RECORD
                                    xc:word;
                                    yc:word;
                                  END;{Record}
                vertexrange     = 1..maxvertices;
                vertices        = array[vertexrange] of coordinates;
                Buildings = RECORD
                                outcode   :string[3];      {e.g. 4a, 15b}
                                building  :string[64];     {building name}
                                n         :integer;        {number of vertices}
                                xy        :vertices;       {vertices}
                                centre    :coordinates;    {for the number}
                            END;

            VAR
                numbuildings   : buildingindex;
                map            : array [buildingrange] of Buildings;
                Orders         : set of buildingrange;
                numorders      : buildingindex;

            PROCEDURE ReadBuildings(var numbuildings : buildingindex);
              CONST
                xscale = 640/28;
                yscale = 480/16;
              VAR
                i, j      : integer;
                mapfile   : text;
                x, y      : real;
              BEGIN
                Assign(mapfile,'builds.dat');
                Reset(mapfile);
                i := 0;
                while not eof(mapfile) do begin
                  i := i + 1;
                  with map[i] do begin
                    readln(mapfile,outcode,building);
                    read(mapfile,n);
                    for j:=1 to n do with xy[j] do begin
                      read(mapfile,x,y);
                      xc := round(x * xscale);
                      yc := round(y * yscale);
                    end;
                  with centre do begin
                    readln(mapfile,x,y);
                    xc := round(x*xscale);
                    yc := round(y*yscale);
                  end;
```

```
      end;
   end;
   close(mapfile);
   numbuildings := i;
   Orders := [ ];
END;{ReadBuildings}


PROCEDURE PlotBuilding(b:buildingrange;colour:integer);
   BEGIN
      SetColor(darkgray);
      SetFillStyle(1,colour);
      with map[b] do
        Fillpoly(n, xy);
      SetColor(white);
      SetTextStyle(smallfont,horizdir,4);
      with map[b] do
        OutTextXY(trunc(centre.xc)-5,trunc(centre.yc),outcode);
   END;{PlotBuilding}


PROCEDURE DrawData(filename:string);
   ... as in Chapter 6
   END;{DrawData}


PROCEDURE ClearOrderBox;
   {Erases old information from the bottom box}
   BEGIN
      DrawData('box.dat');
   END; {ClearOrderBox}


PROCEDURE DrawMap;
   VAR i : buildingrange;

   BEGIN
      DrawData('backgr.dat');
      for i := 1 to numbuildings do
        PlotBuilding(i, lightblue);
      DrawData('Roads.dat');
      DrawData('logo.dat');
      DrawData('names.dat');
      DrawData('menu.dat');
   END;{DrawMap}


PROCEDURE GetInput(VAR reply:string;
           Prompt:string;
           xc:integer;
           Letters:boolean);
   ... as in Chapter 5
   END;{GetInput}


PROCEDURE PlaceOrders;
   VAR
      numorders,
```

```
          code          : integer;
          s             : string;
          i             : buildingrange;
        BEGIN
          Orders := [ ];
          Repeat
            ClearOrderBox;
            GetInput(s,'How many buildings want deliveries? ',
                        320, 450,false);
            Val(s,numorders,code);
          Until ((numorders>0) and (numorders<numbuildings));
          Randomize;
          for i := 1 to numorders do
            Orders := Orders + [random(numbuildings) + 1];

          for i:=1 to numbuildings do
            if i in Orders
            then PlotBuilding(i,LightRed)
            else Plotbuilding(i,lightblue);
        END; {PlaceOrders}

    VAR
      driver, mode   : integer;
      choice         : char;

    BEGIN
      Driver:=detect;
      Initgraph(driver,mode,'');
      ReadBuildings (numbuildings);
      Drawmap;

      Repeat
        Choice:=readkey;
        CASE choice of
          'o','O' : PlaceOrders;
          'r','R' : {Route};
          'q','Q' : ;
        End; {case}
      Until choice in ['q','Q'];
      CloseGraph;
    END.
```

Testing

A program such as this will require much tuning of the data to get it right, but the end product is certainly worth it, as shown in the colour plates.

Summary 7

1.   **Enumerated types** are constructed from lists of identifiers. Input and output are not automatically provided for enumerated types.

2.   **Records** are comprised of fields of different types. **Fields** are selected using a dot operator.

3.   Records as a whole may be **assigned,** but no other facilities are automatically available.

4.   The **with-statement** enables fields of a record to be referred to without the record name.

5.   **Variant records** consist of a section with fixed fields (maybe none) and then a case statement listing various options for a variant section. Only one option is valid for a given variable, and it is determined by the value of the tag field.

6.   **Field names** in a record, as well as across options in a variant record, must be distinct.

7.   **Sets** can be declared on a base type which is integer, boolean, character or enumerated, but not real or string.

8.   Turbo Pascal has a **limit** of 255 for the largest value in a set.

9.   **A set is not initialised** on declaration, and assigning it the value of the empty set or some constant set is necessary before working on it.

10.   Sets cannot be read or written with the predefined read and write statements. Custom-made procedures must be defined for each set type.

11.   The cardinality of the set is the number of elements it contains at any one time.

12.   Pascal provides set operators for membership (*in*), inclusion (< or <=), union (+), intersection (*) and difference (−).

13.   **Abstract data types** link a type definition (usually a record) with the operations that apply to it.

14.   Turbo Pascal provides **units** for putting the declarations and procedures associated with types together.

Self-check quiz 7

1.   Is the following a valid enumerated type? vowels = ('a','e','i','o','u');

2.   If the variable *day* is of an enumerated type *days*, can one say read(days)? write(days)?

3.   Can one record be assigned to another of the same type?

4.   Can fields in different options in a variant have the same names?

5.   Can records be used in write statements?

6.   Can a set of strings be declared?

7.   Find all the errors in the following excerpt.

```
TYPE
   coins = (1, 2, 5, 10, 20, 50);
   coinset = SET OF coins;
```

```
VAR
  n : coins;
BEGIN
  read (n);
  if n in coinset then ....
```

8.   An illness can be identified by possible symptoms, which are catered for by the enumerated type:

```
TYPE
  symptoms = (temperature, headache, stomach ache, cough,
              runny nose, sore eyes, spots);
```

Declare a type called *illness* which is a set of symptoms.

9   Given that *flu* and *cold* are both illnesses, write an expression that represents those symptoms that are common to both.

10.   How is a Turbo Pascal unit brought into a program?

Problems 7

Answers are provided for problems marked with a §.

7.1§ **AD and BC dates** A historian is studying the period of the Roman Empire, which extends either side of 1 AD. He wishes to computerise some of his data and to be able to compare and make simple calculations about the dates. Typical dates and calculations might be:

54 BC – 64 BC = 10 years

33 AD – 4 BC = 38 years

Decide on a method of inputting, storing and outputting such dates, and write procedures to read a date, write a date and subtract two dates.

7.2   **Student marks** Define a record type which contains fields for a student number, a year mark, an examination mark, a total mark and an indicator as to whether the total mark is above a subminimum or not. Assume that:

```
TYPE marks = 0..100;
```

Write a procedure that:

- has parameters for a student and a subminimum;
- reads the student number, year mark and exam mark;
- calculates the total mark as the average of the two marks read in;
- sets the subminimum indicator according to a given subminimum.

Test your procedure with a suitable test program and data.

7.3   **Population increase** Since 1970, the Zanyland population statistics have been stored on a file, with each line containing the year followed by the total people counted for that year. Write a program that will read this file and find the two consecutive years in which there was the greatest percentage increase in population. Use a record to store the year–population pair. Write the program without using any arrays.

7.4   **Inventory** Design a record to hold a typical inventory of wares in a hardware shop. Write a program which will allow inventory data to be read off a text file, and which will print out the complete record of any item whose stock has fallen below its reorder level.

7.5   **Club records**   Choose an activity with which you are familiar and design a record data structure to store information about the people, equipment or events associated with the activity. What operations would be needed for this information?

7.6§   **Prime numbers**   Using the state indicator technique discussed in Example 7.3, write a function to decide whether a given number is prime or not. Test it out by generating random integers.

7.7§   **Sieve of Eratosthenes**   The usual method for finding prime numbers, discussed in the answer to the previous question, seems very inefficient in that division by 9, 15, 21, etc. is still attempted after division by 3 had failed. One of the ancient Greek philosophers, Eratosthenes, discovered a better method. The idea is to put all the numbers in a 'sieve'. The first number is taken out, then all multiples of it removed. Then the next number is taken out, and all its multiples removed. By this process, all of the 'taken out' numbers will be prime. Write a Pascal program to implement the Sieve of Eratosthenes, using sets.

7.8.   **Supermarket competition**   A supermarket is running a competition in which a customer wins a prize for collecting cards with four lucky numbers. The cards are numbered from 1 to 60 and are handed out at the tills. Each Friday the four lucky numbers are announced and any customer holding cards with those numbers may claim a prize. Write a Pascal program which will check a given list of four numbers (from a customer) against a list of four read off a file and indicate whether a prize has been won or not. Use sets and set operations.

7.9§   **Employee training**   Starting with the program in Example 7.8 on employee training schedules, adapt it to print out the names, rather than the numbers, of employees. Also use sets to work out how many employees are doing the same combination of any two courses.

7.10   **Coordinate unit**   Design an abstract data type for coordinates represented as polar or Cartesian, and implement it as a Turbo Pascal unit. Test it out with a suitable example.

7.11   **Time unit**   Design an abstract data type for the 24-hour clock, and implement it as a Turbo Pascal unit. Test it out in the program in Example 4.2.

Advanced topics

This chapter investigates sorting, and then looks at the more advanced aspects of procedures, including procedure variables, recursion, and scope. It concludes with typed files and introduces some of the useful features of Turbo Pascal's DOS unit.

8.1 Sorting

Sorting is a very common operation in computing, and many systems provide high level commands which enable data to be sorted in any specified way. These commands rely on one of a number of sorting algorithms and every programmer should know at least one such sorting algorithm off by heart. Here we introduce a simple one – selection sort – which performs in time proportional to the square of the number of items being sorted. Other algorithms (for example, quicksort) perform faster, but are perhaps more difficult to understand and remember.

Selection sort

Sorting items means moving them around in a methodical way until they are all in order. A method used by some card players is to sort cards by holding them in the right hand, finding the lowest one and taking it out into the left hand, then finding the next lowest and taking it out, until all the cards have been selected, and the left hand holds the cards in order. The following sequence illustrates how this method works.

Left hand	Right hand
	7 3 9 0 2 5
0	7 3 9 – 2 5
0 2	7 3 9 – – 5
0 2 3	7 – 9 – – 5
0 2 3 5	7 – 9 – – –
0 2 3 5 7	– – 9 – – –
0 2 3 5 7 9	– – – – – –

We could implement this by having two arrays and picking the numbers out of one, adding them to the other. However, there is a way of keeping both lists in the same array, the one growing as the other shrinks. Each time an element is picked out, the gap it leaves is moved to one end, thus creating a contiguous gap, which is used to hold the new list. The move is done by a simple swap with the leftmost element of the right hand. So, the example would proceed as follows:

Left hand	Right hand
	7 3 9 0 2 5
0	3 9 7 2 5
0 2	9 7 3 5
0 2 3	7 9 5
0 2 3 5	9 7
0 2 3 5 7	9
0 2 3 5 7 9	

Each time a reduced list is considered, until only one element is left. The algorithm can be phrased more precisely as in Figure 8.1.

Because sorting is clearly going to be useful in many contexts, it makes sense to put it in a procedure from the beginning. The types that it will need are:

```
TYPE
    items   = integer;  {for testing}
    range   = 1..max;
    tables  = array [range] of items;
```

Selection Sort

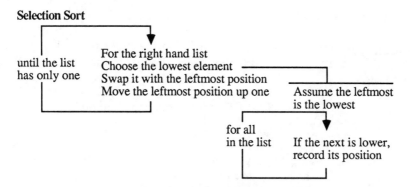

Figure 8.1 Algorithm for selection sort

The parameters would be the array to be sorted, and the number of items that are active in it. (The array may be 100 long, and only have 56 items stored in it, say.)

```
PROCEDURE sort (VAR a : tables;  n : range);
  VAR
    temp      : items;
    i,
    chosen,
    leftmost  : range;

  BEGIN
    FOR leftmost := 1 to n – 1 do begin
      chosen := leftmost;
      for i := leftmost + 1 to n do
        if a[i] < a[chosen] then chosen := i;
      temp := a[chosen];
      a[chosen] := a[leftmost];
      a[leftmost] := temp;
    END;
  END; {sort}
```

Note the interface provided by the parameter list.

Example 8.1 Ocean temperatures sorted

Problem An ocean-going research ship records the sea temperature at each hour of the day. The scientists on board like to see a sorted list of the temperatures in order to get a feel for the spread.

Solution Read in the temperatures, sort them and print them out each day. The sorting procedure above can be used as is.

Program The program starts by defining the types needed by the sort – items, range and tables. The output is in three columns for ease of reading.

```
PROGRAM SortingTemperatures (input, output);
  CONST
    max    = 24;
  TYPE
    items  = real;  {degrees Celsius}
    range  = 1..max;
    tables = array [range] of items;

  VAR
    i      : range;
    temps  : tables;

PROCEDURE readdata (VAR a : tables);
  VAR i : range;
  BEGIN
    writeln('Type in the 24 temperatures');
    for i := 1 to 24 do read(a[i]);
    readln;
  END; {readdata}

PROCEDURE sort (VAR a : tables; n : range);
{As defined above}
END; {sort}

  BEGIN
    writeln('****** Ocean temperatures in order ******');

    readdata(temps);

    sort (temps, max);

    writeln('The temperatures in order are: ');
    for i := 1 to 8 do
      writeln(temps[i]:6:2,'   ',temps[i+8]:6:2,'   ',
          temps[i+16]:6:2,'   ');
    writeln;
  END.
```

Testing

****** Ocean temperatures in order ******
Type in the 24 temperatures
11.1 11.08 11.03 11.56 11.98 12.01 12.0 12.13
12.13 12.5 12.4 12.09 12.5 12.8 13.01 13.1
14.5 14.6 14.51 13.5 13.32 13.04 12.9 12.8

The temperatures in order are

11.03	12.13	13.01
11.08	12.13	13.04
11.10	12.40	13.10
11.56	12.50	13.32
11.98	12.50	13.50
12.01	12.80	14.50
12.01	12.80	14.51
12.09	12.90	14.60

As will be seen in following sections, the sorting algorithm can be applied to arrays of any size, and containing any elements, and can be used to sort in ascending order just by changing the comparison from < to >.

Notice, however, that if we wish to sort from highest to lowest, then the value that moves to the left each time will be the largest, not the smallest.

Example 8.2   Sorting names and marks

Problem   Suppose that the names and marks of a class of students have to be printed in alphabetical order.

Solution   Use a computer. Read all the name–mark pairs into an array, More complex sort them according to the name using selection sort, and then data to sort. print out the contents of the array.

Algorithm   The first step is to define the data and the data structure. The data will look like this:

```
67   Jones K L
51   MacDeedle P
```

with the mark first and then the name. This enables the end of line to be used as a string terminator. We define a record with two fields – one for the name and one for the mark. In the sorting process, the name is used in the comparison part, but when the swapping is done, the whole record is copied. Thus the mark will move around with the name while sorting is proceeding.

Program   The program is really just a rework of the sort given in the previous example, but we give it in full here to emphasise the versatility of the method. Because the types of the array being sorted are different, the sort procedure has had to be changed accordingly.

```
PROGRAM Sortingmarks (input, output, data);
   CONST
      classmax   = 200;
```

```
              namemax    = 24;

          TYPE
            namerange  = 1..namemax;
            names      = string [namemax];
            marks      = 0..100;
            students   = record
                                 name : names;
                                 mark  : marks;
                              end;
            classrange = 0..classmax;
            classes    = array [classrange] of students;

          VAR
            class            : classes;
            noofstudents,
            i                : classrange;
            data             : text;
```

This is the
same as the
previous sort,
but for different
types.

```
          PROCEDURE sortname(var a : classes;  n : classrange);
            VAR
              i,
              chosen,
              leftmost  : classrange;
              temp      : students;  {used in swapping}
            BEGIN
              FOR leftmost := 1 to n – 1 do begin
                chosen := leftmost;
                for i := leftmost + 1 to n do
                  if a[i].name < a[chosen].name
                  then chosen := i;
                temp := a[chosen];
                a[chosen] := a[leftmost];
                a[leftmost] := temp;
              END;
            END; {sortname}


          BEGIN
            writeln('****** Sorting names and marks ******');
            write('For the data file use student.dat');
            assign(data, 'student.dat');
            reset(data);
            noofstudents := 0;
            while not eof(data) do begin
              noofstudents := noofstudents + 1;
              with class[noofstudents] do begin
                read(data, mark);
                readln(data, name);
              end;
            end;

            sortname(class, noofstudents);
```

```
writeln('The class in alphabetical order is: ');
for i := 1 to noofstudents do
   with class[i] do
      writeln(name:namemax,'    ', mark:3);
END.
```

Access tables

Sorting involves a lot of swapping, and if the items being swapped are large records, this can be quite time consuming. There is a technique which can be used with any sorting algorithm to reduce the amount of physical moving of values. *A sorting optimisation.*

For the array to be sorted, we define a companion array, the **access table**, over the same index type, with elements also of the index type thus:

```
TYPE
   accesstables  = array [range] of range;
VAR
   accesstable   : accesstables;
```

The values of this array are initialised to the index values and all references to the array are then made via the access table. When elements have to be swapped, only the access table elements are swapped, which could be very much quicker. Then when the elements are required in sorted order, they are extracted via the access table once again.

For example, if we have values in an array with the corresponding access table as follows:

```
Original array :  D B F E A C G
Access table   :  1 2 3 4 5 6 7
```

and sort them, then the original array remains untouched and the access table becomes:

```
Original array :  D B F E A C G
Access table   :  5 2 6 1 4 3 7
```

To print the original array in sorted order, we would print according to the order in the access table, that is first element 5 then element 2 then 6, and so on. The Pascal to do this is:

```
FOR i := 1 to max do write (table [accesstable [i]]);
```

and would produce, for the above data:

A   B   C   D   E   F   G

This technique is not only useful for avoiding the copying of large items, but also as a means for making a complicated data structure easier to handle.

Example 8.3   Sorting with access tables

| Problem | The Zanyland Weather Department are pleased with the program developed as a result of Example 6.11, and would like to add a further feature: a list of the months in decreasing order of average rainfall.

| Solution | The averages must be stored somewhere as they are calculated. A suitable declaration is:

```
VAR  averagetable : monthlyrains;
```

If this table is sorted, then the average rainfall figures will be in order, but we shall have lost track of their associated months. To keep this information, we maintain the *averagetable* in its original monthly order, and employ the access table technique. Thus we imagine a league table which lists the months in the order required: the corresponding rainfall can then be found in the *averagetable*.

```
TYPE
   leaguetables  = array [months] of months;

VAR
   leaguetable : leaguetables;
```

For example, after sorting, the values in the tables look like this:

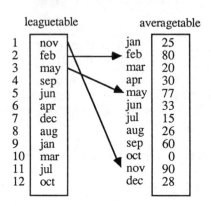

Procedure To perform the sort, we can use the selection algorithm with suitable alterations being made to the comparison and swapping actions. Because we want to look at the values in the average table, but change the values in the league table, we need two array parameters. To prepare for the sort, we shall have to initialise the league table to the straight index values. The sort is:

```
PROCEDURE SortRain (a : monthlyrains;
                          var b : leaguetables;  n : months);
      VAR
        i,
        chosen,
        leftmost : months;
        temp     : months;  {used in swapping}
      BEGIN
        FOR leftmost := 1 to n – 1 do begin
          chosen := leftmost;
          for i := leftmost + 1 to n do
            if a[b[i]] > a[b[chosen]]
            then chosen := i;
          temp := b[chosen];
          b[chosen] := b[leftmost];
          b[leftmost] := temp;
        END;
      END; {SortRain}
```

Program The program of Example 6.11 can be amended to take into account the averages table, and perform the sort. All the other procedures remain the same, and the main program becomes:

```
BEGIN
    writeln('****** Rainfall statistics ******');
    Openfiles;
    readindata(startyear, endyear);
    nyears := endyear - startyear + 1;
    FOR  m := 1 to 12 do begin
      averagetable[m] := monthlyaverage(raintable[m], nyears);
      leaguetable[m] := m;
    end;

    SortRain(averagetable, leaguetable, 12);

    writeln ('The months from wettest to driest are:');
    writeln('Month    Average');
    for m:= 1 to 12 do
      writeln (leaguetable[m]:2,
                averagetable[leaguetable[m]]:12:2);
END.
```

8.2 Procedure variables

In standard Pascal, there is a third form of parameters which allows procedures or functions to be passed, thus enabling the **action** of the procedure as well as the **data** to be varied at the parameter interface.

Turbo Pascal does not directly implement this feature, but provides a more powerful alternative: **procedure types**. A procedure type is defined in the type section, specifying the number, name and types of the parameters it will expect. In the case of a function, the result type must also be specified. Then variables of these types can be declared, and can be assigned and passed as parameters.

Procedure type definition

name = PROCEDURE *(formal parameter declarations)*;

or

name = FUNCTION *(formal parameter declarations)* : *type*;

Uses of procedure types.

Procedure parameters, or procedure types as in Turbo, is not a facility that is often used in programming, partly because many Pascal systems do not support anything like it. The example most often quoted is in numerical analysis where methods for finding roots of functions, integrating them, differentiating them and so on can be written to be independent of any particular function; the function is then passed to the solving procedure as a parameter. This notion of independence is the key to the need for procedures as parameters. In the context of the examples we have seen so far, the sort procedure could benefit from such a feature.

Example 8.4 Multi-way sorting

The selection sorting procedure developed in Section 8.1 is defined to sort in descending order. This aspect of the sort is confined to the single expression in the middle where the comparison is done, that is:

```
if a[i] < a[chosen] then ...
```

If we decide to re-express this comparison as a function, it would read:

```
if inorder (a[i], a[chosen]) then ...
```

The type of the function would be:

```
TYPE
   comparefunc = FUNCTION (a, b : items) : boolean;
```
A procedure
type.

We can then restate the interface of the sort procedure to include a parameter
of this type:

```
PROCEDURE sort (var a : somearray;  n : range;
                inorder : comparefunc);
```
Using it as a
parameter.

Calling the sort procedure needs actual parameters for the three formals
listed, and the following would satisfy:

```
TYPE
   range      = 1..50;
   somearray = array [range] of items;

VAR
   table  : somearray;
   size   : range;

FUNCTION descending (x, y : items) : boolean;
   BEGIN
     descending := x > y;
   END; { descending}
```

The resulting call would then be:

```
sort (table, size, descending);
```
Passing a
procedure
variable as a
parameter.

The power of this facility becomes apparent when we define:

```
FUNCTION ascending (a,b : items) : boolean;
   BEGIN
     ascending := a < b;
   END; {ascending}
```

and can call on the same procedure to order the names in the other direction:

```
sort (table, size, ascending);
```

Notice that the names of the formal parameters in the procedure type
declaration are unimportant: there is no requirement that those of any
procedure of that type have the same formal names.

Procedure types do not occur in all languages, as they are considered
difficult to implement at runtime. However, it is a good idea to gain practice
with them, as the concept of parameterised action is central to proper
programming in advanced languages.

8.3 Recursion

We now consider an aspect of procedures and functions which renders them very powerful indeed.

Solutions to problems that involve iteration can often be expressed in the following general terms:

> **The operation**
>   Do something
>   If the data is not 'finished',
>   then do the same operation on amended data.

An example of this kind of thinking would be counting people for party invitations. If a party list is written out as:

> John
> Mary & Peter
> David & Anne & Catherine & Thomas
> George
> William & Harry
> Aunt Edith
> Granny & Grandpa

and we wish to count both the people who are coming and the number of invitations needed, then we can express the algorithm as:

A recursive algorithm.

> **Count a person**
>   Read a name
>   Add one
>   If an ampersand follows, count a person

Essentially, we are reusing the operation by calling it from itself. This is known as **recursion**. In Pascal, the above operation could be part of another procedure as follows:

```
PROCEDURE partyplan;
VAR
   people, invitations : 0 .. 1000;
```

A recursive procedure.

```
PROCEDURE countaperson;
BEGIN
   readname;
   people := people + 1;
   if ampersandfollows then
      countaperson;
END; {countaperson}

BEGIN
   people := 0;
```

```
            invitations := 0;
            while not eof do begin
               countaperson;
               invitations := invitations + 1;
            end;
            writeln('For the ', people:1,' people, you will need ',
                      invitations:1, ' invitations.');
         END.
```

where *ampersandfollows* and *readname* are suitably defined.

If the recursive call comes at the very end of the operation, then the recursion can be replaced directly by a loop. For example, we could have just as easily written:

```
         PROCEDURE countaperson;
         BEGIN
            repeat
               readname;
               people := people + 1;
            until not ampersandfollows;
         END; {countaperson}
```

Recursion usually only becomes preferable to looping when parameters are involved. Recursive algorithms share with loops the two essential properties that:

- there must be a stopping condition, and

- some variables must change their values each time.

Recursion with parameters

When a recursive call is made on a procedure with parameters, it follows the same execution pattern as an ordinary call. The parameters and local variables of the caller are remembered (or 'stacked') and the new procedure is entered with the new parameters. At the end of the call, the program returns to where it was, and the caller's parameters and variables become visible again. With a recursive procedure, the parameters and variables have the same name and meaning each time, though they may have different values, and thus they can give the effect of an array that is constructed as time goes by, and then disappears. By deftly altering the order of the 'do something' and 'do the operation again' in the general algorithm above, we can obtain the effect of looking at the array in reverse. This is aptly illustrated by the next example.

Example 8.5 Based number writing

Problem Write a procedure to print out positive integers of any size to a given base.

Solution If we knew that the number had exactly, say, three digits, then we could calculate the hundreds first, the tens next and finally the units. But if we express the solution like this:

> Print the left part of the number; write the rightmost digit

and consider that printing the left part is exactly the same operation again, then it is not necessary to know in advance how long the number is. When we eventually get down to a single digit then printing the left part does nothing, the rightmost digit is written, and we return to the previous piece of the number.

Example Suppose we print 102 to base 8. This proceeds in steps as follows:

Tracing a recursive algorithm.

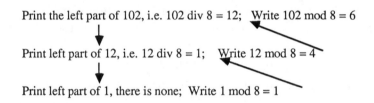

Print the left part of 102, i.e. 102 div 8 = 12; Write 102 mod 8 = 6

Print left part of 12, i.e. 12 div 8 = 1; Write 12 mod 8 = 4

Print left part of 1, there is none; Write 1 mod 8 = 1

and the digits printed out are 146, in that order.

Algorithm The stopping condition here coincides with the left part running out. We can confirm that the variables will change because the procedure is called with the value of parameter *number* being the *number div base*. In algorithmic terms, the solution becomes:

> **Print number to a base:**
>   If number < base, then write it out
>   Otherwise
>   Print number div base to base
>   Write out number mod base

The procedure, together with a test program, follows on easily.

Program

```
PROGRAM Basetester (input, output);
VAR number, base : 0 .. maxint;
```

```
PROCEDURE print (n, b : integer);
  BEGIN
    if n < b then write(n:1)
    else begin
      print (n div b, b);
      write(n mod b:1);
    end;
  END; {print}

BEGIN
  writeln('****** Testing printing to a base ******');
  write ('Number and base (positive only): ');
  readln(number, base);
  write(number:1,' to ', base:1,' is ');
  print(number, base);
  writeln;
END.
```

Backtracking with recursion

Recursion effectively enables us to build up a history of values and then go back and use them again. It is very effective if there is a choice of paths to follow at a given time. One can travel recursively down one, find it no good, come back up to the crossroads with everything restored to what it was before, and proceed down some other path. This technique is used widely in game playing programs, for chess, noughts and crosses, or any situation where there are choices to be made. A full discussion of this fascinating area is beyond the scope of this book, but is sure to be taken up again in future courses in advanced programming, recursive techniques or data structures.

The full power of recursion.

Recursive data types

A data type which is still to be discussed (in Chapter 9) is the **pointer**. The structures that can be built with pointers are inherently recursive. Hence many of the algorithms to create and manipulate such structures are excellent examples of recursion at work.

8.4 Finer points about procedures

Levels of nesting

A program with procedures is said to consist of several **levels**. The outermost level is level 1, which is that of the program itself. Thus all declarations made under the program header are at level 1. Level 1 is also

Procedure is used to mean both procedure and function.

known as the **global** level, and the variables and procedures declared there are called **globals**.

Globals and
locals defined.

Within these outer procedures at level 1, further declarations can be made. These would then be at level 2. Procedures inside them would be at level 3, and so on, for as many levels of nesting as are required. Declarations within a procedure are called **local** declarations, and the identifiers that they introduce are known as local to that procedure. Parameters acquire the same level as the locals, not as the procedure. Thus if we had the little skeleton program:

```
PROGRAM skeleton (input, output);

    VAR i, j : integer;

    PROCEDURE order (VAR n, m : integer);

    VAR temp : integer;
    ...
    END; {order}

    BEGIN
    ...
    END.
```

then *i*, *j* and *order* are at level 1, but *n*, *m* and *temp* are considered to be declared inside *order* and therefore are all at level 2.

Scope and visibility

With all these places where declarations can be made, it is necessary to sort out which identifiers are visible where, and what happens if the same name is used more than once. The **scope** of an identifier is the extent of the procedures over which the identifier is visible and can be used. This leads to Pascal's rule of scope.

Pascal's Rule of Scope

An identifier is visible in the block (i.e. program, procedure or function) in which it is first declared *and* in all enclosed blocks in which it is not redeclared.

The term 'enclosed blocks' refers to the nesting. If we view nested procedures as a set of nested boxes, then what the rule is saying is that the inner boxes can see outwards, but not vice versa. One way of remembering this is to imagine all the boxes being built with one-way glass: someone in a box can see out, but no one outside can see in.

The forward directive

The order in which declarations are made also affects visibility. Pascal requires that any use of an identifier must be preceded by its declaration. Thus if two procedures are declared at the same level, their order of declaration will dictate who can call whom. The procedure currently being declared cannot actually see the following ones. This problem can be overcome by declaring the procedure as *forward*, then giving its details later on. For example, if procedure *A* calls *B* and vice versa, then we could declare them as follows:

Use of the
forward clause.

```
PROCEDURE B;  forward;

PROCEDURE A;
  BEGIN
    ...
    B;
  END;

PROCEDURE B;
  BEGIN
    ...
    A;
  END;
```

Occlusion

As stated in the Rule of Scope, an identifier is not visible if it is redeclared in an inner block. The effect of this is that if two variables in the same scope have the same name, only the innermost one is visible. The proper name for this phenomenon is **occlusion**. The identifier which is hidden because of the inner declaration is said to be **occluded**.

Names can hide
each other.

The external directive

In many Pascal systems, including Turbo, there is a facility for linking up to procedures written in other languages. These procedures must be declared in the Pascal program with the external directive. In Turbo, linking to

Linking up to
other
languages.

assembler routines is provided and a typical declaration would be:

```
PROCEDURE MoveWord (var source, dest; count : word); external;
```

8.5 Typed files

The text files that we have used up to now consist of items of type character and include special end-of-line markers. Pascal actually permits new file types to be declared. These files can consist of items of any type, and in particular of records. This means that programs that process many items of data and then have to store the processed form, can do so efficiently. Typed files can be accessed sequentially, as well as randomly, and a file opened for reading can also be used for writing, and vice versa. Thus typed files are far more flexible than text files.

Form of a file declaration

A file type is declared as follows:

```
┌─────────────────────────────────────────────────────┐
│ File type declaration                                 │
├─────────────────────────────────────────────────────┤
│   TYPE  identifier = FILE OF type identifier ;        │
└─────────────────────────────────────────────────────┘
```

Variables of this type can then be defined. For example, in Section 7.2, a record for type *Roomdimensions* was defined. A corresponding file would be declared as in:

```
TYPE Roomfiles   = FILE of Roomdimensions;

VAR  Roomfile    : Roomfiles;
```

In Turbo Pascal, a file can be declared without a type. This facility is used for connecting to low-level input/output devices, and is also useful for parameter passing, as seen in the standard procedures Turbo provides (below).

Properties of files

Files must be opened, assigned and closed as already described in Section 5.3. The procedures and function that can be used are:

assign(F,name)   connects F to the file of that name
reset (F)   opens the file for reading
rewrite(F)   opens the file for writing
eof(F)   returns true if the file is positioned past its end

Both typed files and text files do not actually have to exist on some external device: Pascal does allow the concept of a **local file**. Thus it is possible to declare and use a file within a program, without connecting it to any device. At the end of the program, then, no record of the file would remain.

Reading and writing the file is done by the read and write statements. Thus to read a value from a file we have:

read(F, X);

and to write a value we use simply:

write(F, X);

As with text files, several items can be listed as parameters, so that the following are also valid:

read(F, X, Y);
write(F, P, Q, R);

Typed files consist of a sequence of items of that type. Therefore read and write operations must refer only to variables of that type. This is in contrast to text files which are files of characters, but for which the read and write procedures are equipped to convert numbers to and from characters as well. Text files can be examined via the Turbo Pascal editor, but typed files cannot.

Differences between text and typed files.

The other major difference between text and typed files is that typed files do not have to be accessed strictly in sequence, but can be accessed by record number using the following procedures:

PROCEDURE Seek (var F; N : longint);
FUNCTION Filepos (var F) : longint;
FUNCTION Filesize (var F) : longint;
PROCEDURE Truncate (var F);

A typed file consists of elements numbered from 0. *Seek* enables movement about the file based on these indices. Thus *Seek*(6) will position us at the seventh element. *Filepos* will return the number of the current element and *Filesize* will determine how many elements the file currently contains. *Truncate* is used to delete the rest of the file from the current position onwards.

These routines enable fairly sophisticated file handling to be accomplished through Turbo Pascal, but further expansion of this topic is beyond the scope of an introductory text.

8.6 Turbo Pascal's DOS unit

Like most languages intended for development of sophisticated applications, Turbo Pascal provides an interface to the operating system of the computer, in this case DOS. The interface is implemented as a unit, called DOS.

The DOS unit has many facilities which enable one to get at the low-level features and parameters of the computer and its filing system. We shall concentrate on a few of the more widely applicable features. For full details consult the manual.

Date and time

An obvious need in a program is to be able to report the current date and time. To do this, we can call the following procedures:

Getting the date and time.

```
PROCEDURE GetDate (var year, month, day, dayofweek : word);
PROCEDURE GetTime (var hour, minute, second, sec100 : word);
```

where the parameters have the usual ranges, except *dayofweek* which returns 0 .. 6 where 0 corresponds to Sunday.

For example, to include the date and time a program is run, along with the little title that we usually print out, we could write the following procedure:

```
PROCEDURE Header(title : string);
VAR y, m, d, w, h, m, s, s100 : word;
BEGIN
  GetDate (y,m,d,w);
  GetTime(h,m,s,s100);
  writeln('***** ',title, ' on ',d,'/',m,'/',y,' at 'h,':',m,':',s' *****');
END; {Header}
```

There are other procedures in the category which enable one to set the date and time and interrogate the age of files, and so on. Consult the manual for more information.

Interrogating the directory

A second group of procedures in the DOS unit concerns file handling. There are many of these, but we shall just look at the ones that relate to the file directory.

A DOS directory keeps details of all its files, which Turbo collects into a record of the following type:

```
TYPE                                                   The file
   SearchRec = record                                  information
      Fill    : array [1..21] of byte;                 record.
      Attr    : byte;
      Time    : Longint;
      Size    : Longint;
      Name    : string[12];
   end;
```

We shall concern ourselves only with the name of the file; the use of the other fields is beyond the scope of this book.

Assuming that we wished to scan a directory to find the names of all the files in it, we could use one of the following:

```
PROCEDURE FindFirst (Path : string;  Attr : word; var s : SearchRec);
PROCEDURE FindNext (var S : SearchRec);
```

Findfirst will search the current or specified directory for a file with the given attribute, and return the details of the first one it finds in *s*. There are several attributes relating to hidden files, directories, and so on. For our purposes, we would just want to look at normal files, and so will supply *Archive* for the *Attr* parameter.

For the *Path*, we can specify *.* to get all files, or if a data file is expected, one could restrict the path to *.DAT, say.

After having done a *Findfirst*, we can proceed with calls to *FindNext*. When there are no more files to find, a DOS unit variable, *DosError* is set to a non-zero value. We can therefore see how a list of files could be made available to the program, and thence to the user. This is explored in the example.

Example 8.6   A file selection facility

| Problem | In many of the programs since Chapter 5, the user has been asked to supply a file name for data to the program. It is quite possible that the user will have forgotten the precise form of the file name, and would like the opportunity to review the files in the directory before answering the question.

| Solution | Access the DOS unit to print out a list of files on request. We could also provide a facility to change the path, which would enable files in other directories to be listed as well.

Given that we shall be able to display a list such as this:

The output
required.

Files in the directory c:\user\peter\project1*.dat

class1.dat
class2.dat
temp.dat
final.dat
p.dat

it may be nice to supply in addition a facility to enable the desired file to be chosen by moving the cursor, rather than by entering the name. We shall tackle this issue as well.

The first task, therefore, is to get the list of files and store their names in an array. They can then be displayed and selected.

| Procedure |

```
CONST
  dirmax = 40;

TYPE
  filenames  = string[12];
  dirindex   = 0..dirmax;
  dirrange   = 1..dirmax;
  directories = array [dirrange] of filenames;

CONST
  fx1      = 10;   fx2      = 66;
  fy1      = 5;    fy2      = 17;
  perline  = 4;    column = 14;

PROCEDURE GetFileNames (var n : dirindex;
        var D : directories; var path : string);
  VAR
    S : SearchRec;
  BEGIN
    border (fx1, fy1, fx2, fy2, true);
    window (fx1, fy1, fx2, fy2);
    writeln('Give the path and file group required ');
    writeln(' for example *.dat or *.* or C:\users\peter');
    write('? ');
    readln(path);
    Findfirst (path, Archive, S);
    n := 0;
    while (n<dirmax) and (DosError = 0) do begin
      n := n+1;
      D[n] := S.name;
      FindNext (S);
    end;
    if n = 0 then begin
      writeln('No such files.      Press return to continue.');
      readln;
```

```
      end;
END; {GetFileNames}
```

Calling this procedure will result in the array being given the available names, and *n* being set with the number there are (even if it is zero). We also return the path so that it can be printed out later.

Notice that we chose to write the request for the path in a central window, complete with a border (from Example 5.1): this may not be convenient in all cases, and could be altered.

| Procedure | Now to print out the filenames in this window, ensuring that each has a defined position which we can afterwards interpret when the user moves the cursor. Given that there may be many files (we've allowed for up to 50), we shall arrange them five per line as follows:

```
┌─────────────────────────────────────────────────────────────┐
│                                                               │
│  Files in the directory c:\user\peter\project1\*.dat          │
│                                                               │
│  class1.dat   class2.dat   temp.dat    final.dat    p.dat     │
│  cm131.dat    cm101.dat    cm333.dat                          │
│                                                               │
│                                                               │
│                                                               │
│                                                               │
│                                                               │
│                                                               │
└─────────────────────────────────────────────────────────────┘
```

The procedure to do this is:

```
PROCEDURE DisplayFiles (n : dirindex; D : directories;
         path : string);
  var i : dirindex;
  BEGIN
    border(fx1, fy1, fx2, fy2, true);
    window(fx1, fy1, fx2, fy2);
    writeln('Files in the directory ',path);
    gotoxy(1, 4);
    i := 0;
    while i < n do begin
      i := i + 1;
      write(D[i],'   ':column-length(D[i]));
      if i mod perline = 0 then writeln;
    end;
  END; {DisplayFiles}
```

Algorithm | Now we turn to the choosing part. We position the cursor at
the first file, and set the chosen file to 1. We allow the user to
use the four cursor keys and the space bar, interpreting them as follows:

up	Move up one line and subtract 5 from the file number
down	Move down one line and add 5 to the file number
right	Move to the next file and add one to the file number
left	Move to the previous file and subtract 1 from the file number
space	Stop, returning this current file number.

Of course, we shall need to handle the boundary conditions carefully, not
allowing movement outside the window.

The question is: how do we read the cursor keys? Turbo provides a
ReadKey function which will record the value of the special keys, which have
extended key codes. These cannot be represented by the standard ASCII codes
(see Appendix F) and so start off with character zero, and are followed by a
second code. The full list is given in Appendix F, but for our purposes, we
will use:

up	71
down	80
left	75
right	77

All of the other special keys on an extended keyboard can be read in in the
same way, and obviously, our procedure could be much extended to take
account of <PgUp>, <Home> and so on.

Procedure | At the start of this procedure, we set up the boundaries for the
files when displayed, so that movement of the cursor can be
curtailed. The InitBoundaries procedure makes extensive use of sets. Note
that we redraw the border and window, but do not overwrite the contents.

```
PROCEDURE ChooseFile (n : dirindex; var f : dirrange);

  CONST
    up     = 72;
    down   = 80;
    left   = 75;
    right  = 77;
    space  = ' ';

  TYPE
    indexsets = set of dirrange;

  VAR
    ch          : char;
```

```
x              : 1..80;
y              : 1..25;
ymax, ymin ,
xmin, xmax  : indexsets;

PROCEDURE InitBoundaries;
   var  i : dirindex;
   BEGIN
     if n > perline then ymin := [1..perline]
     else ymin := [1..n];
     if n > perline then ymax := [n-perline+1..n]
     else ymax := [1..n];
     xmin := [ ];
     xmax := [ ];
     for i := 1 to n div perline do begin
       xmin := xmin + [(i-1)*perline+1];
       xmax := xmax + [ i*perline];
     end;
     if n mod perline <> 0
     then begin
       xmin := xmin + [(n div perline)*perline+1];
       xmax := xmax + [n];
     end;
   END; {InitBoundaries}

BEGIN
  if n <> 0 then begin
    Initboundaries;
    f := 1;
    gotoxy (1, 2);
    writeln('Use cursors then space to select.');
    clreol;
    gotoxy (1,4);
    x := 1;
    y := 4;
    repeat
      ch := readkey;
      if ch = chr(0) then begin
        ch := readkey;
        case ord(ch) of
          up     : if not (f in ymin) then begin
                         f := f-perline; y := y-1; end;
          down  : if not (f in ymax) then begin
                         f := f+perline; y := y+1; end;
          left    : if not (f in xmin) then begin
                         f := f-1;  x := x-column; end;
          right   : if not (f in xmax) then begin
                         f := f+1; x := x+column; end;
        end;
        gotoxy (x,y);
      end;
    until ch = space;
```

```
          end;
          END; {ChooseFile}
```

Testing Putting this all together, we would imagine that a program would make the following calls:

```
VAR
    path      : string;
    MyDir     : directories;
    filename  : string[12];
    fileno    : filerange;
    n         : fileindex;
    data      : text;
```

A versatile
sequence.

```
GetFileNames (n, MyDir, path);
DisplayFiles(n, MyDir, path);
ChooseFile (n, fileno);
assign (data, MyDir[fileno]);
reset (data);
```

This trio of procedures is not confined to use with text files: they can equally well be used for general files.

Unit Since the procedures all perform a joint function, and have common types and so on, it would be a good idea to group them together into a unit. This could have an interface such as:

```
UNIT fileunit;
INTERFACE

    USES crt, dos;

    CONST
      dirmax = 40;

    TYPE
      filenames  = string[12];
      dirindex   = 0..dirmax;
      dirrange   = 1..dirmax;
      directories = array [dirrange] of filenames;

      PROCEDURE OpentextFile (var f : text);
      PROCEDURE GetFileNames (var n : dirindex;
                     var D : directories; var path : string);
      PROCEDURE DisplayFiles (n : dirindex;
                     D : directories; path :string);
      PROCEDURE ChooseFile (n : dirindex; var F : dirrange);
```

The *OpenTextFile* procedure would then be:

```
PROCEDURE OpenTextFile(var f : text);
  VAR
    n      : dirindex;
    D      : directories;
    path   : string;
    fileno : dirrange;

  BEGIN
    repeat
      GetFileNames (n, D, path);
    until n <> 0;
    DisplayFiles (n, D, path);
    ChooseFile(n, fileno);
    assign(f,D[fileno]);
  END; {OpenTextFile}
```

Manipulating the directory

Turbo Pascal also provides a set of procedures which mimic the DOS directory handling facilities. These are:

```
PROCEDURE ChDir (s : string);
PROCEDURE Erase (var F);
PROCEDURE GetDir (drive : byte; var s : string);
PROCEDURE MkDir (s : string);
PROCEDURE Rename (var F; newname : string);
PROCEDURE RmDir (s : string);
```

If any errors occur during the execution of one of these, for example, if *MkDir* finds that that name already exists, then an internal error flag is set, and this can be tested by calling the function:

```
FUNCTION IoResult : word;
```

However, in order to recover from such an error, we must first turn off the input/output error checking using {$I–}. When there is a chance that a file procedure will cause an error, we bracket it by {$I–} and {$I+} and then immediately look at *IoResult*. If it is 0 then all is well, otherwise some alternative action can be taken.

Example 8.7   A safe file opener

| Problem | We would like to have a way of opening files that takes account of mistyped names. |

Solution   The procedures developed in the previous example to some extent avoid the problem of a user typing in the name of a file that is not there. However, a simpler file opening procedure can be specified, which still protects the program from crashing. We use {$I–} and *IoResult* as described above.

Algorithm   The algorithm consists of several choices in an overall loop. Note that the loop also provides the option of cancelling the opening altogether.

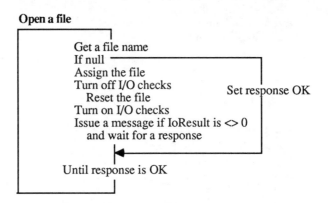

Open a file

Get a file name
If null
Assign the file
Turn off I/O checks
   Reset the file
Turn on I/O checks
Issue a message if IoResult is <> 0
   and wait for a response

Set response OK

Until response is OK

The point about waiting for the response, is that an appropriate message can be issued if the file is not there, such as:

The file does not exist, is this OK?

When opening for reading, the user would regard this as an error, but when opening for writing, it is more than likely that this is the correct state. Either way, the user has the option of trying another file instead.

As before, separate file openers for text and typed files will have to be developed: this is left as an exercise for the reader.

Summary 8

1. The data in an array can be **sorted** by various methods, one of which is selection sort.

2. Sorting large records can be done via **access tables**, so that the records themselves are not moved.

3. **Procedure types** can be declared which enable routines be passed as parameters, allowing considerable versatility of action at runtime.

4. Pascal procedures and functions can be defined in terms of themselves using **recursion**. Recursive procedures, like loops, must be careful to specify a stopping condition.

5. **Scope:** an identifier is visible in the block in which it is first declared and in all enclosed blocks in which it is not redeclared.

6. **Occlusion** occurs if an identifier is redeclared in an inner scope. The outer identifier is made invisible at the inner scope.

7. **Files** of any type can be declared in Pascal. They can be accessed via the usual read and write procedures.

8. Typed files can be **accessed randomly** using the *seek* procedure.

9. The Turbo Pascal DOS unit provides access to the filing system, in particular for accessing the **file directories**.

Self-check quiz 8

1. Why does the main loop of the sorting algorithm specify $n - 1$ as the upper bound?

2. When sorting data, why is the record the most useful type for the items?

3. How would we sort the student records in Example 8.2 on either name or mark?

4. What are the advantages of using access tables?

5. Work through the Basetester program of Example 8.5 for the following data: 123 to base 5.

6. What is *DosError* and how is it used when interrogating a directory?

7. What output would be produced by the following program when given the input AB123CDE69F?

```
PROGRAM Printing (input, output);

  PROCEDURE sift;
  VAR ch : char;
  BEGIN
    read(ch);
    if ch in ['0' .. '9'] then begin
      sift;
      writeln(ch);
    end;
  END; {sift}

BEGIN
  while not eof do begin
```

```
            sift;
            writeln('*');
        end;
    END.
```

8. Can two procedures in a program have the same name?

9. Can a procedure nested inside another 'see' the global variables of the program?

10. Can a typed file be examined through the Turbo editor?

Problems 8

Answers are provided for problems marked with a §

8.1§ **Sorting strings** Add to the *Searchingtables* program of Example 7.4 a sorting procedure which is defined for arrays of names. Use it to sort each table of words after it is read in. Given that the tables are then in alphabetical order, can you think of a way in which the search procedure could be optimised to detect more quickly that a word is not in the table?

8.2§ **Sorting names or marks** In the *Sortingmarks* program of Example 8.2, it would be useful to be able to sort on the name field or on the marks field of the table of students. Using a function as a parameter, as described in Section 8.2, extend the program to print out two lists – one in alphabetical order of name, and one in descending order of marks.

8.3§ **Palindromes** A palindrome is a word or sentence that reads the same forwards as backwards, disregarding punctuation. Famous palindromic sentences are:

> Madam, I'm Adam!

> Able was I, ere I saw Elba.

Checking for a palindrome involves successively comparing pairs of characters, one from each end of the input. This can be expressed nicely as a recursive check:

> It is a palindrome if the leftmost and rightmost chars are the same
> and the inner portion of the sentence is a palindrome.

Write a recursive function which tests whether a given string (stripped of all punctuation and spaces) is a palindrome or not. Test the function in a short program.

8.4 **Recursive functions** Define and test simple recursive functions for the following:

- factorial;
- the Fibonnacci sequence;
- the length of a string;
- the highest common factor of two numbers.

8.5 **File opener** Complete Example 8.7 by writing a general file opening procedure which gives the user the option of trying another file before making a commitment.

Dynamic data

In this chapter we introduce pointers and show the basic algorithms for list processing. Turbo Pascal's features for object oriented programming and animation are examined, and the chapter closes with a case study based on pointer manipulation.

9.1 Pointers

In Pascal, every variable declared in the VAR section is given a name – its **identifier**. Identical items can be grouped in an array, so that one name can stand for a whole list of items. Each item is known by a **designator** comprising the array name and a subscript to that array, and can be accessed directly by its designator. The drawback of arrays is that the number of items must be known in advance, and, once set, it cannot be expanded. This can lead to situations such as shown in Figure 9.1 where much of the array is empty.

Pascal provides for lists of varying size to be created. Each item in a list is created separately and linked to the next by means of a pointer. A pointer by itself can point to the first item. The example list would then be represented as in Figure 9.2.

The shaded
areas are
wasted.

list

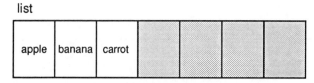

Figure 9.1 Array with unused items

No waste – but
an overhead for
the pointers.

list

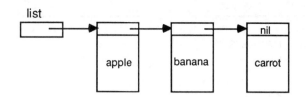

Figure 9.2 Linked list with pointers

If another item needs to be added to the list, another **node** and pointer are created and linked up. When no longer required, nodes can be removed from lists. Moreover, this adding and removing does not have to be done at the start or end of the list – it can be done anywhere within the list, simply by reorganising the pointers.

The cost of
using pointers.

The price that one pays for such flexibility is twofold. Firstly there is the **overhead** of one pointer per node, plus one for the start of the list. A pointer usually takes up at least as much space as an integer. If the data in the nodes requires more space than the pointer – and it usually does – then the overhead is not significant. However, one would not use pointers to hold lists of characters, say: it would be more economical to waste characters at the end of a packed array than to provide a pointer per character.

The second part of the cost of pointers is a **lack of accessibility**. Each element of an array is directly accessible by means of its subscript; not so for nodes in a pointer list. They can only be accessed by starting at the name of the list and following a chain of pointers until the required node is reached. Thus, once again, one would not use pointers if diverse items in the list need to be accessed all the time, as is the case in a sort. But if the list is to be processed sequentially most of the time, then a linked list is not a drawback.

The form of pointer declarations

The syntax for declaring a pointer type is simply:

Pointer type
identifier = ^ *type*;

The carat symbol ^ serves to indicate that pointers are involved. Turbo Pascal also defines a special type called *pointer* which can be used in conjunction with another operator, @, and the *ptr* function for low-level programming. An example of the use of the *pointer* type is given in Section 9.5 when animation is discussed.

9.2 Linked lists, stacks and queues

There are four steps to setting up and accessing a linked list using pointers. We give them all in general form here and then explain them using an example. Throughout the forms, the term *nodes* in italics stands for whatever record type is to constitute the list. Consequently, the term *tonodes* is used for the type that points to *nodes*. Other identifiers in italics have a similar importance, that is, they convey the general sense of the item, but could be any identifier required by the particular circumstances.

1.   **Define the node and pointer types.**

Four steps in defining a linked list.

```
TYPE
  tonodes = ^ nodes;
  nodes   = RECORD
              link : tonodes;
              other data fields
            END;
```

The nodes are records with an extra field for the link to the next node.

2.   **Declare the header.**

```
VAR
  list : tonodes;
```

This will define a variable which can be used to point to a dynamically created node. As yet it has no value, that is:

list

Pascal has a special pointer value called *nil* which can be assigned to pointer variables to indicate specifically that they point nowhere. This value can be tested for, and is conventionally used as the link value for the last node in a list. Pointers are considered to be bound to their node type, but *nil* is a pointer literal and is compatible with all pointer types.

3.   **Create space for a new node.**

         new (*list*);

Space large enough for a node of the correct type is taken from an area in the Pascal system known as the **heap**. The address of this area is put into the pointer variable mentioned. This produces:

list

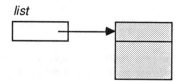

4.   **Access fields in the node.** If the node is a record, access to a field is via the dot notation, plus the carat, to indicate that a pointer must be followed first.

         listt^.field

Example 9.1   Party people

In the example in Section 8.3, various people were to be invited to a party, and they were listed as families, for example:

         Tom & Pat
         Nigel & Judy & William & Michael

Each family, therefore, is a list of people, and the list is of variable size. We could set up such a list with the declarations:

```
TYPE
  topeople = ^people;
  people   = record
        next   : topeople;
        name : names;
      end;
```

```
VAR
   head, guest : topeople;
```

As each name is read in, a space for a new name can be created (together with its pointer), and linked up to the others. The loop to do this would be:

```
head := nil;
repeat
  new(guest);
  readname (guest^.name);
  guest^.link := head;
  head := guest;
until nomoreampersand;
```

Working through this sequence for Nigel, Judy, William and Michael, we see that the list is created looking like this:

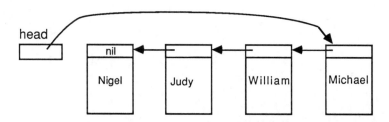

The names have been inserted in the list in reverse order. A means of linking them in a more obvious order is discussed after the quick resumé of the properties of pointers.

Pointer values and operators

Pointer values are generated identifiers. The nodes that a pointer may point to are kept in the area of memory called the **heap**. Therefore a valid pointer value is any address in the heap. It is not possible to have pointers pointing to a variable or area of memory, other than one created through the procedure *new*. There is no notation for pointer literals except for the special value *nil*. *The heap defined.*

Pointer values can be assigned and compared for equality. They can also be followed down to their nodes, or **dereferenced**, by using the up-arrow. Thus if *head* is a pointer, *head^* represents the node it points to. Such indirect names are legitimate wherever variables of that type are legitimate. Thus given the two pointers and nodes:

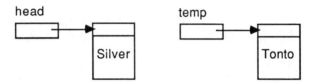

the assignment:

head^ := temp^;

will copy the entire contents of the node pointed to by *temp* into the node pointed to by *head*. Pictorially, we have:

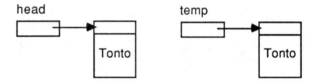

This is quite different to saying:

head := temp;

which would only copy the pointer, giving:

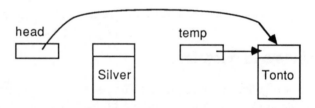

In this case, note that the node originally pointed to by *head* would be inaccessible after the assignment, unless the pointer to it had previously been copied somewhere.

Use of *new* and *dispose*.   There are two special procedures for pointers: *new* and *dispose*. *New* acquires an area from the heap, as already described, and *dispose* can be used to return unwanted nodes to the heap. The system may then be able to reuse that space. In addition, Turbo Pascal provides *mark* and *release* which allow the heap to be marked at a certain point and then cut back to that point. This method of retrieving space is more efficient than disposing. For full details see the Turbo Manual.

Pointer values cannot be read or written. Input and output of fields of nodes they point to are subject to the input and output provisions of their own types.

Stacks and queues

The list that was built up in Example 9.1 is known as a **stack**, since new nodes are added at the top or front of the list. Sometimes it is essential that the nodes be added at the end, maintaining the chronological order of arrival. This structure is a great British institution, known as a **queue**.

In order to create a list of nodes in the order in which they are provided, it is necessary to know at all times where the end of the list is. Nodes can then be linked using this pointer. The appropriate loop for creating a list of names, as described above, in order is:

```
VAR
  head, last, guest : topeople;

  head := nil;
  repeat
    new (guest);
    readname (guest^.name);
    guest^.link := nil;
    if head = nil
      then head := guest
      else last^.link := guest;
    last := guest;
  until nomoreampersand;
```

This sequence will create the following list:

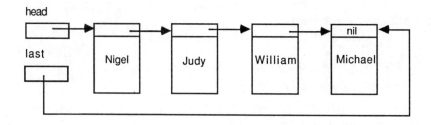

Scanning a list

Once a list is created, it can be scanned by following the pointers. Notice that we can only scan the list in the direction in which the pointers were created. Thus for the loop just created above, we could print out the names with the following loop:

```
VAR
  head, current : topeople;

current := head;
while current <> nil do begin
  writename(current^.name);
  current := current^ .next;
end;
```

There are many variations on the basic stack and queue, depending on whether deletions can occur at the front or back or both. In the most general case, nodes can be added anywhere in the list, which would be useful, for example, if they had to be maintained in alphabetical order.

9.3   More complex data structures

Stacks and queues are **linear lists**: all such lists have the property that they have only one pointer to another node. There is no reason why a node should not branch off into several sublists, and these do not even have to be of the same type. The following example is a simple illustration of this facility. Even more complex and formalised structures can be developed, as would be covered in a course on data structures. The following example illustrates such a typical build up of links.

Example 9.2   Holiday camp data

Problem   The Zanyland Holiday Camp Recreation Section likes to keep track of the interests of people who are attending the camp. For each family, it records:

- the surname,
- the sex, sports and hobbies of each adult, and
- the sex and age of each child.

Children are assumed to be interested in everything, but knowing their age helps to group them with their peers. Since families can vary a lot in size, a dynamic means of storing this data is needed.

| Solution | Use pointers. We can set up a structure for a family as follows:

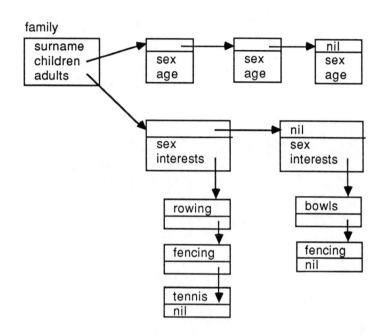

Then the structure can be processed for all adults, or all children, or all those interested in tennis, say, just by following the appropriate pointers.

| Algorithm | The data type definitions are the most important part of this example. Once a diagram, such as here, has been drawn, it is relatively simple to write down the corresponding Pascal types. Then to test that the structure is as required, and to have basic processes for accessing, we devise procedures to read in a family and print out its details again.

There are actually three kinds of list here – the adults, children and the interests. In each case, the principle of creating nodes and linking them up is the same, but it is not possible to use a single procedure to read in all three, as the types are different. What still remains to be decided is the form of the input data. We shall assume that it is entered interactively, with prompts for each field. A 'Q' will end a group of adults or children and an empty string will signal the end of the group of hobbies. The complete program follows.

Program

```
PROGRAM Holidaydata (input, output);
  CONST
    namemax    = 24;
    empty      = ' ';

  TYPE
    namerange  = 1..namemax;
    names      = string[namemax]
    sexes      = (male, female);
    ages       = 0 .. 16;
    hobbies    = names;
    tochildren = ^ childnode;
    childnode  = record
                     next  : tochildren;
                     sex   : sexes;
                     age   : ages;
                 end;
    tohobbies  = ^ hobbynode;
    hobbynode  = record
                     next    : tohobbies;
                     hobby   : hobbies;
                 end;
    toadults   = ^ adultnode;
    adultnode  = record
                     next      : toadults;
                     sex       : sexes;
                     interests : tohobbies;
                 end;
    families   = record
                     surname  : names;
                     children : tochildren;
                     adults   : toadults;
                 end;
  VAR
    family : families;

  PROCEDURE readhobbies (VAR head : tohobbies);
    VAR
      temp, last    : tohobbies;
      hobbyname : hobbies;
    BEGIN
      head := nil;
      last := nil;
      repeat
        write('Interest (return for none)? ');
        readln (hobbyname);
        if hobbyname <> empty then begin
          new(temp);
          temp^.hobby := hobbyname;
          temp^.next := nil;
```

```
            if head = nil
              then head := temp
              else last^.next := temp;
            last := temp;
          end;
      until hobbyname = empty;
    END; {readhobbies}


PROCEDURE readadults (VAR head : toadults);
  VAR
    temp, last  : toadults;
    ch          : char;
    finished    : boolean;
  BEGIN
    head := nil;
    last := nil;
    finished := false;
    repeat
      repeat
        write('Sex? (M, F, or Q for no more): ');
        read(ch);
      until ch in ['M','m','F','f','Q','q'];
      readln;
      if ch in ['Q','q'] then finished := true else
      begin
        new(temp);
        if ch in ['M','m']
          then temp^.sex := male
          else temp^.sex := female;
        temp^.next := nil;
        readhobbies(temp^.interests);
        if head = nil
          then head := temp
          else last ^.next := temp;
        last := temp;
      end;
    until finished;
  END; {readadults}


PROCEDURE readchildren (VAR head : tochildren);
  VAR
    temp, last : tochildren;
    ch         : char;
    finished   : boolean;
  BEGIN
    head := nil;
    last := nil;
    finished := false;
    repeat
      repeat
        write(Children? (M, F, or Q for no more): ');
        read(ch);
```

```
                        until ch in ['M','m','F','f','Q','q'];
                        readln;
                        if ch in ['Q','q'] then finished := true else
                        begin
                          new(temp);
                          if ch in ['M','m']
                            then temp^.sex := male
                            else temp^.sex := female;
                          temp^.next := nil;
                          write('Age ');
                          readln(temp^.age);
                          if head = nil
                            then head := temp
                            else last^.next := temp;
                          last := temp;
                        end;
                      until finished;
                    END;  {readchildren}

            PROCEDURE printhobbies (head : tohobbies);
              VAR scan : tohobbies;
              BEGIN
                scan := head;
                while scan <> nil do begin
                  write(scan^.hobby, ' ');
                  scan := scan^.next;
                end;
              END; {printhobbies}

            PROCEDURE printadults (head : toadults);
              VAR scan : toadults;
              BEGIN
                scan := head;
                while scan <> nil do begin
                  case scan^.sex of
                    male : write('male');
                    female : write('female');
                  end;
                  write(' with interests ');
                  printhobbies (scan^.interests);
                  writeln;
                  scan := scan^.next;
                end;
              END;  {printadults}

            PROCEDURE printchildren (head : tochildren);
              VAR scan : tochildren;
              BEGIN
                scan := head;
                while scan <> nil do begin
                  case scan^.sex of
                    male    : write('boy');
```

```
              female : write('girl');
           end;
           write(' age ');
           writeln(scan^.age);
           scan := scan^.next;
         end;
      END;  {printchildren}

   BEGIN
      writeln('***** Reading holiday data *****');
      writeln('Testing for one family only');
      write('Surname: ');
      readln(family.surname);
      writeln('Adults');
      readadults(family.adults);
      writeln('Children');
      readchildren(family.children);
      writeln;
      writeln('The ', family.surname, ' family''s data is: ');
      writeln('Adults:');
      printadults(family.adults);
      writeln('Children:');
      printchildren(family.children);
   END.
```

Testing

***** Reading holiday data *****
Testing for one family only
Surname: Jones
Adults
Sex (M, F or Q for no more): m
Interest (return for no more)? bowling
Interest (return for no more)? swimming
Interest (return for no more)? tennis
Interest (return for no more)?
Sex (M, F or Q for no more): f
Interest (return for no more)? swimming
Interest (return for no more)?
Sex (M, F or Q for no more): q
Children
Sex (M, F or Q for no more): m   **Age** 6
Sex (M, F or Q for no more): f   **Age** 3
Sex (M, F or Q for no more): q

The Jones family's data is:
Adults:
male with interests bowling swimming tennis
female with interests swimming
Children:
boy aged 6
girl aged 3

9.4 Objects

In the history of programming, there have been various movements which have changed the way people wrote programs, and which led to new and better languages. Some of these were:

- the **structured programming** movement in the 1970s, which promoted the control and data structures we find in Pascal;

- the **modular programming** movement, which emphasised modules or units; and

- the **data abstraction** movement, which concentrated on abstract data types and endeavoured to make them as general as possible.

The latest of these is **object-oriented programming** which looks at solutions to problems in terms of the objects that need to be defined and manipulated. Turbo Pascal provides quite powerful features for OOPS, and has an excellent treatise on how to use them in the manual. We shall look at them briefly here, and construct a small example.

There are three facets to Turbo's OOPS facility:

- **objects** which are records with data and method fields;

- **inheritance** of properties from one object to another;

- **late binding** of methods to reflect the latest circumstances.

Defining an object

An object is defined as a type which has data fields and **method** fields. The method fields consist of the procedures and functions which operate on the data fields. There are two special kinds of method fields called **constructors** and **destructors**, which, as their names suggest, are used to create and destroy individual objects. The form for a simple object definition is:

Object type

OBJECT *(heritage)*
    data field list
    methods list
END

Following on from the type definition, each of the methods is then expanded as an ordinary procedure or function declaration. An example of an object is:

```
TYPE
  Lists = OBJECT
    head, last : tonodes;
    constructor Init;
    procedure Add (n : tonodes);
    procedure Print;
    destructor Done;
  end;
```

The object type *Lists* has two data fields and four methods. The two data fields are intended to point to the first and last nodes of the list; they are of a pointer type, *tonodes*, which will be defined appropriately later. The constructor method *Init* will be used to initialise the data fields. The body of *Init* could be:

```
constructor Lists.Init;
  begin
    head := nil;
    tail := nil;
  end;
```

Notice that the object name precedes the method name in the declaration, thus distinguishing it from other methods of the same name.

The *Add* procedure will link the given node onto the list. Its body is as follows:

```
PROCEDURE Lists.Add (n : tonodes);
  begin
    if head = nil
      then head := n
      else last^.next := n;
    last := n;
  end;
```

Print will be defined similarly. The destructor, *Done*, can be defined to tidy up and delete all the nodes for a list.

Creating and using objects

Having defined an object type, we can then declare variables of this type, and call the methods to manipulate them. To create two lists, we would say:

```
VAR
  List1, List2 : lists;
```

The effect of the variable declaration is to create a record on the stack with the appropriate data fields, as well as pointers to the methods. As we shall see later, these methods can be made to vary in powerful ways.

Inheritance

Given an object type, we can define a new type which is based on it, but which has additional fields and methods added to it. The new type inherits all the methods of the old type, although it may replace some of them. In particular, with new data fields, the new object will need a new constructor method.

Consider now the definition of the *nodes* type:

```
TYPE
  tonodes = ^ nodes;

  nodes = OBJECT
    next : tonodes;
    constructor Init;
    procedure Display; virtual;
    destructor Done;
  end;
```

Each node will have a link field called *next*, a constructor and destructor and a procedure to display the values of the data in the node. What data? Well, this is where inheritance comes in. The *nodes* object defines the bare bones of a node, giving just the ability to link nodes together. We can now inherit this ability and add to it data fields of numerous kinds. So, for example, we could define new objects as follows:

```
TYPE
  charnodes = OBJECT (nodes)
    data : char;
    constructor Init;
    procedure Display; virtual;
  end;

  numnodes = OBJECT (nodes)
    num : integer;
    constructor Init;
    procedure Display; virtual;
  end;
```

Both are based on the original *nodes* type, but each has added its own particular data field.

Character node objects will have two data fields – *data*, defined by itself, and *next* inherited from *nodes* . It will also have four methods: its own *Init* and *Display* methods, and the *Init* and *Done* methods inherited from *nodes* . Why are there two *Init* methods and only one *Display*?

Virtual methods

The two *Init* methods would be expanded as follows:

```
constructor Nodes.Init;
  begin
    next := nil;
  end;

constructor charnodes.Init;
  begin
    Nodes.Init;
    read(ch);
  end;
```

In other words, *charnodes.Init* initialises its own fields, and can also call on *Nodes.Init* to initialise the inherited fields. However, in the case of displaying a node, the new object may wish to replace the old method altogether. This is achieved by declaring the method as **virtual**. When the new object is declared, a Virtual Method Table is created for it, and the latest versions of any virtual methods are inserted here, and used thereafter for this object.

Consider now the *Print* method from the list object. It is expanded as:

```
procedure Lists.Print;
  var node : tonodes;
  begin
    node := head;
    while node <> nil do begin
      node^.Display;
      node := node^.next;
    end;
  end;
```

If we created a list object which uses character nodes, then whenever this list is printed, each individual node will be displayed using the display method defined for *charnodes*. In other words, because *Display* is declared as virtual, the compiler knows when compiling the *Print* procedure that the actual version of *Display* required will only be settled (or **bound**) later.

Dynamic objects

Objects are often used in conjunction with pointers. Dynamically created objects must be initialised with a constructor call, and so Turbo Pascal has extended the syntax of the *new* and *dispose* procedures to include the name of an appropriate constructor or destructor. To create a linked list of *charnodes* we would use:

```
VAR
  charlist : lists;
  ch : ^ charnodes;

charlist. Init;
while not eoln do begin
  new(ch, Init);
  charlist.Add (ch);
end;
```

Similar sequences can be constructed for other types of lists.

Example 9.3 Lists using objects

| Problem | We would like to create an object framework for manipulating lists of many different kinds.

| Solution | The basis for the necessary objects has been developed in the foregoing discussion. We can declare the list and node objects in a unit, and use them from the programs that require the facility. To test the unit, we can write a short program with two sorts of node lists, read data into them in and print it out.

| Unit | In the unit that follows, the destructors have not yet been fully expanded: this is left as an exercise for the reader. Notice, too, that *Nodes.Display* is a null procedure, but is there for completeness.

```
UNIT Listunit;

INTERFACE
TYPE
tonodes = ^ nodes;

Lists = object
  head, last : tonodes;
  constructor Init;
  destructor Done; virtual;
  procedure Add (n : tonodes);
  procedure Print;
end; {Lists}

Nodes = object
  next : tonodes;
  constructor Init;
  destructor Done;
  procedure Display; virtual;
end; {Nodes}
```

```
IMPLEMENTATION
  constructor Lists.Init;
    begin
      head := nil;
      last := nil;
    end;

  destructor Lists.Done;
    begin
    end;

  procedure Lists.Print;
    VAR node : tonodes;
    BEGIN
      node := head;
      while node <> nil do begin
        node^.Display;
        node := node^.next;
      end;
    END;

  procedure Lists.Add (n : tonodes);
    begin
      if head = nil
        then head := n
        else last^.next := n;
      last := n;
    end;

  constructor Nodes.Init;
    begin
      next := nil;
    end;

  destructor Nodes.Done;
    begin
    end;

  procedure Nodes.Display;
    begin
    end;
END.
```

Program Now we can test this out with a program as follows:

```
PROGRAM TestObjects;
  USES listunit;

  TYPE
    charnode = OBJECT (nodes)
      data : char;
      constructor Init;
```

```
        procedure Display; virtual;
      end;

  numnode = OBJECT (nodes)
    number : integer;
    constructor Init;
    procedure Display ; virtual;
  end;

procedure charnode.Display;
 BEGIN
   write(data);
 END;

constructor charnode.Init;
 BEGIN
   nodes.Init;
   read(data);
 END;

procedure numnode.Display;
 BEGIN
   writeln(number);
 END;

constructor numnode.Init;
 BEGIN
   nodes.Init;
   readln(number);
 END;

VAR
  charlist : lists;
  ch       : ^charnode;
  numlist : lists;
  num      : ^numnode;

BEGIN
  writeln('***** Testing objects *****');
  charlist.Init;
  writeln('Type in characters for the list, ending with <return>');
  while not eoln do begin
    new(ch,Init);
    charlist.Add(ch);
  end;
  readln;
  writeln('The list is:');
  charlist.Print;
  writeln;

  numlist.Init;
  writeln('Type in numbers for a list, ending with cntl-Z');
```

```
         while not eof do begin
           new(num, Init);
           numlist.Add(num);
         end;
         writeln('The numbers are:');
         numlist.Print;
       END.
```

| Testing |

A typical run of the program would be:

***** Testing objects *****
Type in characters for the list, ending with <return>
hgtfry
The list is:
hgtfry
Type in numbers for a list, ending with cntl-Z
67
34
52
^Z
The numbers are:
67
34
52

Objects are a very powerful programming technique and Turbo Pascal provides considerable support for them. In addition to the extra syntax, there is also a whole object library of user interface routines called Turbo Vision. Objects for windows, menus, buttons, status lines and so on are defined and can be used to enhance the quality of Turbo Pascal programs with suprisingly little effort. However, Turbo Vision is beyond the scope of this introductory book, and the reader is referred to the excellent manual provided by Borland.

9.5 Turbo Pascal and animation

The final aspect of the Turbo Pascal Graph unit that we shall consider is animation, or the ability to move images around on the screen. Moving images can be used to demonstrate the progress of an algorithm, to provide amusement, or to enhance the quality of a user interface. In the latter case, we could for example have a menu move sideways off the screen, or fade into a central point, rather than just disappear.

The routines that we need from the Graph unit are:

```
       PROCEDURE GetImage (x1, y1, x2, y2 : word; var BitMap);
       PROCEDURE PutImage (x, y : word; var BitMap; Bitop : word);
```

The Graph unit maintains a complete pixel image of the screen, known as a bit map. *GetImage* will extract a specific rectangle from that map into the *BitMap* parameter. *BitMap* is an untyped parameter which is usually a pointer to space on the heap for the data being extracted. We avoid knowing too much about its requirements by collecting the necessary information through the following routines:

```
FUNCTION ImageSize (x1, y1, x2, y2 : word ) : word;
PROCEDURE GetMem (var p : pointer; size : word);
```

ImageSize will work out how much memory is needed to store the image at the given coordinates, and *GetMem* will allocate memory on the heap for the image.

PutImage, then, can be given this pointer and successive top left corner starting points to draw the image at different places on the screen. The *BitOp* parameter provides the final touch, by enabling a previous image to be overwritten or added to. The available bit operations are:

```
CopyPut   = 0;
XorPut    = 1;
OrPut     = 2;
AndPut    = 3;
NotPut    = 4;
```

To overwrite what was on the screen before, we use *XorPut* (exclusive or). So, to move an image called *Picture* around the screen, we need the following sequence of calls:

```
VAR
   Picture      : pointer;
   size         : word;
   x1, y1,
   x2, y2, X, Y : word;

BEGIN
   Draw the image

   {Capture the bit map}
      size := imagesize(x1, y1, x2, y2);
      Getmem (picture, size);
      GetImage (x1, y1, x2, y2, picture^);

   PutImage(x1,y1,picture^,XorPut);    {Erase the image}

   X := GetMaxX div 2;
   Y := GetMaxY div 2;                 {Start in the centre}

   REPEAT
      PutImage(X,Y, Picture^, XorPut);   {Draw the image}
```

```
      Delay(100);
      PutImage (X, Y, Picture^, XorPut);   {Erase the image}
      Move to a new position
   UNTIL Keypressed;

      FreeMem (picture, size);
   END;
```

The *FreeMem* procedure releases the memory obtained through *GetMem*.

Example 9.4   Bouncing ball

| Problem | To illustrate the use of animation, we would like to bounce a red ball around the screen.

| Solution | The animation sequence above can be used as is, with the drawing of the ball (a flood-filled circle) and the calculating of the new position being the only new parts. When calculating a new position, we shall allow the ball to move in a straight line until it hits a side of the screen, and then to bounce off at an angle.

| Algorithm | Bouncing the ball off the sides of the screen follows simple rules. If the ball hits a side, then reverse the direction of x; if it hits the top or bottom, then reverse the direction of y. In both cases, we choose a new angle for the line. This is illustrated in Figure 9.3, where the signs indicate the x and y directions before and after the ball hits a boundary.

We shall make the x step a fixed amount, say 20 pixels, and vary the y step by a random amount between 0 and 1 times the x step. In this way, the ball will bounce in diagonal lines most of the time.

| Program | By writing *DrawBall* and *MoveBall* procedures, we can use the animation sequence to construct a bouncing ball program.

```
PROGRAM BouncingBall (input, output);
USES Graph, Crt;
CONST
  radius = 20;

VAR
  Picture         : pointer;
  size            : word;
  yratio          : real;
  MaxX, MaxY,
  X, Y, xdir,
  x1, x2, y1, y2  : word;
  driver, mode    : integer;
```

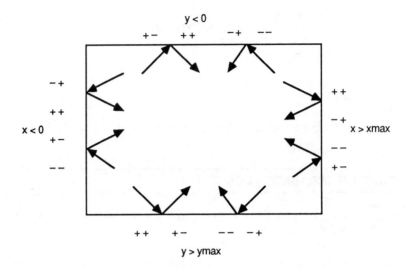

Figure 9.3 Changing directions for bouncing balls

```
PROCEDURE DrawBall (var x1, y1, x2, y2 : word);
 CONST
  start = 200;

 BEGIN
   SetColor(DarkGray);
   SetFillStyle(Solidfill,red);
   SetLineStyle(SolidLn,0,NormWidth);
   Circle(start,start,radius);
   Floodfill(start,start,Darkgray);
   x1 := start-radius;
   x2 := start+radius;
   y1 := start-radius;
   y2 := start+radius;
 END; {Drawball}

PROCEDURE MoveBall
            (var x,y : word; var xdir : word; var yratio : real);
    CONST step = 20;

    FUNCTION incline : real;
     BEGIN
       incline := random + 0.1;
     END;

   BEGIN
     x := x +xdir*step;
     y := y + round(step*yratio);
```

```
     if (x + 2*radius + 1> maxx) then begin
       {Reset x and reverse direction}
       X := maxx - 2*radius - 1;
       xdir := -xdir;
       {Alter yratio but keep same direction}
         if yratio > 0 then yratio := incline else yratio := -incline;
     end;

     if x < radius then begin
       {Reset X and reverse direction}
       x := 0;
       xdir := -xdir;
       {Alter yratio but keep same direction}
       if yratio > 0 then yratio := incline else yratio := -incline;
     end;

   if (y + 2*radius +1 > maxy) then begin
   {Reset Y and reverse direction}
   yratio := -incline;
   y := maxy - 2*radius - 1;
 end;

   if (y < radius) and (yratio < 0) then begin
   {Reset Y and reverse direction}
     y := 0;
     yratio := incline;
   end;
END; {MoveBall}

BEGIN
 Randomize;
 driver := detect;
 InitGraph(driver, mode, ");

 MaxX := GetMaxX;
 MaxY := GetMaxy;
 SetLineStyle(SolidLn,0,Thickwidth);
 Rectangle(0,0,MaxX,MaxY);
 DrawBall(x1, y1, x2, y2);

 size := imagesize(x1, y1, x2, y2);     {Capture the bit map}
 Getmem (picture, size);
 GetImage (x1, y1, x2, y2, picture^);

 PutImage(x1,y1,picture^,XorPut);      {Erase the image}

 X := MaxX div 2;
 xdir := 1;
 yratio := -0.5;

REPEAT
   PutImage(X,Y, Picture^, XorPut);   {Draw the image}
```

```
                    Delay(100);
                    PutImage (X, Y, Picture^, XorPut);  {Erase the image}
                    MoveBall(X, Y, xdir, yratio);
                 UNTIL Keypressed;

                 FreeMem (picture, size);

                 END.
```

| Testing | This will be fun!

9.6   Case study 4: Electronic diary

Problem

Students studying computer science at Zanyland University have to undertake a group project in their second year. The number of groups and the number of students in each project group varies from year to year. One of the difficult tasks at the beginning of the course is establishing when members of a particular group can meet to discuss their project, since they may be taking different courses and have different timetables. They would like to get computer assistance in arranging meetings.

Solution

We can write a program which will read in:

- a list of course numbers and their lecture days and times;
- lists of the courses taken by students in each project group;

and then print out for each group the times when they could possibly meet. We ought to consider carefully the data structures that are most appropriate for this problem. Will linked lists be best, or sets or arrays?

Algorithm

There is a good deal of design work that needs to be done for this program. Let us start with the overall structure of the program. We need to read in the course timetable and then, for each project group, the individual students' timetables. The main program could therefore look like this:

```
PROGRAM MeetingTimes (input, output);

BEGIN
  writeln('*** The meeting time organiser *****');
  Initialise;
  SetUpFiles;
  ReadTimetable;
  WHILE not eof do begin
    StartProject;
    while not ABlankLine do
      ReadaStudent(some parameter?);
      ComputeandPrintFreetimes;
  end;
END.
```

The next design decision concerns the data structures. The main computation is one of finding intersections of times, which points us to sets. However, Pascal sets can only handle small numbers and characters, not complex records like a day–time pair, so we would need to convert each block on the timetable into a numeric code. This is easy enough if the timetable is regarded as having five days and eight, say, periods per day. A student's timetable can therefore be represented as a set of numbers between 1 and 40. To work out the free times, we can do the following:

```
freetimes := [1..maxperiods];
student := project.first;
while student <> project.last do begin
  freetimes := freetimes – student↑.timetable;
  student := student^.next;
end;
```

In other words, we start off with all the periods in the *freetimes* set and work through the list of students in the project, subtracting out the timetables. What is left is the free time for all.

We have therefore assumed that the students in a project will be represented by a linked list. This is sensible, because we do not know how many students there will be per group. The *project* type will have a pointer to the first and last student in the group, and the handling of the list is just as explained in Section 9.2.

What about the timetable itself? The data for a student will include course numbers, presumably, and this has to be looked up in the list of courses read in initially. If we want to look up a number, then an array is ideal, but in this case, that may be very wasteful. Course numbers may be in the thousands, and the students doing the projects may only take a small selection of these. Therefore, once again, we shall use a linked list for the courses. Each course will keep its number and the set of periods that it uses. Notice that the number of elements in the set is quite variable, so that one course may have three periods and another six, without any trouble.

Program

A first stab at the timetable data structures, main program, and the procedure to read in the information is:

```
PROGRAM MeetingTimes (input, output);
  CONST
    space          = ' ';
    periodsperday  = 8;
    periodmax      = 40;  {5 x periodsperday}
  TYPE
    coursenos = 000..999;
    periods   = ^periodmax;
    periodset = set of periods;
    tocourses = ^courses;
    courses = record
      number : coursenos;
      pattern : periodset;
      next     : tocourses;
    end;
    courselists = record
      first, last : tocourses;
    end;

  VAR
    courselist : courselists;

  FUNCTION ABlankLine : boolean;
  BEGIN
    ABlankline := eoln;
  END;

  PROCEDURE ReadTimetable;
  VAR course : tocourses;

  PROCEDURE readpattern(var course : tocourses);
  VAR
    ch     : char;
    n      : integer;
    period : periods;

  FUNCTION converttoperiod
          (day : char; period : integer) : periods;
  VAR p : integer;
  BEGIN
    case day of
    'M', 'm' : p := 0;
    'T', 't' :  p := periodsperday;
    'W', 'w' : p := periodsperday*2;
    'H', 'h' : p := periodsperday*3;
    'F', 'f' :  p := periodsperday*4;
```

```
    end;
      converttoperiod := p + period;
    END; {converttoperiod}

  BEGIN
    with course^ do begin
     pattern := [ ];
     next := nil;
     read(number);
      while not eoln do begin
       repeat read(ch) until ch <> space;
       read(n);
       period := converttoperiod(ch,n);
       pattern := pattern + [period];
      end;
      readln;
    end;
    END; {readpattern}

  BEGIN
    writeln('Type in a course number, followed by ');
    writeln('the periods given as days and slots');
    writeln('where days are MTWHF and slots are 1..8');
    writeln('e.g.');
    writeln('301  M1  T1   H3');
    courselist.first := nil;
    courselist.last := nil;
    while not ABlankLine do begin
      new(course);
      readpattern(course);
      if courselist.first = nil
      then courselist.first := course
      else courselist.last^.next := course;
      courselist.last := course;
    end;
    END; {Readtimetable}
```

You can take the rest of it from here!

Summary 9

1. **Pointers** to dynamically created variables (usually records) enable lists and structures to be built up.

2. The **pointer symbol** ^ is used when declaring a pointer type and to dereference from the pointer to the variable it is pointing to.

3. Pointer variables are declared as usual in the VAR declarations; the **dynamic variables** they point to are created on the heap at run time using the *new* procedure.

4. Linear lists such as **stacks** and **queues,** as well as more complex structures, can be built up by making use of pointers.

5. Turbo Pascal's objects consist of data fields and **method fields**. Methods are used to manipulate the data.

6. An object can inherit fields from another object. The type of the descendant is compatible with the type of its ancestor.

7. Virtual methods enable descendants to decide how to manipulate objects.

8. Dynamic objects must be created with a constructor call before any other methods are called.

9. Turbo Pascal's Graph unit has routines to simulate **movement of images** on the screen.

10. **Memory** for storing images must be explicitly allocated and freed.

Self-check quiz 9

1. What are the advantages of using pointers for structures?

2. What are the disadvantages?

3. What does the *new* procedure do?

4. What is the difference between a stack and a queue?

5. What is the difference between nested records and inherited objects?

6. Can *Init* constructors have parameters?

7. In Example 9.3, explain how the association between *Display* in the *Lists.print* procedure and *NumNode.Display* is set up.

8. Write a suitable destructor for *Lists.Done*.

9. Give a truth table for the *XOR* operator.

10. In the following sequence, explain why one mention of *picture* has pointer dereference symbol ^ and the other does not.

```
Getmem (picture, size);
GetImage (x1, y1, x2, y2, picture^);
```

Problems 9

Answers are provided for problems marked §.

9.1§ **Class timetables** The two types of data in case study 4 have different life spans: the course timetable will be set for a year, and probably change little between years, while the students' timetable could change every term. Reading in the course days and times every time we need to set up meetings could be tedious. It would be better to have one program to do this, and another to read the students' data. To connect these two, we need a file.

Write a program which will read in the class timetable interactively and store the information in a general file. Then modify the program in case study 4 to read this file in, prior to requesting the students' timetables.

9.2 **Airline seating** The seating on large airplanes consists of ten seats in a row of the form:

Seat letter: A B C   D E F G   H I J

W S S S A S S S S A S S W

where **W** indicates a window, **S** a seat and **A** an aisle. Different airplanes have different arrangements of seats, but the seat letters always reflect their position, even if some letters have to be missed out. For example, a small plane with only four seats across might have the following arrangement:

Seat letter: A C   H J

W S S A S S W

Rows of seats are also divided into between one and three cabins for first, business and economy class. For example, in a 100 row plane, there could be rows 1 – 12 for first class, rows 14 – 40 for business class and rows 41 – 101 for economy. (Notice that it is customary in aviation not to use the number 13 for a row, as it is deemed unlucky.) Devise a way of storing the seating information for various types of planes so that it can be readily used by a seat reservation program. Then write the reservation program, which accepts seats requests for a certain type of plane and a number of seats of a given class. The program should allocate seats using two simple rules: a group of people should be seated in the same row, preferably with no aisle intervening; and window and aisle seats should be allocated before centre seats.

9.3   **Graphic airplanes** Design a way of showing the seating plans of an airplane on the screen. Use the graphical facilities you have to best advantage, including colour for the classes, and so on.

9.4§   **Object-oriented holidays** Convert the program in Example 9.2 to use objects. Include the List unit from Example 9.3, and derive new objects for the three types of lists: adults, children and hobbies.

10

Projects

At the end of a course on programming in Pascal, there is usually an opportunity to test your new-found knowledge by writing a fairly lengthy program. The following problems are of the right size and complexity to be tackled over four to six weeks and should result in Pascal programs of about 500 to 800 lines. The chapter starts by outlining what to look for in a project, and how to approach it so as to get the most out of it.

10.1 Getting the most out of a project

The primary aim of a major project at the end of a course is to give one the opportunity to put into practice all one has learnt. The project topic should be carefully chosen so as to be manageable, and at the same time instructive and interesting. Many students like to feel that they are achieving something of lasting value when they take on a major project, and so it is often attractive to give a project a real life flavour. In the following sections are a selection of good projects which fulfill these objectives.

What to avoid in a project

If devising one's own project, there are factors to consider, to avoid falling into the trap of doing a lot of work without exercising much skill.

Keep the data volume down

The purpose of a project is to program, not to type in data. Therefore, avoid problems that require a large amount of data to be entered before the program can sensibly do anything. Such problems include inventory and stock control systems, employee or student record systems, bank statement and payroll systems, and theatre or airline reservation systems. For all of these, one would have to both invent the data and type it in, which is time-consuming and does not add anything to one's programming experience. Moreover, Pascal is probably not the best language for solving these types of problems. A language specifically designed for data processing or transaction processing, such as COBOL, would be more suitable.

Keep the output simple

The second characteristic to watch out for is excessive output, and in particular, displayed or graphic output. Getting a pleasing format on a screen can take hours of one's time, but is not a challenging or learning activity. Therefore, it is best at this stage to go for problems that have fairly routine output, or at least for those that can have two levels of output, as described in Section 10.2.

Avoid interactive testing

Testing is an essential part of ensuring that one has grasped the principles of good programming. If the program does not perform correctly, then it is not worth much. In order to test effectively, one must be able to take the program through predefined paths repeatedly. If a certain place in the program can only be reached via a long dialogue, then there will be quite a temptation to omit testing it. Programs that need a lot of interactive testing are games (with the user as one of the players), computer aided instruction (CAI) and spreadsheets. These are popular systems on PCs, but they are not trivial to write well, and the testing problem really rules them out at this stage.

Know the answers

Given the above bias against excessive input and output, it is clear that much of the program's efforts will be in calculating some results. Ensure that the expected result is well known. In other words, do not at this stage tackle a problem with a result that you could not produce yourself on paper. Statistical and mathematical problems fall into this category.

Where to start

Once you have decided on a project with a definable goal, the steps to follow are familiar, viz:

- define the problem,
- consider solutions,
- do examples and decide on the input and output,
- devise the data structures and algorithms,
- write the program(s),
- test the system.

In the projects that follow, the first three are better defined than the others, and also include specifications for input and output. In all cases, however, you should expect to spend roughly half of your allotted time on the first four steps, and only start writing programs and testing once everything is thoroughly thought out on paper.

Test data

During the design phase, set up one or more files of test data, and use them repeatedly. Do not rely on entering data interactively, as you will make mistakes and take up far too much time. In most cases, a project can be almost wholly completed with a basic input scheme, and then have a more fancy input procedure added at the end.

Generating sensible values for test data can also be a problem sometimes, and it may help to invoke a random number generator to do this automatically.

Narrative versus graphic output

The user-friendliness and effectiveness of a computer system can be greatly enhanced by a good use of graphics and colour on the screen. At the same time, it is also important that a printed record of the progress of a session be available. Unfortunately, screens and printers are seldom compatible and what works well on one does not easily transfer to the other, although this is changing as laser printers become more common.

One way of reconciling the capabilities of screens and printers is to go for narrative output. This gives the facts of what is happening as the program progresses, without any pictorial aids. Such narrative output can be the first record of the program's actions, and then later more exciting forms can be introduced.

A further advantage of narrative output is that it can be used during debugging. Printing to a file the state of important data structures at the start of each procedure can provide a valuable aid in deciding where to start looking for the cause of errors. If carefully designed, such output need not impact on any future graphics, and can remain in place as a back up.

10.2 Game simulations

This project involves simulating a game by means of a program. Three games are described below. They are:

- Battleships,
- Rat Race,
- Racing Demon.

These are all games of chance and no skill is involved. Therefore it will not be necessary to build any strategy into the program. For this reason, it is not required that a person be able to interact with the computer and play against the program. There is no interaction once the game is under way. Before starting to design the program, it would be useful to play the game a few times to make sure that the rules are understood.

Each game has been divided into two parts – the basic game and the advanced game. The intention is that one would tackle the basic game first and then go on to the advanced game. In two of the games – Battleships and Rat Race – the basic game consists of reading in a board and playing according to the full rules; the advanced game involves generating new boards in the program. In Racing Demon, the basic game consists of generating the hands and playing according to simplified rules; the advanced game adds in the full rules.

Being games of chance, Battleships, Rat Race and Racing Demon require the services of a random number generator to generate firing positions, thows of the die or cards in a pack, respectively. Random numbers can be generated by using the predefined Turbo function *Random* (see Section 3.6).

Battleships

The game of Battleships is played by two players. Each player has a 10 by 10 board on which 10 warships are secretly placed. The warships occupy 1 to 4 squares each and may not touch each other, even at corners. The number and size of each kind of ship is fixed as:

- one battleship of four squares,
- two cruisers of three squares,
- three frigates of two squares,
- four submarines of one square.

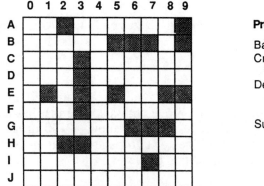

Figure 10.1 A Battleships Board

A typical board, and the dialogue required to set it up, is shown in Figure 10.1.

The game is played as follows. Each player in turn calls a square by giving its row and column, say B7, and the other player replies whether water or a ship has been hit, and which kind of ship. If a battleship, cruiser or destroyer is hit, then the player must in successive turns endeavour to sink the ship by hitting all its squares, before going on to another random guess. Once a player has sunk a ship, all the surrounding squares can be marked off on the copy of the opponent's board, since they could not contain any ships. The winner of the game is the first to sink all opposing ships.

Basic game

Write a program to simulate the game of Battleships for two players. Your program should:

1. Read in two boards, with each ship given as a starting square (letter and number) and an orientation (except for submarines). A sample input is shown above.

2. Set up blank boards for each player to record the hits.

3. Play the game by repeatedly for each player:
   - generating a firing position,
   - answering what was hit,
   - marking the hit,

- checking for a win,
- outputting the state of play.

Advanced game

Add to your working program a procedure to generate boards correctly, instead of reading them in.

Suggested narrative output

The ships occupy 20 squares in total. Writing all these squares will fit on one line. The line can be written for each move with a square that has been hit indicated by a blank. A typical game will take about 40–50 turns, which corresponds to a maximum of 100 lines or two pages of output per game. This would not be unreasonable for testing purposes.

Suggested graphic output

Put the boards next to each other on the screen and show the ships and hits with suitable symbols.

Rat Race

Rat Race is a board game in which four players each move a coloured counter around a board until the first reaches the cheese at the end. The board consists of a 7 by 7 matrix and on each square is a picture of one of:

- a running rat,
- a sleeping rat,
- a trapped rat,
- the cheese.

The running rats are of the same four colours as those used for the counters and each one's nose points in one of four directions. A sample board with typical interactive input is shown in Figure 10.2.

Each player throws a die to move and then proceeds along the board as follows:

sleeping rat	– stops there;
trapped rat	– stops there and misses next turn;
running rat own colour	– throws again and moves anew;
running rat other colour	– follows noses until a sleeping or trapped rat is reached.

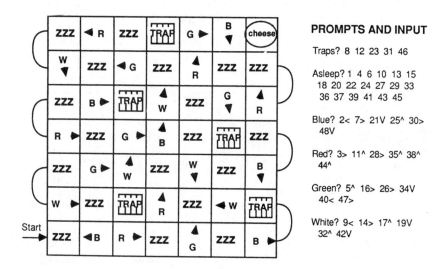

PROMPTS AND INPUT

Traps? 8 12 23 31 46

Asleep? 1 4 6 10 13 15
18 20 22 24 27 29 33
36 37 39 41 43 45

Blue? 2< 7> 21V 25^ 30>
48V

Red? 3> 11^ 28> 35^ 38^
44^

Green? 5^ 16> 26> 34V
40< 47>

White? 9< 14> 17^ 19V
32^ 42V

Figure 10.2 A Rat Race Board

A last throw must take the player exactly to the cheese to win.

Basic game

Write a program to simulate the game of Rat Race for four players. The program should:

1. Read in the position on the board of 5 traps, 19 sleeping rats and 6 running rats of each colour, their noses pointing in the directions given. Assume that the data is arranged so that the directions will not point off the board. An example of input is given above.

2. Play the game by repeatedly for each player:
   - rolling a die;
   - moving a counter;
   - checking for the type of square landed on, and acting accordingly;
   - checking for a win;
   - outputting the state of play.

Advanced game

Add to the working program a procedure to generate new boards with the characteristics as described above. The program must ensure that the nose directions do not point off the board.

Suggested narrative output

The important information for each player at each turn is the starting point, the die throw, ending point, and progress in getting there. This can be printed in tabular form, allowing for a variable number of steps in the Progress column. Headings and sample values might be:

TURN	PLAYER	POSITION	DIE THROW	PROGRESS
1	blue	0	5	to 5, ^ to 10, sleep
1	red	0	3	to 3, throw again
	red	3	4	to 7, > to 8, trap

This will take four or more lines per turn. If the game takes 25 moves, about 100 lines of output will be generated, which is reasonable for testing.

Suggested graphic output

The board will fit on the screen with a squeeze. Choose suitable symbols for the traps, rats and cheese (those above are only a suggestion) and don't forget that the counters have to appear somehow as well. When testing, don't print out the board for every move – use the narrative output for that and only print the board every now and then.

Racing Demon

This is a card game for any number of players, but we shall restrict it to two. Each player has a pack of cards and sets up a **hand** as follows. Thirteen cards are placed face down as a **kitty**, four cards are placed face up in a **row** next to this. The remaining cards are kept as the **stock**. Once everyone is ready, play proceeds simultaneously. Players put out into the centre any aces and then try to build on them in suit with any of the cards from their row or the top of their stock. If a card from a row is played out, then one from the kitty is turned up in its place. When no more cards can be played, the top of the stock is put to the bottom and the process repeated. Thus after a few turns, the game might be as shown in Figure 10.3.

The game ends when one player has exhausted the kitty. All players then stop and the winner is the one who has put out the most cards, with the player who finishes the game getting a bonus of 10.

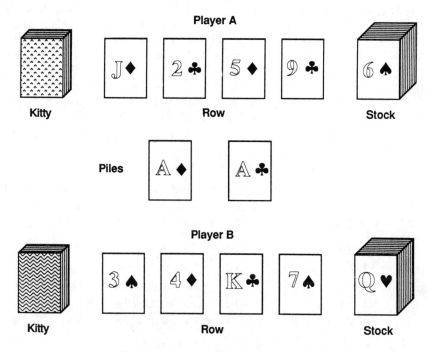

Figure 10.3 A Racing Demon hand

Basic game

Write a program to simulate the game of Racing Demon for two players. In this form, the game may end in a draw, which is detected when all the stock cards have been leafed through without any moves being possible. The program should:

1. Shuffle each of the two packs and deal out the hands.

2. Play the game by repeatedly for each player:
    *   checking if any row card can be played and if so, replenishing it from the kitty;
    *   checking if the top stock card can be played and if not, putting it at the bottom;

- checking for a win or draw;
- outputting the state of play.

Advanced game

The real game of Racing Demon allows a further kind of play. If a player cannot put anything out, then the rows can be built on with cards in decreasing face value, alternating black (clubs or spades) on red (hearts or diamonds). If this is done, then only the last of any sequence on a row card can be played. For example, in the position above, Player B could put the three of spades on the four of diamonds and thus get another kitty card out. If there is still nothing to go in the centre, the queen of hearts could be put from the stock onto the king of clubs, and so on.

Add a further procedure to the running program to take this into account.

Suggested narrative output

All the visible cards (the four in the row and the top of the stock) should be written for each move. The number of cards in the kitty and the state of the eight possible piles are also relevant. A possible output might be:

TURN	PILES	PLAYER	KITTY	ROW	STOCK	PLAY
5	A♦ A♣	1	13	J♦ 2♣ 5♦ 9♣	6♠	2♣
	A♦ 2♣	2	11	3♠ 4♦ K♣ 7♠	Q♥	none
6	A♦ 2♣	1	12	J♦ A♥ 5♦ 9♣	6♠	A♥
	A♦ 2♣ A♥	2	11	3♠ 4♦ K♣ 7♠	2♥	2♥

Suggested graphic output

An arrangement of the cards on the screen is fairly easy, and the stock and rows can be displayed and changed as needed. On the PC, symbols for the card suits are available as part of the character set (as shown above).

10.3 Organiser systems

This group of projects concerns reconciling certain sets of changing information against a fixed data file. The three projects are:

- Examination Timetabler,
- References Lister,
- Meeting Arranger.

In each case there is a data file with information that remains fairly permanent. This is read into the computer when the program starts running.

Then sets of data are read in which refer to the permanent information, and the program is required to come up with some arrangement of the data in accordance with certain criteria.

The permanent data file need not be more than about forty lines long, which is reasonably easy to set up, and the sets of varying data can be of a similar length, and still exercise the system adequately.

Examination Timetabler

Examinations have to be arranged so that students do not have two at the same time. In universities where students may opt for a variety of courses, the number of combinations can be quite large, and the timetabling of the exams can be a lengthy process. The aim of this project is to produce a feasible timetable given the basic information of room and class sizes and the varying information of a clash list. A clash list contains one entry for each course on offer, and a list of all those courses with which it clashes. Such a list is computed from the student registration file and is a standard starting point for timetable programs.

Input design

There are two streams of input. The permanent input consists of room sizes and class sizes. We have to decide how to identify rooms and courses. Let us suppose that rooms have codes that are short strings, such as Chem 4.5 or Maths 5B. Their sizes will be between 20 and 1000 seats. Courses are usually identified by codes as well, such as MA301 or CS105. However, we are going to have to work with these codes, so a simplification may be to go for all numeric codes at first.

The data for the clash list is simple, and if the course codes are numeric, can be generated automatically by using random numbers as described in the previous section. If the full codes are required, then it would still be best to work with numbers internally, and provide a translation to the more meaningful names on input and output.

Output design

The output would ideally be a table, with the dates down the side, AM and PM across the top, and the rooms and courses in each box. Initially, though, it would be sufficient to output the list of courses, together with the calculated date and time of each examination.

Extensions

The program must ensure that courses are not split over rooms and that no examinations clash. It should also endeavour to make life a bit better for students by not setting two examinations on the same day for anyone. This can easily be done if there is an unlimited period for the examinations, so a further refinement would be to try to make the total examining period as short as possible.

References Lister

Scientific works refer to other works by giving a list of references. Each reference contains a name, title, source of the paper or book, and a year. In different circumstances, one would want a file of references to be printed out in different orders, and perhaps in different formats. The aim of this project is to produce lists of references in a standard format, and sorted on any one of the items (name, title, source, date). The sources in each reference will be coded, and will refer to a standard list of references which is kept separately.

Input design

Suprisingly, this project does not break the above rule about difficult data. In any journal, there will be be plenty of references listed, and a number of these can be copied out as data. Fifty would suffice to test the system. The format for each reference must be decided, and the reading in could be quite tricky. Typical references would be:

Jones P, How to clean disks, JC 12 (4) 35-67, 1989.
Smith R W, Devices and their uses, Addison-Wesley, 1988.

A simple input scheme will put each item for a reference on a separate line; more compact schemes will need to devise special separators for the items (commas won't do).

The permanent information consists of journal codes with their full names, such as:

JC   Journal of Cleanology

With this project, there is a third stream of input – the choices of the user. By means of a dialogue, the system must enquire as to what sort of list is required, and in what format if alternatives are offered.

Output design

The output consists of lists of references sorted by one or other of the items. The output format is simply that used by the journal from which the data came.

Extensions

A useful extension to the system is to select items on certain criteria, such as all books by Jones or all references after 1985. This requires further dialogue to be designed. It would be nice to select also on keywords within titles, such as all titles about programming.

Meeting Arranger

See exercises 9.1 and 9.4 for this one.

10.4   Text processing

Text processing projects are very popular, because they produce a satisfying amount of output from input which is generally on file already. The two described here can also turn into useful little programs to keep.

Report Formatter

Although most computer systems have applications that will format a report very nicely, these are usually designed with general documents in mind, and may have far more features than needed just to get something out looking neat.

The simplest text formatter collects words into lines (as many in a line as possible subject to a given width limit). When a line is complete it is output 'right justified', that is, spaces are inserted to ensure that the final character appears at the right margin. The only event that can interrupt this formatting is the presence of a seemingly blank line. If the line is completely empty, then any text that has not yet been output is forced out, and if the line has n spaces then the current line is forced out as before, and a new line indented by n spaces is begun.

This process continues, while at the same time, the lines are gathered into pages of a specified length.

Extensions

For reports, there are two further essential features. The first is the 'as is' mode: there must be a way of suspending the right-justification, for headings, tables and so on. The second is the ability to skip to a new page. Design a simple way of indicating these.

Profiler

When programs are going wrong, it is often helpful to know when and how often procedures are called. This information can also be of use in tuning large programs that run for a long time. The aim of this project is to take an existing program and to add Pascal write statements to it so that it will output to a file a log of the time each procedure is called, and then go back and process this log, producing a table of the percentage of time spent in each procedure.

Output design

We need to decide on a fixed form for the added statements to use. This must include a code for the procedure called, and the start and end times. The procedure codes can be assigned internally, by keeping a list of procedure names as they come in. This list can then be used in reverse to print out the names in the percentage table.

Extensions

For debugging purposes, it is also important to have the values of parameters printed: only value parameters on entering a procedure, but all parameters on exit. If this is done, then the system will assume two different modes: profiler mode, which outputs raw coded data to a file for processing by the table program, and more readable data which can go to the screen while the program is running.

Appendix A Standard declarations

Reserved words

and	file	object	then
asm	for	of	to
array	function	or	type
begin	goto	packed	unit
case	if	procedure	until
const	implementation	program	uses
constructor	in	while	var
destructor	inline	record	while
div	interface	repeat	with
do	label	set	xor
downto	mod	shl	
else	nil	shr	
end	not	string	

Predefined types

Boolean
Byte
Char
Comp
Double
Extended
Integer
LongInt
Pointer
Real
ShortInt
Single
Text
Word

Directives

absolute
assembler
external
far
forward
interrupt
near
private
virtual

Predefined variables

Variable	Type
Input	Text file
Output	Text file
Exitcode	Integer
FileMode	Byte
InOutRes	Integer
RandSeed	LongInt
StackLimit	Word

Plus various interrupt locations,
overlay and pointer variables

Predefined Constants

true
false
maxint

Devices

CON
PRN
AUX

Appendix B   Standard procedures

Exit	*Flow of control*	Ofs	
Halt		Ptr	
RunError		Seg	
		SPtr	
Dispose	*Dynamic allocation*	SSeg	
FreeMem			
GetMem		Fillchar	*Miscellaneous*
Mark		Move	
New		Randomize	
Release		Hi	
MaxAvail		Lo	
MemAvail		ParamCount	
		ParamStr	
Chr	*Transfer*	Random	
Ord		SizeOf	
Round		Swap	
Trunc		UpCase	
Abs	*Arithmetic*	Eof	*All Files*
ArcTan		FilePos	
Cos		FileSize	
Exp		IOResult	
Frac		Assign	
Int		ChDir	
Ln		Close	
Pi		Erase	
Sin		GetDir	
Sqr		MkDir	
Sqrt		Rename	
		Reset	
Dec	*Ordinal*	Rewrite	
Inc		RmDir	
Odd		Seek	
Pred		Truncate	
Succ			
		Append	*Text files*
Delete	*String*	Flush	
Insert		Read	
Str		Readln	
Val		SetTextbuf	
Concat		Write	
Copy		Writeln	
Length		Eoln	
Pos		SeekEof	
		SeekEoln	
Addr	*Pointer*		
CSEg		BlockRead	*Untyped files*
DSeg		BlockWrite	

Appendix C   The Crt unit

Constants

Black	0
Blue	1
Green	2
Cyan	3
Red	4
Magenta	5
Brown	6
LightGray	7
DarkGray	8
LightBlue	9
LightGreen	10
LightCyan	11
LightRed	12
LightMagenta	13
Yellow	14
White	15
Blink	128

Plus various monitor constants

Variables

Variable	Type
Checkbreak	Boolean
CheckEof	Boolean
CheckSnow	Boolean
DirectVideo	Boolean
LastMode	Word
TextAttr	Byte
WindMin	Word
WindMax	Word

Functions

KeyPressed
ReadKey
WhereX
WhereY

Procedures

AssignCrt
ClrEol
Delay
DelLine
GotoXY
HighVideo
InsLine
LowVideo
NormVideo
NoSound
Sound
TextBackGround
TextColor
TextMode
Window

Appendix D   The DOS unit

Constants

Readonly
Hidden
SysFile
VolumeID
Directory
Archive
AnyFile

Types

FileRec	record
TextBuf	array
TextRec	record
Registers	record
DateTime	record
SearchRec	record
ComStr	string[127]
PathStr	string[79]
DirStr	string[67]
NameStr	string[8]
ExtStr	string[4]

Variables

DosError =	**Meaning**
0	No error
2	File not found
3	Path not found
5	Access denied
6	Invalid handle
8	Not enough memory
10	Invalid environment
11	Invalid format
18	No more files

Plus various flags and file modes

Procedures and functions

GetDate	*Date and Time*
GetFTime	
GetTime	
PackTime	
SetDate	
SetFTime	
SetTime	
UnpackTime	
GetIntVec	*Interrupt support*
Intr	
MsDos	
SetInvVec	
DiskFree	*Disk status*
DiskSize	
FindFirst	*File handling*
FindNext	
FSplit	
GetFAttr	
SetFAttr	
FExpand	
FSearch	
Exec	*Process handling*
Keep	
SwapVectors	
DosExitCode	
EnvCount	*Environment handling*
EnvStr	
GetEnv	
GetCBreak	*Miscellaneous*
GetVerify	
SetCBreak	
SetVerify	
DosVersion	

Appendix E   The Graph unit

Constants

Detect	0	ClipOn	True
		ClipOff	False
Plus many adapter specific constants		TopOn	True
		TopOff	False

grOK
grNoInitGraph
grInvalidMode
grError
plus other error values

Plus colours as for the Crt

Plus special colours for an IBM 8514 adapter

SolidLn	0
DottedLn	1
CentreLn	2
DashedLn	3
UserBitLn	4
NormWidth	1
ThickWidth	3
DefaultFont	0
TriplexFont	1
SmallFont	2
SansSerifFont	3
GothicFont	4
HorizDir	0
VertDir	1
UserCharSize	0
LeftText	0
CenterText	1
RightText	2
BottomText	0
TopText	2

EmptyFill	0
SolidFill	1
LineFill	2
LtSlashFill	3
Slashill	4
BkSlashFill	5
LtBkSlashFill	6
HatchFill	7
XHatchFill	8
InterleaveFill	9
WideDotFill	10
CloseDotFill	11
UserFill	12
CopyPut	0
XorPut	1
OrPut	2
AndPut	3
NotPut	4
MaxColors	15

Types

PaletteType	record
LineSettingsType	record
TextSettingsType	record
FillSettingsType	record
FillPatternType	array
PointType	record
ViewPortType	record
ArcCoordsType	record
Variables	
GraphGetMemPtr	
GraphFreeMemPtr	

Functions

GetBkColor
GetColor
GetDefaultPalette
GetDriverName
GetDriverMode
GetMaxColor
GetMaxMode
GetMaxX
GetMaxY
GetModeName
GetPaletteSize
GetPixrel
GetX
GetY
GraphErrorMsg
GraphResult
ImageSize
InstallUserDriver
InstallUserFont
RegisterBGIDriver
RegisterBGIfont
TextHeight
TextWidth

Procedures

Arc
Bar
Bar3D
Circle
ClearDevice
ClearViewPort
CloseGraph
DetectGraph
DrawPoly
Ellipse
FillEllipse
FillPoly
FloodFill
GetArcCoords

GetAspectRatio
GetFillPattern
GetFillSettings
GetImage
GetLineSettings
GetModeRange
GetPalette
GetTextSettings
GetViewSettings
GraphDefaults
InitGraph
Line
LineRel
LineTo
MoveRel
MoveTo
OutText
OutTextxy
PieSlice
PutImage
PutPixel
Rectangle
RestoreCrtMode
Sector
SetActivePage
SetAllPalette
SetAspectRatio
SetBkColor
SetColor
SetFillPattern
SetFillStyle
SetGraphBufSize
SetGraphMode
SetLineStyle
SetPallete
SetRGBPalette
SetTextJustify
SetTextStyle
SetUserCharSize
SetViewPort
SetVisualPage
SetWriteModes

Appendix F   ASCII character codes

Dec	Hex		Char	Dec	Hex	Char	Dec	Hex	Char	Dec	Hex	Char
0	0	^@	NUL	32	20		64	40	@	96	60	'
1	1	☺	SOH	33	21	!	65	41	A	97	61	a
2	2	●	STX	34	22	"	66	42	B	98	62	b
3	3	♥	ETX	35	23	#	67	43	C	99	63	c
4	4	♦	EOT	36	24	$	68	44	D	100	64	d
5	5	♣	ENQ	37	25	%	69	45	E	101	65	e
6	6	♠	ACK	38	26	&	70	46	F	102	66	f
7	7	●	BEL	39	27	'	71	47	G	103	67	g
8	8	◘	BS	40	28	(	72	48	H	104	68	h
9	9	○	TAB	41	29	)	73	49	I	105	69	i
10	A	■	LF	42	2A	*	74	4A	J	106	6A	j
11	B	♂	VT	43	2B	+	75	4B	K	107	6B	k
12	C	♀	FF	44	2C	,	76	4C	L	108	6C	l
13	D	♪	CR	45	2D	-	77	4D	M	109	6D	m
14	E	♫	SO	46	2E	.	78	4E	N	110	6E	n
15	F	¤	SI	47	2F	/	79	4F	O	111	6F	o
16	10	►	DLE	48	30	0	80	50	P	112	70	p
17	11	◄	DC1	49	31	1	81	51	Q	113	71	q
18	12	↕	DC2	50	32	2	82	52	R	114	72	r
19	13	‼	DC3	51	33	3	83	53	S	115	73	s
20	14	¶	DC4	52	34	4	84	54	T	116	74	t
21	15	§	NAK	53	35	5	85	55	U	117	75	u
22	16	■	SYN	54	36	6	86	56	V	118	76	v
23	17	↨	ETB	55	37	7	87	57	W	119	77	w
24	18	↑	CAN	56	38	8	88	58	X	120	78	x
25	19	↓	EM	57	39	9	89	59	Y	121	79	y
26	1A	→	SUB	58	3A	:	90	5A	Z	122	7A	z
27	1B	←	ESC	59	3B	;	91	5B	[	123	7B	{
28	1C	∟	FS	60	3C	<	92	5C	\	124	7C		
29	1D	↔	GS	61	3D	=	93	5D	]	125	7D	}
30	1E	▲	RS	62	3E	>	94	5E	^	126	7E	~
31	1F	▼	US	63	3F	?	95	5F	_	127	7F	⌂

Dec	Hex	Char	Dec	Hex	Char	Dec	Hex	Char	Dec	Hex	Char
128	80	Ç	160	A0	á	192	C0	└	224	E0	α
129	81	ü	161	A1	í	193	C1	┴	225	E1	β
130	82	é	162	A2	ó	194	C2	┬	226	E2	Γ
131	83	â	163	A3	ú	195	C3	├	227	E3	π
132	84	ä	164	A4	ñ	196	C4	─	228	E4	Σ
133	85	à	165	A5	Ñ	197	C5	┼	229	E5	σ
134	86	å	166	A6	a	198	C6	╞	230	E6	μ
135	87	ç	167	A7	o	199	C7	╟	231	E7	τ
136	88	ê	168	A8	¿	200	C8	╚	232	E8	φ
137	89	ë	169	A9	⌐	201	C9	╔	233	E9	θ
138	8A	è	170	AA	¬	202	CA	╩	234	EA	Ω
139	8B	ï	171	AB	½	203	CB	╦	235	EB	δ
140	8C	î	172	AC	¼	204	CC	╠	236	EC	∞
141	8D	ì	173	AD	¡	205	CD	=	237	ED	Φ
142	8E	Ä	174	AE	«	206	CE	╬	238	EE	∈
143	8F	Å	175	AF	»	207	CF	╧	239	EF	∩
144	90	É	176	B0	░	208	D0	╨	240	F0	≡
145	91	æ	177	B1	▒	209	D1	╤	241	F1	±
146	92	Æ	178	B2	▓	210	D2	╥	242	F2	≥
147	93	ô	179	B3	│	211	D3	╙	243	F3	≤
148	94	ö	180	B4	┤	212	D4	╘	244	F4	⌠
149	95	ò	181	B5	╡	213	D5	╒	245	F5	⌡
150	96	û	182	B6	╢	214	D6	╓	246	F6	÷
151	97	ù	183	B7	╖	215	D7	╫	247	F7	≈
152	98	ÿ	184	B8	╕	216	D8	╪	248	F8	°
153	99	Ö	185	B9	╣	217	D9	┘	249	F9	∙
154	9A	Ü	186	BA	║	218	DA	┌	250	FA	·
155	9B	¢	187	BB	╗	219	DB	█	251	FB	√
156	9C	£	188	BC	╝	220	DC	▄	252	FC	ⁿ
157	9D	¥	189	BD	╜	221	DD	▌	253	FD	²
158	9E	Pt	190	BE	╛	222	DE	▐	254	FE	■
159	9F	ƒ	191	BF	┐	223	DF	▀	255	FF	

Extended key codes are returned by those keys or key combinations that cannot be represented by the standard ASCII codes listed above. These codes must be read by the *ReadKey* procedure. If a character value of 0 is detected, then an extended key code follows. (See Section 5.6 and Example 8.6 for more details.) The meaning of the second code is given in this table.

Second code	Meaning
3	NUL
15	Shift Tab
16–25	Alt-Q/W/E/R/T/Y/U/I/O/P
30–38	Alt-A/S/D/F/G/H/I/J/K/L
44–50	Alt-Z/X/C/V/B/N/M
59–68	Keys F1–F10
71	Home
72	↑
73	PgUp
75	←
77	→
79	End
80	↓
81	PgDn
82	Ins
83	Del
84–93	F11–F20 (Shift-F1 to Shift-F10)
94–103	F21–F30 (Ctrl-F1 to Ctrl–F10)
104–113	F31–F40 (Alt-F1 to Alt–F10)
114	Ctrl-PrtScr
115	Ctrl ←
116	Ctrl →
117	Ctrl-End
118	Ctrl-PgDn
119	Ctrl-Home
120–131	Alt-1/2/3/4/5/6/7/8/9/0/-/=
132	Ctrl-PgUp
133	F11
134	F12
135	Shift-F11
136	Shift-F12
137	Ctrl-F11
138	Ctrl-F12
139	Alt-F11
140	Alt-F12

Appendix G   Syntax diagrams

program

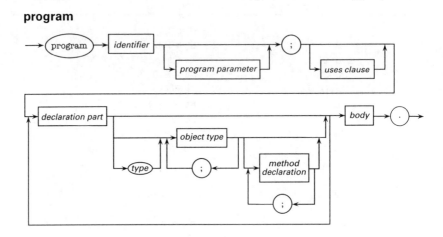

program parameters

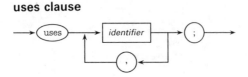

body

uses clause

unit

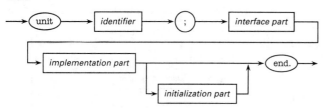

implementation part

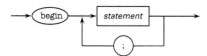

initialization part

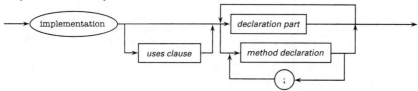

interface part

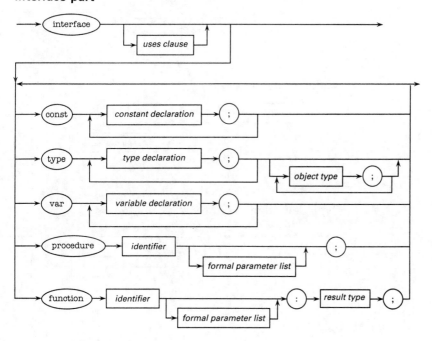

declaration part

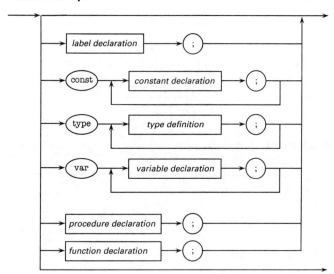

label declaration

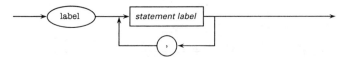

constant definition

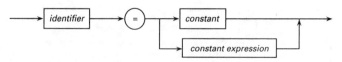

type definition

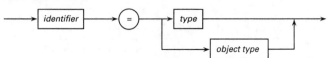

variable declaration

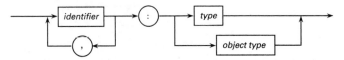

statement label

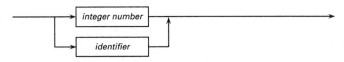

constant

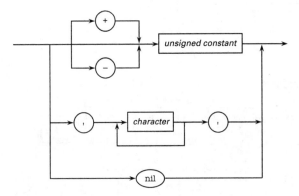

unsigned constant

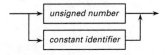

identifier

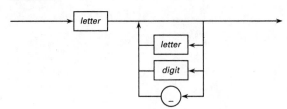

function declaration

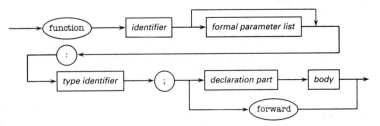

result type

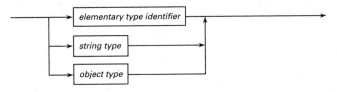

procedure declaration

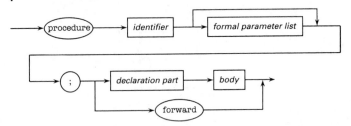

formal parameter list

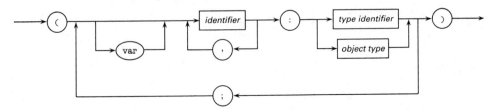

type

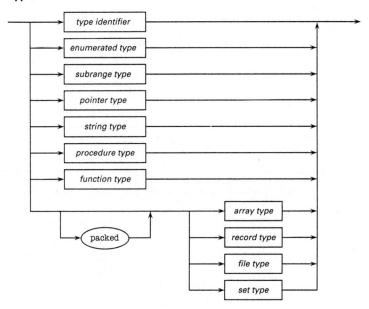

enumerated type

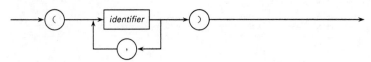

subrange type

string type

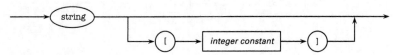

procedure type

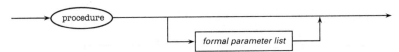

function type

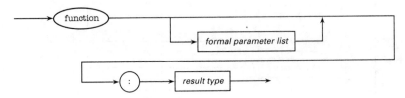

array type

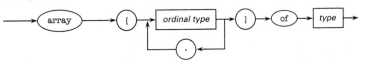

record type

field list

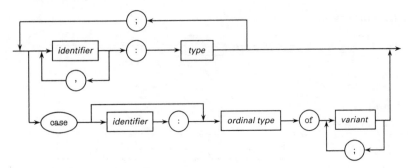

variant

file type

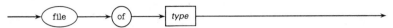

set type

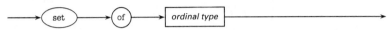

compound statement

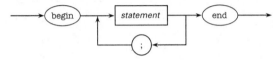

statement

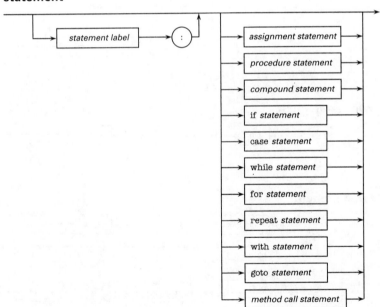

assignment statement

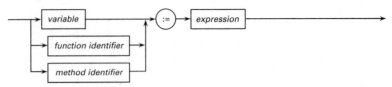

procedure call statement

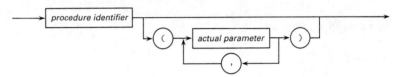

if statement

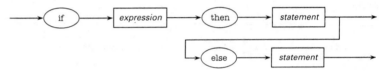

while statement

for statement

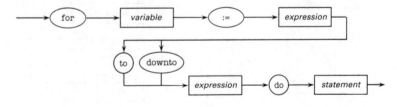

case statement

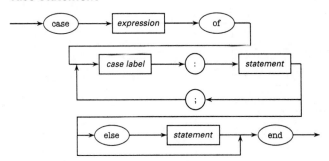

case label

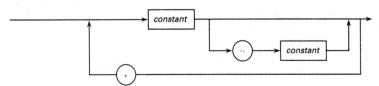

repeat statement

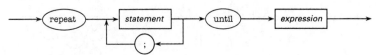

with statement

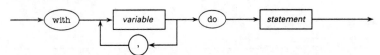

goto statement

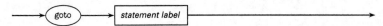

actual parameter

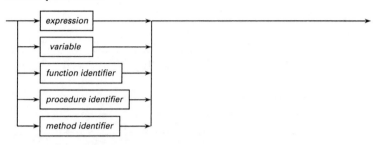

expression

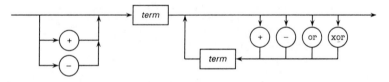

simple expression

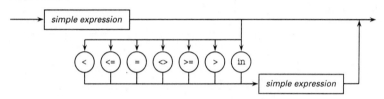

term

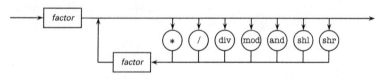

factor

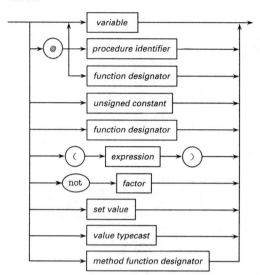

function designator

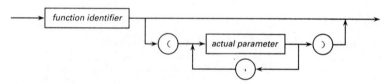

set value

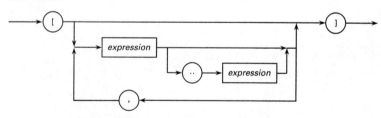

value typecast

variable

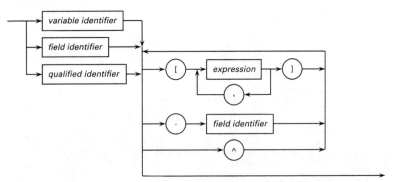

qualified identifier

unsigned number

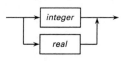

signed number

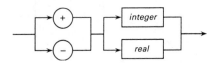

integer

real

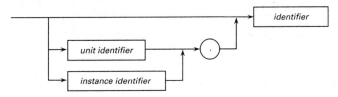

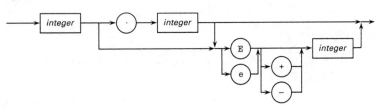

object type

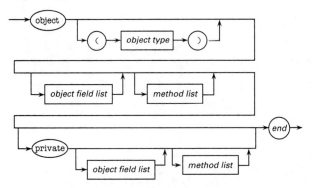

object field list

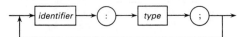

method list

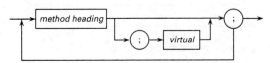

method heading

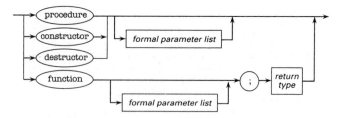

method declaration

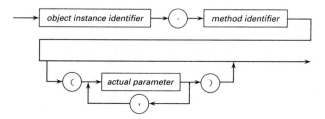

method call statement

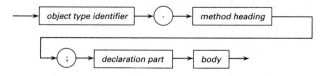

method function designator

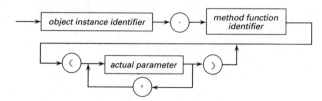

Answers to quizzes

Quiz 1

1. The hardware, software and devices that are available.
2. Several programs sharing a single (large) computer.
3. A microcomputer usually has all the necessary software and devices to make it a general purpose tool; a microprocessor is usually designed and programmed for a single embedded application; a personal computer is another name for a microcomputer, but with the emphasis being on software which is used in the home and office (such as spreadsheets, word processors, games, and so on); there are different sorts of chips – memory chips, processor chips and so on, and several go into a single microprocessor.
4. Mips (millions of instructions per second) or Megaflops (millions of floating point operations per second) are most usual.
5. RAM is random access memory for reading and writing, whereas ROM is for read-only access.
6. A compiler translates a program in a high-level language like Pascal into the machine code of the computer.
7. An editor, debugger, on-line help, and access to the DOS filing system.
8. Unambiguous, precise, finite, self-checking and brief notation.
9. The codes which directly drive the hardware instructions of the computer.
10. A compilation error indicates an error in the formulation of a construct in a language, whereas an execution error indicates an error in the logic of the program.

Quiz 2

1. After a write statement, output will proceed directly after the last item written; after a writeln statement, output will proceed at the start of a new line.
2. Yes, but they must be in different procedures.

3. Ah ha! A for-statement cannot print an infinite sequence! We must know when to stop. If we assume that we must stop at 100, then the answer is:

```
VAR i : 0 .. 10;
FOR i := 0 to 10 do
    write(i * 10, ' ');
```

4. Errors are:

VAR not VARIABLE

BEGIN needed for PROCEDURE Tops

FOR loop :=, not =

1 to 10 not 1 .. 10

writeln('!') – remember the quotes around a character.

END. – fullstop at the end of a program.

5. The declaration always comes first.

6. Although the statements under the for-statement are indented, there is no *begin-end* bracketing them. Therefore the loop applies only to the first statement, and we get:

5 times 5 times 5 times 5 times 5 times 5 times 5 times 5 times 5 times 5 times 5 times 5 times ******* is *******

where the ******* indicates that the value is indeterminate because the loop variable *multiple* does not have a defined value at the end of the loop. The two ways of correcting the loop are:

- put the statements in a procedure and let the loop call the procedure; or
- bracket the statements with *begin-end*.

7. Six stars would be printed, for the loop values 10, 9, 8, 7, 6, 5.

8. There is an interval of 8 between the seven numbers and an offset of -13. Therefore we can run a loop from 0 to 6, multiplying the loop variable by 8 and subtracting 13.

```
VAR i : 0 .. 6;
FOR i := 0 to 6 do
    write( i * 8 – 13, ' ');
```

9. The effect will be 'Hello' written in the top left corner of a window starting at (1,1), so it will be in the top left of the screen.

10. The centre is approximately at (40, 12). Therefore, we can use a window around this as follows:

```
window(38,12,48,12);
Textcolor(yellow);
write('Hello');
```

Quiz 3

1.
K = 1,000	cannot use a comma in a number.
Prize = D50	D50 is not a valid constant – must just use 50.
2ndPrize = D25	Identifier must start with a letter. D25 not valid.
i,j,k	k is being redefined.

start, end   end is a keyword.

2.   Yes, comments can extend over several lines.

3.   Integer, real, boolean, char, string and text.

4.   *ClrEol* erases any text on the rest of the line after the current cursor position.

5.   • State in advance how many items there will be.

        • Precede the data with a count.

        • Put a special terminator after the items.

        • Make use of an end-of-file property.

6.   **67 98 91**

7.   *Pre* can only have one of the values, so once one is found, there is no sense in checking further; the statements should be connected with *else* :

```
if pre = 'm' then write('milli') else
if pre = 'c' then write('centi') else
if pre = 'K' then write('kilo');
```

8.   The then-part consists only of the statement *temp := x*, since there is no *begin-end* bracketing the indented statements. So *temp* will sometimes get set to *x* and the other two statements will always be executed, the last with unpredicatable results in some cases.

9.   Named constants contribute towards the readability of a program. Changes to constants need only be made in one place, reducing the chance of errors.

10.   The random function gives numbers between 0 and a specified limit. We want 212+32+1=245 different values. Thus the limit is 244, and we subtract 32 to get the required range, as in:

```
random(244)-32
```

Quiz 4

1.   Range of values; notation for constants; input and output capabilities; operators; procedures and functions.

2.   *write(-maxint)* will get close.

3.   Assuming that the field width for integers is 10 characters, we have:

```
1948~~~~~~194800
```

Notice that the values are written close up to each other, unless field indicators or explicit spaces are inserted.

4.   *mod* is not defined for negative divisors.

        exp cannot raise a negative number to a real power.

        ln is not defined for negative values.

        arctan – no restriction.

5.
```
possiblyleap := (day = 29) and (month = 2);
```

6.   The expression does not constrain the interval as required. We need *and* not *or*.

7.   *Temp* has not been initialised to zero.

8. To adapt the for-loop, we must run it over all the readings, expressed as integers from 1 to 600, and divide by ten when printing.

```
total := 0;
for sec := 1 to 600 do begin
    write(sec / 10:4:1);  read(temp);
    total := total + temp;
end;
```

Other possibilities using conditional loops are:

```
total := 0;                          total := 0;
sec := 0.1;                          sec := 0.1;
while sec < 60.1 do begin            repeat
    write(sec:4:1);  read(temp);         write(sec:4:1);  read(temp);
    total := total + temp;               total := total + temp;
    sec := sec + 0.1;                    sec := sec + 0.1;
end;                                 until sec > 60.0;
```

Notice that equality on real numbers is avoided.

9. In a computer with 11 digits of precision, the 9-digit constant can be stored comfortably. Writing it out with a field width of 10:6 will give ~~3.141593. However, in a 4-digit computer, the full constant will not even be stored. Only 3.141 will fit. Therefore, writing it out with 10:6 will yield ~~3.141000.

10.
```
shift := trunc(time) div + 1;
```

Quiz 5

1. By writing out the character with the appropriate value, that is, ASCII 7, as in write(chr(7)).

2. For-loops only operate on discrete types such as characters. Strings do not qualify.

3. ord(ch) – ord('0')

4.
```
read(ch);
while not (ch in ['0'..'9'] do begin
    write(ch);  read(ch);
end;
```

5. <cntrl-z>

6. The assign procedure associates a Pascal file name with a disk file or a device such as a printer.

7. Yes, provided it is a file that is being used for output!

8. 'gr' is not a valid key-value. 'a' appears twice. The end-statement is followed by a comment as in end {case}.

9. The program continues executing at the next statement.

10.
```
SetTextStyle(Triplexfont,horizdir,4);
OutTextxy(300,200,'My name');
```

Quiz 6

1.   PROCEDURE P (a, b : integer; var r : real; x : real);

2.   Yes, and it is sometimes convenient to do so.

3.   No, they are both in the same declaration level.

4.   No, we cannot have subranges of reals.

5.   Yes, subscripts can extend over the whole range of the discrete types.

6.   Provided the $R+ option is on, the program will stop with an error message.

7.   A compilation error occurs.

8.   Provided the $R+ option is on, the program will stop with an error message.

9.   Yes, any part of the matrix that has been defined as its own type, for example a row.

10.   No, only scalar values can be returned.

Quiz 7

1.   No, values of an enumerated type must be identifiers.

2.   No, unfortunately.

3.   Yes.

4.   No, they must be distinct.

5.   Not the whole record, only fields that are of the simple types for which write is defined.

6.   No, only sets of discrete values are allowed.

7.   Enumerated types cannot consist of integers – only newly declared identifiers.

Enumerated types cannot be read with the read procedure.

Coinset is a type, so we cannot use it with the in operator. We must define, declare and initialise a set for the coins, such as:

```
TYPE
   change = set of coins;
VAR
   pocket : change;
pocket := [ ];

if n in pocket then ...
```

8.

```
TYPE
   illness = set of symptoms;

{Assumes the existence of a writesymptom procedure}
PROCEDURE writeillness ( bug : illness);
   VAR s : symptoms;
   BEGIN
     for s := temperature to spots do
        if s in bug then writesymptom (s);
   END;
```

9.   flu * cold

10.   By the USES statement.

Quiz 8

1. The main loop takes i to $n-1$ so that the inner loop always has at least one value to compare a_i to.

2. The record can contain a key value as well as other information.

3. Include a function type parameter to do the actual sorting, and then provide an appropriate actual function such as:

```
FUNCTION nameorder (a,b : students) : boolean;
  BEGIN
    nameorder := a.name < b.name;
  END; {nameorder}
```

4. If the records to be sorted are very large, then access tables avoid a lot of expensive swapping while sorting is going on. We can also have several different access tables providing different 'sorts' of the same data, which remains untouched.

5. The answer is 443, as worked out in the following trace:

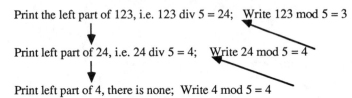

Print the left part of 123, i.e. 123 div 5 = 24;   Write 123 mod 5 = 3

Print left part of 24, i.e. 24 div 5 = 4;   Write 24 mod 5 = 4

Print left part of 4, there is none;   Write 4 mod 5 = 4

6. *DosError* is a variable in the DOS unit which is set to a non-zero value when one of the DOS unit routines fails. It is therefore used by *FindNext* to signal the end of file names in the given directory.

7. The program reads a character, and if it is a digit it holds and calls the *sift* procedure recursively. As soon as a non-digit is found, the recursive calls *unwind* and the digits are printed in reverse order. If the data is typed on a screen and interspersed with the output, we would have:

```
A*
B*
123C321*
D*
E*
69F96*
```

8. Only if they are in different scopes, that is, nested inside different procedures or units.

9. Yes indeed.

10. No. Only text files can be examined by an editor.

Quiz 9

1. The structures can grow as the data dictates, and elements can be connected in many different ways.

2. There is a storage overhead for the pointers providing the links, and a lack of direct accessibility by name to the nodes being pointed at.

3. It creates space on the heap for a variable of the type referenced by the pointer parameter, and sets the parameter to point to this space.

4. A stack is a first-in-first-out structure, whereas a queue is a last-in-first-out structure.

5. If a record B declares a field of type A, then B includes fields of A, but B and A are different types. If an object D inherits an object C, then D and C are compatible types.

6. Yes.

7. When the *Lists.Print* procedure is compiled, the compiler notes that *Display* is a virtual procedure, and delays binding it to any actual procedure. When the *NumNode* object type is declared, a virtual method table is set up for all variables of this type, and the display method points to *NumNode.Display*, being the most recent one. Thus when Print is executed for a *NumList*, *NumNode.Display* is picked off the VMT.

8.
```
destructor Lists.Done;
  var n : tonodes;
  begin
    n := head;
    while n <> nil do begin
      dispose(n.Done);
      n := n^.next;
    end;
  end;
```

9. XOR   T   F

    T   F   T

    F   T   F

10. *Getmem* is given the address of where the allocated memory is. Therefore it is provided with the pointer variable in which to place the address. *GetImage*, on the other hand, is interested in the contents of the memory pointed to by *picture*.

Answers to selected problems

Chapter 1

This set of problems is intended to lead you into a greater awareness of the size and capabilities of the computer hardware and software you will be using. There are no common answers to the questions, but some help on Question 1.5 is offered.

The number of bytes in this text book is approximately (418 pages by 50 lines by 70% full on average by 85 characters per line) = 1243K. This will fit comfortably on two 800K diskettes.

Chapter 2

2.1 **Printing names** As a sample, the procedure for 'm' would look like this:

```
PROCEDURE m;
  BEGIN
    writeln('******');
    writeln('      *');
    writeln('  ****');
    writeln('      *');
    writeln('******');
  END; {m}
```

Given that the other letters' procedures are similarly defined, then the program might look like this:

```
PROGRAM William (input, output);
  BEGIN
    W; i; l; l; i; a; m;
  END.
```

The important point to grasp in this example is the concept of the identifier for a procedure. We have assumed that the procedures have single letter names. This might be confusing if we wanted to use these names somewhere else (for example, as a loop variable), so instead we could choose names such as *printm*, *printi* and so on. Then the program would be:

```
PROGRAM William (input, output);
  BEGIN
    printW; printi; printl; printl; printi; printa; printm;
  END.
```

Can you see whether there would be a problem with writing the name 'Susan' in this way? *Two* procedures for 's' would have to be defined, and they would have to have different names. *Prints* and *printS* are the same name, since Pascal does not regard cases as different.

2.2 **Mystery output** The program prints two dumbbells, one under the other. Each has the form:

2.3 **One man went to mow** The way of tackling this problem is to take a verse from the output and underline those parts that change each time, that is:

<u>3</u> men went to mow, went to mow a meadow,
<u>3</u> men, <u>2</u> men, <u>1</u> man and his dog, went to mow a meadow.

We set up one loop for the verses, based on how many men there are, and one loop to repeat all the men in reverse order. A first attempt at a program for five men is:

```
PROGRAM MowaMeadow (output);
  VAR
    man, companions : 1 .. 5;
  BEGIN
    writeln('****** One man went to mow ******');
    FOR man := 1 to 5 do begin
      writeln(man,' men went to mow, went to mow a meadow,');
      FOR companions := man downto 2 do
        write(companions, ' men, ');
      writeln('1 man and his dog, went to mow a meadow. ');
    end;
  END.
```

A point to note is that the inner loop is skipped when the loop variable *man* is one. If you run the program, you will notice that it has one defect: the first line is written as '1 men ...' rather than '1 man ...'. How would the program have to be altered to display correct grammar?

2.4 **Times tables** There are three nested loops here. The outermost one runs down the page for each group of tables. It goes from 1 to 4, there being 4 groups of 3. The next loop goes down the lines of each group, from 1 to 12. The final loop goes across the page for the three tables in a group. In addition, each group must have three headings printed. It therefore makes sense to parcel up the printing of a group into a procedure, with two parameters indicating the first and last tables. A suitable program would be:

```
PROGRAM OldenDays (input, output);
VAR
  down : 1..4;

  PROCEDURE PrintThreeAcross (first, last : integer);
  VAR
    across, line : 1..12;
  BEGIN
    for across := first to last do
      write(across:2, ' times table   ');
    writeln;
    for line := 1 to 12 do begin
      for across := first to last do
        write(line:2, ' x ',across:2, ' = ', line*across:3,' ':5);
      writeln;
    end;
  END; {PrintThreeAcross}

BEGIN
  writeln('******* Times Tables up to 12 *****');
  for down := 1 to 4 do begin
    PrintThreeAcross ((down-1)*3+1,down*3);
    writeln; writeln;
  end;
END.
```

2.6 **Number triangle** Nested loops are needed here, very similar to those in the *Mountain* procedure of Example 2.5. To print the triangle centred, we regard the blanks as one of the 'tones' and have two loops, one after the other, inside the loop for the rows. To print it upside down, a *downto* could be used.

Chapter 3

3.1 **Large class symbols** The pattern for the else-if sequence for class marks was given in Section 3.4. The point to remember when amending it for printing each symbol in a large format is that **compound statements** are needed to group more than one procedure call after each *then* or *else*.

```
if mark >= 75
then eye
else
  if mark >= 70  then begin
    eye; eye; dash; one;
  end else
  if mark >= 60  then begin
    eye; eye; dash; two;
  end else
  if mark >= 50 then begin
    eye; eye; eye;
  end else
    eff;
```

The handling of the two second classes could have been grouped as follows:

```
if mark >= 60 then begin
  eye; eye; dash;
```

```
                              if mark >= 70 then one else two;
                           end
```

3.2   **Rainfall figures** The solution to this problem involves a mixture of the algorithms for summing numbers and for finding the largest one, and the mixture is all wrapped up in loops for the weeks and days. It is vital to have a clear picture of the algorithm before proceeding to the program. The positioning of the checks and loops is shown in the pseudo-code chart:

Calculate rainfall
Initialise wettest day total and number
Initialise driest week number

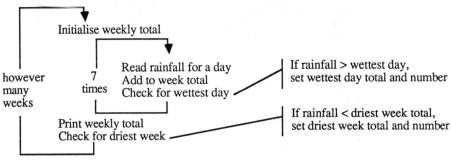

Print wettest day number
Print driest week number

Notice that the checking for the wettest day and driest week involves keeping track of two variables – the actual rainfall and the day or week number. In order to find the maximum rainfall for the wettest day, the total can be initialised to zero; for the driest week, the initialising is not so clear and it is necessary to choose something impossibly large.

Recording the wettest day also has its problems because in the loop, the day number will run from 1 to 7, but ultimately, the wettest day must be recorded in the range 1 to 28. To perform this mapping, the week number must be taken into account.

3.3   **Golf scores** The solution to the Golf Course problem is based on finding the lowest number; the handling of the handicap and par are very much side issues. Obviously, the algorithm for finding the highest number (Section 3.4) can be adapted to find the lowest. A point to note is how the question suggests that the prompts, data and results should all appear on a single line. This will require deft use of write, read, and writeln. What follows is a suitable main program, omitting the procedures that it calls. Notice how the use of procedures makes the main program really easy to read.

```
PROGRAM GolfScorer (input, output);
CONST
    noofplayers =4;
    par         = 30;
    NoofHoles   = 9;
    maxplayers  = 6;
    maxscore    = 100;
```

```
VAR
  player,
  winner              : 1 .. maxplayers;
  handicap,
  total,
  result,
  winningresult       : 0 .. 100; {say}

BEGIN
  writeln('***** Golf Scoring Program ******');
  writeln;
  PrintHeading;
  player := 1;
  ReadHandicap;
  ReadandTotalShots;
  PrintOutcome;
  winner := player;
  winningresult := result;
  FOR player := 2 to Noofplayers do begin
    ReadHandicap;
    ReadandTotalShots;
    PrintOutcome;
    CheckforWinner;
  END;
  AnnounceWinner;
END.
```

Chapter 4

4.1 **Examination marking** First consider the rules that can be broken. They are:

- too many questions answered overall (>5);
- too many questions answered from A (>3);
- too many questions answered from B (>3).

To monitor whether the rules are being obeyed we use three counters. As soon as a section counter exceeds its quota, a boolean is set. After all the marks have been read, the booleans are tested in order to write out any message regarding a rule being broken. The algorithm is shown overleaf.

4.2 **Rabbits!** Two things happen every three months: the children become adults, and new children are born. As formulated here, everything happens in pairs, so we can base our calculations on pairs, too. The program is centred around a simple while loop, which stops when we run out of room. The results you should get are:

***** Rabbit populations *****

We assume that a pair of rabbits of 3 months or over produces 2 more rabbits every 3 months.

In 27 months there will be more than 500 rabbits.

4.3 **Pattern making** The solution to this problem will bear some similarity to that for controlling the apparatus discussed in Example 4.5. As each of the numbers is read, it must be checked against the previous one, and when they are no longer equal, something must be done. The action required is the writing out of the instruction $(n*m)$, where m is the number and n is the count of the occurrences of that number.

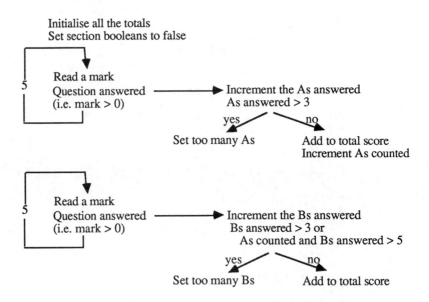

4.11 **Conversion tables**   There are two problems here – the conversion and the tabulation. For the conversion, we shall need some assignment statements, and conversion from reals to integers. The tabulating is more difficult. Probably three columns per line on the card will be easy to read, and we assume that the engineers will supply the starting value for the card, for example, 10 kg. However, we should also try to devise a program that is not tied to a 20 by 3 card, but one that can be adapted to print a table of any reasonable size.

Tackling the conversion first, we know that one kilogram is 2.2046 lbs, and a lb has 16 oz. Therefore for k kilograms, we can calculate the lbs as $k * 2.2$. This could be a real number. For example, 4.3 kg gives 9.46 lbs. We need to isolate the fraction and multiply it by 16. This can be done using the trunc function to get the integer part of the lbs and subtracting this from the original, that is $9.46 - 9 = 0.46$. Multiplying by 16 gives 7.36, which in whole numbers, rounded, is 7 oz. The complete sequence of steps, in Pascal, would be:

```
VAR  kg, whole, frac  : real;
       lbs, oz          : integer;

whole := kg * 2.2;
lbs := trunc (whole);
frac := whole – lbs;
oz := round (frac * 16);
```

The tabulation part draws on the experience of Example 2.7, to get several values across the line. Putting three columns across, with 20 lines down, we have 60 values. At 0.1 kg intervals, this enables us to print 6 kg per page. Unlike Example 2.7, though, we would like to print the values downwards in columns, as in:

kg	lb	oz	kg	lb	oz	kg	lb	oz
0.0	0	0	2.0	4	7	4.0	8	13
0.1	0	4	2.1	4	10	4.1	9	1
0.2	0	7	2.2	4	14	4.2	9	4

Two nested loops will satisfy this as shown in the algorithm (assuming we number the rows and columns from 0):

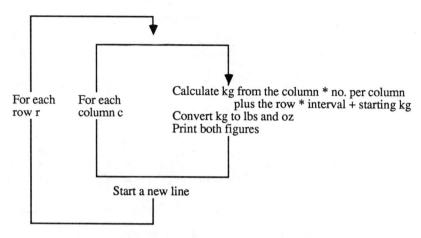

For each   For each   Calculate kg from the column * no. per column
row r   column c   plus the row * interval + starting kg
                                    Convert kg to lbs and oz
                                    Print both figures

Start a new line

Do a few examples yourself to check that the formula is correct. The complications are that we are dealing in tenths of a kg and that there is a variable starting point. The program should now follow easily.

Chapter 5

5.1   **Converting names** It is surprisingly easy to perform this conversion. Each character is read in and checked and then written out either as is or converted to lower case. The checks depend both on the character itself and on the previous character. Looking at the previous character enables initials and the first letter of double surnames to remain in capitals.

```
PROGRAM Convert (input, output, oldfile, newfile);
  {Copies a file of names in capitals to a new file with
  names in both cases}
  VAR oldfile, newfile : text;

  PROCEDURE CopyandConvert;
    CONST
      space = ' ';
    VAR
      ch, previous : char;
    BEGIN
      previous := space; {to force a capital to start with}
      WHILE not eoln(oldfile) do begin
        read(oldfile,ch);
        if previous in [' ', '.', '-', '"']
        then write(newfile,ch)
        else
          if ch in ['A'..'Z']
          then write(newfile, chr(ord(ch) – ord('A') + ord('a')))
          else write(newfile,ch);
      END; {while}
      readln(oldfile);
      writeln(newfile);
    END; {CopyandConvert}
```

```
              BEGIN
                writeln('****** Converting from capitals ******');
                writeln;
                write('For the old file connect to old.file');
                write('For the new file connect to new.file');
                reset(oldfile, 'old.file');
                rewrite(newfile, 'new.file');
                WHILE not eof(oldfile) do
                   CopyandConvert;
                close(newfile);  {if necessary}
              END.
```

5.2 **Word length profile** The extension to the existing program will involve closing the file, resetting it again, and then processing it in a similar way, making use of the *readaword* and *skipagap* procedures as before. Each time a word is read, its length (*letters*) is compared with the average in order to decide whether to increment the counter or not.

5.3 **Splitting a file** Here we give the full Turbo Pascal version of the program.

```
              PROGRAM Splitter (input, output, all, pos, neg);
              VAR
                all, pos, neg : text;

              PROCEDURE printfile (VAR f : text);
                VAR n : integer;
                BEGIN
                  reset(f);
                  WHILE not eof(f) do begin
                    read(f, n);
                    write(n, '   ');
                  END;
                  writeln;
                END; {Printfile}

              PROCEDURE Connectfile (var f : text);
                VAR filename : string[20];
                BEGIN
                  write('For the ',s,' file? ');
                  readln(filename);
                  assign(f, filename);
                END; {Connectfile}

              BEGIN
                writeln('****** Splitting a file ******');
                writeln;
                writeln('For the data file'); connectfile(all);  reset(all);
                writeln('For the positives file'); connectfile(pos);  rewrite(pos);
                writeln('For the negatives file '); connectfile(neg);  rewrite(neg);
                WHILE not eof(all) do begin
                   read(all, n);
                   if n >= 0
                   then write(pos, n, '   ')
                   else write(neg, n, '   ');
                END;
                close(pos);  close(neg);
                printfile(pos);
                printfile(neg);
              END.
```

Since the printing is done for both files, it is profitable to put it in a procedure.

corrected.

Notice, however, that the parameter, which is the name of the file, has to be declared with the keyword VAR. This is further explained in Chapter 6.

If the separate files are not needed later on, they could be left as local files, unconnected to any device and existing only during the run of the program.

5.4 **Comments** This, and Problem 5.5, are typical character processing programs. Characters are read from a file, one by one, examined, processed and written out again. The programs are made more interesting by the introduction of the notion of a paragraph; at each new paragraph, after a blank line, the counters and conditions can begin anew.

The body of the comments program is governed by a single boolean variable, *inacomment*, which records whether we are processing a comment or not. Depending on the value of this condition, the occurrence of a { or } at specific points will either be correct or an error. This is all shown in the program.

```
PROGRAM Comments (input, output, data, results);
VAR
  data, results      : text;
  ch                 : char;
  inacomment,
  endofparagraph     : boolean;
  commentcount,
  noncommentcount : 0 .. maxint;

PROCEDURE CheckforOpenComment;
BEGIN
  if ch = '{' then
    if inacomment {already}
    then writeln(results, '*** { found in a comment'
    else inacomment := true;
END; {CheckforOpenComment}

PROCEDURE CheckforCloseComment;
BEGIN
  if ch = '}' then
    if not inacomment
    then writeln(results, '*** } no opening comment')
    else inacomment := false;
END; {CheckforCloseComment}

PROCEDURE CountandWrite;
BEGIN
  if inacomment
  then commentcount := commentcount + 1
  else begin
    noncommentcount := noncommentcount + 1;
    write(results, ch);
    if eoln(data) then writeln(results);
  end;
END; {CountandWrite}

PROCEDURE CheckforParagraph;
{Detects a blank line}
BEGIN
  if eoln(data) then readln(data);
  if eoln(data) then begin
    readln(data);
    endofparagraph := true;
    if inacomment then writeln(results, '*** No ending bracket');
    writeln(results);
  end;
```

```
                      END; {CheckforParagraph}

                      BEGIN
                        writeln('****** Comment checker ******');
                        writeln;
                        write('For data file, assign to comments.dat');
                        write('For results file assign to comments.out');
                        assign(data,'comments.dat');
                        reset(data);
                        assign(results,'comments.out');
                        rewrite(results);
                        WHILE not eof(data) do begin
                          endofparagraph := true;
                          commentcount := 0;
                          noncommentcount := 0;
                          inacomment := false;
                          while not endofparagraph do begin
                            read(data,ch);
                            CheckforOpenComment;
                            CountandWrite;
                            CheckforCloseComment;
                            CheckforParagraph;
                          end;
                          writeln('Comment is ', trunc(commentcount * 100 /
                                    (commentcount + noncommentcount)):1,
                                    '% of the text');
                        END;
                        close(results);
                      END.
```

Chapter 6

6.1   **Sum of squares** The function is:

```
            FUNCTION SumofSquares (n, m : integer) : integer;
            VAR
              i, sum : integer;
            BEGIN
              sum := 0;
              for i := n to m do
                sum := sum + sqr(i);
            END; {Sum of squares}
```

To call it we would say something like:

```
            writeln(SumofSquares(1,10));
```

6.2   **Parameter passing** The output from *picture* would be:

```
            1   0
            2   2 2 2
            3   6 3 3 3 3 3 3
            4   12 4 4 4 4 4 4 4 4 4 4 4 4
```

The parameters to *modify* are listed separately because one is a value parameter and the other is VAR.

6.5   **Exam marks revisited** The structure of the program is defined by the loop which looks at each student in turn, viz:

```
WHILE not eof(data) do begin
    EchoName;
    Clear;
    while not eoln (data) do begin
        ReadSubjectandMark;
        CheckandTotal;
    end;
    readln(data);
    AssessResult;
    n := n + 1;
END;
```

There are five procedures that are called by the main program and together they access all the 11 variables which are needed to read and perform the calculations. These have all been declared globally, which is not good practice. A better structure would be to declare a procedure in which the 11 variables are defined, and which perform the mechanics of the loop. The five procedures will then be declared inside this procedure, and can access their common data quite safely. Between students, the variables will be inacessible. Thus the loop above becomes:

```
WHILE not eof(data) do begin
    Processstudent;
    n := n + 1;
END;
```

As for the use of parameters, there really does not seem to be any need here. No action is repeated with differently named variables from different places, so nothing is gained by adding parameters. Notice also that there is a basic 'charge' for parameters in that there still has to be an actual parameter to pass to the formal, so having parameters does not cut down on global variables.

Chapter 7

7.1   **AD and BC dates**   For the input, it would be nice if the dates could remain in the traditional format. However, if the read statement is used for the number, the BC or AD part will have to be separated from the year by a space. Alternatively, the number could be read character by character and converted to an integer by a procedure.

For storing the dates, there are two possibilities. Either the year can be an integer, and a separate field of, say,

```
TYPE eras = (BC, AD);
```

could indicate what era it refers to, or we could investigate storing BC dates as negative numbers. Either way, there will be an impact on the operations. Using negative numbers might make the arithmetic easier, but the other option might be easier for writing. Try them both!

7.6   **Prime numbers**   The method for deciding whether a number is prime is to divide it by successive smaller numbers and if any divides evenly, then the number is not prime. There are several well-known refinements to this outline:

- 1, 2 and 3 are prime;
- Try dividing by 2 first;
- Then start dividing from 3, and skip all even numbers as divisors;
- Stop dividing when the divisor exceeds the square root of the number.

To explain the last refinement note that if the number has a divisor, and that divisor is greater than the square root, then a divisor smaller than the square root must already have been found. So once all the smaller numbers have been tried, the process can stop.

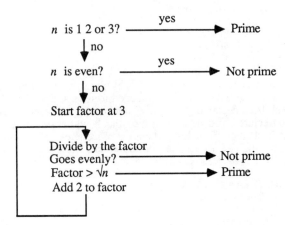

There are two points at which the loop can stop, and neither is at the start or end of the loop, so a while statement or repeat statement is not immediately applicable. What we do is regard the loop as having **states**, which can be expressed in the symbolic type

        TYPE states = (stilldividing, factorfound, nofactors);

The state of the loop starts off as *stilldividing*. Then when one of the stopping conditions becomes true, the state changes. After the loop, the state

```
PROGRAM Primetesting (input, output);
    VAR  number : integer;

    FUNCTION prime (n : integer) : boolean;
        TYPE
            natural  = 0..maxint;
            states   = (stilldividing, factorfound, nofactors);
        VAR
            factor   : integer;
            root     : natural;
            state    : states;
        BEGIN
        if (n <= 3) then prime :=true else
        if not odd(n) then prime := false else
        BEGIN
            root := trunc(sqrt(n));
            write('Square root is approx: ', root:1,
                '    Trial factors are: ');
            factor := 3;
            state := stilldividing;
            REPEAT
                write(' ', factor:1);
                if n mod factor = 0 then state := factorfound else
                if factor > root then state := nofactors else
                factor := factor + 2;
```

```
            UNTIL state <> stilldividing;
            writeln;
            prime := not (state = factorfound);
        END;
    END; {prime}

BEGIN
    writeln('****** Prime testing program ******');
    write('Type in a number (greater than 0): ');
    readln(number);
    case prime(number) of
        true     : writeln(number:1, ' is prime');
        false    : writeln(number:1, ' is not prime');
    end;
END.
```

Sample test runs might be:

```
****** Prime testing program ******
Type in a number (greater than 0): 211
Square root is approx: 14   Trial factors are: 3  5  7  9  11  13  15
211 is prime

****** Prime testing program ******
Type in a number (greater than 0): 213
Square root is approx: 14   Trial factors are: 3
213 is not prime

****** Prime testing program ******
Type in a number (greater than 0): 12343
Square root is approx: 111   Trial factors are:  3  5  7  9  11  13  15  17  19  21  23
25  27  29  31  33  35  37  39  41  43  45  47  49  51  53  55  57  59  61  63  65  67
69  71  73  75  77  79  81  83  85  87  89  91  93  95  97  99  101  103  105  107  109
111  113
12343 is prime
```

It may seem wasteful in this last example to be dividing by multiples of 3, when we know that 3 doesn't go. The same applies to multiples of 5 and 7 and so on. However, recognising multiples in order to exclude them as divisors will take a division operation in itself, which will not save anything. There are other methods of testing for primes, and a good one is discussed in the next problem.

7.7   **Sieve of Eratosthenes**   The algorithm will use set difference to take values out of the sieve, and set union to construct the set of primes.

Sieve of Eratosthenes

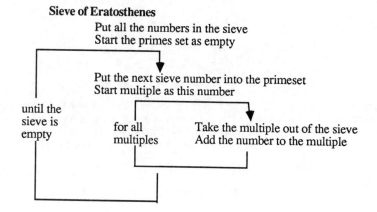

Although we know the size of the base set, conditional rather than counting loops will be needed. In the outer one, the stopping condition will be the sieve being empty, which may occur before the last number needs to be considered.

Of course, the primes do not have to be put into a set themselves – they could just be written out, but this way there is more illustration of set manipulation!

```
PROGRAM Eratosthenes (input, output);
  CONST
    maxset = 255;
  TYPE
    baserange  = 0..maxset;
    sets       = set of baserange;
  VAR
    sieve, primes    : sets;
    n, next,
    multiple, count  : baserange;

  BEGIN
    writeln('****** Primes using a sieve ******');
    write('Primes up to (<= ', maxset:1, ')? ');
    repeat
      readln(n);
    until  (n >= 2) and (n <= maxset);
    sieve := [2..n];
    primes := [ ];
    next := 2;
    count := 0;
    REPEAT
      if next in sieve then begin
        primes := primes + [next];
        count := count + 1;
        multiple := next;
        while multiple <= n do begin
            sieve := sieve – [multiple];
            multiple := multiple + next;
        end;
      end;
      next := next + 1;
    UNTIL sieve = [ ];
    writeln('The ', count:1, ' primes up to ',n:1, ' are:');
    for next := 2 to n do
      if next in primes then write(next:1,' ');
    writeln;
  END.
```

Running the program gives the expected output:

```
****** Primes using a sieve ******
Primes up to (<= 255)? 50
The 15 primes up to 50 are:
2  3  5  7  11  13  17  19  23  29  31  37  41  43  47
```

7.9   **Employee training**   The major sticking point for this extension is that we cannot use Pascal sets to store names. There are two ways of going about the solution. We could abandon sets as inadequate, and use linked lists or arrays of strings instead. Adding each employee onto the class list is then no longer the simple:

```
classlist[c] := classlist[s] + [employee]
```

but will necessitate extending the list or array. Printing is not really more difficult.

However, if we are to work out how many employees are doing the same combination of any two courses, then we want to hold on to the sets, because they will enable us to use intersection to ascertain the answers.

The second approach is to keep the employee numbers and use them in the class lists, but to maintain an additional list of names for each number. All the calculations are done on the numbers, and only the printing process need change to print out names instead. If the names list is kept as an array, indexed by number, then in fact the only change will be in *printset* where *write(n:8)* becomes:

```
write(namelist[n]:8);
```

Chapter 8

8.1   **Sorting strings**   A sorting procedure for an array of names defined as strings would be declared as:

```
PROCEDURE sortnames (VAR T : stringtables; n : stringindex);
```

The procedure would then be called by:

```
sortnames (daytable);
sortnames (seasontable);
sortnames (depttable);
```

If the tables being searched are known to be in alphabetical order, then as soon as the search has gone past the possible place for x, it can stop. The change comes in the loop as follows:

```
REPEAT
  if x = T[i] then state := found else
  if (x > T[i]) or (i = high) then state := notthere else
  i := succ(i);
UNTIL state <> searching;
```

8.2   **Sorting names or marks**   Following the method outlined in Section 8.2, we need to declare a function for each type of ordering that we want, and link these in to a function type parameter in the sort. The type is:

```
TYPE compares = function (a,b : students) : boolean;
```

and the actual functions will be:

```
FUNCTION namesordered (s1, s2 : students) : boolean;
BEGIN
  namesordered := s1. name < s2.name;
END;

FUNCTION marksordered (s1, s2 : students) : boolean;
BEGIN
  marksordered := s1.mark > s2.mark;
END;
```

The sort procedure is delared as:

```
PROCEDURE sortclass (VAR C : classes; n : classrange;
                     inorder  : compares);
```

and the comparison statement in the inner loop becomes:

```
if inorder(C[i], chosen) then ...
```

The calls to the sort would be:

```
sortclass (class,n,namesordered);
sortclass (class,n,marksordered);
```

If we wanted to keep the different lists, then we could declare some new variables and sort into them instead, for example:

```
VAR
    namelist: classes;

namelist := class;
sort (namelist, n, namesordered);
```

8.3 **Palindromes** The recursive function is:

```
FUNCTION IsPalindrome (s : phrase; left, right : range) : boolean;
    BEGIN
      if left >= right  {the stopping condition}
      then IsPalindrome := true
      else
        if s[left] = s[right]
           then IsPalindrome := IsPalindrome(s,left+1,right−1)
           else IsPalindrome := false;
    END; {IsPalindrome}
```

It would be called by an expression such as *IsPalindrome(data, 1, n)*.

Chapter 9

9.1 **Class timetables** The program has to take a linked list and store it on a file. Unfortunately, pointer values cannot be meaningfully reinstated from a file. Therefore, we have to write out the records one by one, without the pointers, and when we read them back, we add the pointers again. The file definition would be something like this:

```
storedcourses = record
    number : coursenos;
    pattern : periodset;
  end;
coursefiles = file of storedcourses;
```

9.4 **Object-oriented holidays** The conversion follows the line of Example 9.3. The following program retains the same user interface as Example 9.2, but illustrates the advantages of factoring most of the list processing statements into a unit with objects.

```
PROGRAM HolidaywithObjects (input, output);
  USES ListUnit;

  CONST
    namemax  = 24;
```

```
    empty      = ";

TYPE
 namerange  = 1..namemax;
 names      = string[namemax];
 sexes      = (male, female);
 ages       = 0 .. 16;
 hobbies    = names;

 tochildren = ^ childnode;
 childnode  = object (nodes)
    sex  : sexes;
    age  : ages;
    constructor Init (var nomore : boolean);
    procedure Display; virtual;
 end;

 tohobbies  = ^ hobbynode;
 hobbynode  = object (nodes)
    name  : hobbies;
    constructor Init(var nomore : boolean);
    procedure Display; virtual;
 end;

 toadults = ^ adultnode;
 adultnode = object (nodes)
    sex  : sexes;
    interests  : lists;
    constructor Init (var nomore : boolean);
    procedure Display; virtual;
 end;

 families = record
        surname  : names;
        children : lists;
        adults   : lists;
 end;

VAR
 family : families;

procedure readhobbies (var hobbylist : lists); forward;

{--------- Methods for the three objects ---------------}

 constructor hobbynode.Init(var nomore : boolean);
  begin
    next := nil;
    nomore := false;
    write('Interest (return for none)? ');
    readln (name);
    if name = empty then
      nomore := true;
    end; {hobbynode.Init}

 constructor adultnode.Init(var nomore : boolean);
 var ch : char;
     ahobby : tohobbies;
  begin
    next := nil;
    nomore := false;
```

```
            repeat
              write('Sex? (M, F, or Q for no more): ');
              read(ch);
              until ch in ['M','m','F','f','Q','q'];
            readln;
             if ch in ['Q','q'] then
               nomore := true
             else begin
               if ch in ['M','m']
               then sex := male
               else sex := female;
               readhobbies(interests);
             end;
          end; {adultnode.Init}


          constructor childnode.Init(var nomore : boolean);
          var ch : char;
          begin
          next := nil;
          nomore := false;
          repeat
            write('Sex? (M, F, or Q for no more): ');
            read(ch);
            until ch in ['M','m','F','f','Q','q'];
          readln;
           if ch in ['Q','q'] then
             nomore := true
           else begin
             if ch in ['M','m']
             then sex := male
             else sex := female;
             write(' Age ');
             readln(age);
           end;
        end; {childnode.Init}

    PROCEDURE hobbynode.Display;
    BEGIN
       write(name, ' ');
       END; {hobbynode.Display}

    PROCEDURE adultnode.Display;
    BEGIN
       case sex of
         male : write('male');
         female : write('female');
       end;
       write(' with interests ');
       interests.print;
       writeln;
       END; {adultnode.Display}

    PROCEDURE childnode.Display;
    BEGIN
       case sex of
         male : write('boy');
         female : write('girl');
       end;
       write(' age ');
       writeln(age);
       END; {childnode.Display}
```

```
{------------- Main procedures and program -----------}

PROCEDURE readhobbies(var hobbylist: lists);
 VAR
   hobby    : tohobbies;
   finished : boolean;
 BEGIN
   hobbylist.Init;
   repeat
     new(hobby,Init(finished));
     if not finished then hobbylist.Add(hobby)
     else dispose(hobby,Done);
   until finished;
 END; {readhobbies}

PROCEDURE readadults(var adultlist: lists);
 VAR
   adult    : toadults;
   finished : boolean;
 BEGIN
   adultlist.Init;
   repeat
     new(adult,Init(finished));
     if not finished then adultlist.Add(adult)
     else dispose(adult,Done);
   until finished;
 END; {readadults}

PROCEDURE readchildren(var childlist: lists);
 VAR
   child    : tochildren;
   finished : boolean;
 BEGIN
   childlist.Init;
   repeat
     new(child, Init(finished));
     if not finished then childlist.Add(child)
     else dispose(child,Done);
   until finished;
 END; {readchildren}

BEGIN
 writeln('***** Reading holiday data *****');
 writeln('Testing for one family only');
 write('Surname: ');
 readln(family.surname);

 writeln('Adults');
 readadults(family.adults);

 writeln('Children');
 readchildren(family.children);

 writeln;
 writeln('The ', family.surname, ' family"s data is: ');
 writeln('Adults:');
 family.adults.print;
 writeln('Children:');
 family.children.print;
END.
```

Index to procedures and programs

Note: Turbo Pascal procedures are referred to in the main index

Index

A

abs 98, 119
abstract data types 252
access tables 287
accuracy 118, 125
actual parameters 185, 189
Ada 10
algorithm 9
    development 13
and 105
Arc 219
arctan 119
arithmetic limits 123
array 207
    and security 211
    constants 211
    multi-dimensional 214
    properties 210
    untyped 220
ASCII 363
aspect ratio 184
assembly language 11
assign 152
AssignCrt 154
assignment 60
    statement 61
average 217

B

backtracking 295
Bar 219
Bar3D 219
base type 254
based number writing 294
BASIC 10

BEGIN

    for compound statements 77, 109
    for procedures 30
    for programs 24
binding 324
bit map 332
bits 5
blank lines 25
    checking for 199
boolean 60, 102
    input/output 107
    operators 105
    precedences 106
    properties 105
borders 142
bottom-up 19
byte 95
bytes 5

C

C language 10
cardinality 257
case, lower and upper 53
case-statement 74, 164
CGA 5
changing directories 28, 307
char 60, 139
character set 142, 363
character type 139
    codes 363
    functions 141
    input/output 140
    operators 141
    sizes 179
    values 140
checksums 194
chips 4